THE FLETCHER JONES FOUNDATION
HUMANITIES IMPRINT

The Fletcher Jones Foundation has end-
innovative and enduring s

The publisher and the University of California Press Foundation
gratefully acknowledge the generous support of the Fletcher Jones
Foundation Imprint in Humanities.

Black Handsworth

BERKELEY SERIES IN BRITISH STUDIES
Edited by James Vernon

1. *The Peculiarities of Liberal Modernity in Imperial Britain*, edited by Simon Gunn and James Vernon
2. *Dilemmas of Decline: British Intellectuals and World Politics, 1945–1975*, by Ian Hall
3. *The Savage Visit: New World People and Popular Imperial Culture in Britain, 1710–1795*, by Kate Fullagar
4. *The Afterlife of Empire*, by Jordanna Bailkin
5. *Smyrna's Ashes: Humanitarianism, Genocide, and the Birth of the Middle East*, by Michelle Tusan
6. *Pathological Bodies: Medicine and Political Culture*, by Corinna Wagner
7. *A Problem of Great Importance: Population, Race, and Power in the British Empire, 1918–1973*, by Karl Ittmann
8. *Liberalism in Empire: An Alternative History*, by Andrew Sartori
9. *Distant Strangers: How Britain Became Modern*, by James Vernon
10. *Edmund Burke and the Conservative Logic of Empire*, by Daniel I. O'Neill
11. *Governing Systems: Modernity and the Making of Public Health in England, 1830–1910*, by Tom Crook
12. *Barbed-Wire Imperialism: Britain's Empire of Camps, 1976–1903*, by Aidan Forth
13. *Aging in Twentieth-Century Britain*, by Charlotte Greenhalgh
14. *Thinking Black: Britain, 1964–1985*, by Rob Waters
15. *Black Handsworth: Race in 1980s Britain*, by Kieran Connell

Black Handsworth

Race in 1980s Britain

Kieran Connell

UNIVERSITY OF CALIFORNIA PRESS

University of California Press, one of the most distinguished university presses in the United States, enriches lives around the world by advancing scholarship in the humanities, social sciences, and natural sciences. Its activities are supported by the UC Press Foundation and by philanthropic contributions from individuals and institutions. For more information, visit www.ucpress.edu.

University of California Press
Oakland, California

© 2019 by Kieran Connell

Library of Congress Cataloging-in-Publication Data

Names: Connell, Kieran, author.
Title: Black Handsworth : race in 1980s Britain / Kieran Connell.
Description: Oakland, California : University of California Press, [2019] |
    Series: Berkeley Series in British Studies ; 15 | Includes bibliographical
    references and index. |
Identifiers: LCCN 2018036127 (print) | LCCN 2018037563 (ebook) |
    ISBN 9780520971950 (ebook) | ISBN 9780520300668 (cloth : alk. paper) |
    ISBN 9780520300682 (paperback)
Subjects: LCSH: Blacks—England—Birmingham—Social conditions—
    20th century. | Handsworth (Birmingham, England)—Social
    conditions—20th century. | Handsworth (Birmingham, England)—
    Race relations—History—20th century.
Classification: LCC DA690.B6 (ebook) | LCC DA690.B6 C76 2019 (print) |
    DDC 305.896/042496—dc23
LC record available at https://lccn.loc.gov/2018036127

Manufactured in the United States of America

26 25 24 23 22 21 20 19
10 9 8 7 6 5 4 3 2 1

*For A. S. F.
and
in memory of K. H. C.*

CONTENTS

List of Illustrations — ix
Acknowledgments — xi
Abbreviations — xiii

Introduction: Black Handsworth — 1

1. Shades of Black: Political and Community Groups — 18
2. Visualizing Handsworth: The Politics of Representation — 53
3. Dread Culture: Africa in Handsworth — 91
4. Leisure and Sociability: The Black Everyday — 119

Epilogue — 157

Notes — 163
Bibliography — 191
Index — 217

ILLUSTRATIONS

1. Demolition site in Handsworth, 1979   *63*
2. Handsworth Self-Portrait Project, 1979   *65*
3. Tabloid front-page article, "War on the Streets," 1985   *75*
4. Baptism, ca. late 1970s   *78*
5. Band rehearsal, ca. late 1970s   *78*
6. Couple dancing, ca. late 1970s   *80*
7. Boy with a flag, ca. 1970s   *81*
8. African Liberation Day, 1977   *82*
9. "A day trip to Skegness"   *83*
10. Confrontation between the police and two black men, 1985   *85*
11. Cover of Steel Pulse's *Handsworth Revolution*, 1978   *92*
12. Kokuma Dance Company performing *The History of the Drum*, 1992   *99*
13. Kokuma Dance Company, 1992   *101*
14. Francis Nation (r.), Handsworth Continental Cricket Club, ca. early 1980s   *125*
15. Handsworth Continental Cricket Club, ca. early 1980s   *128*
16. Men playing dominoes in the Bull's Head pub, ca. early 1980s   *135*
17. Photograph taken at Earnest Dyche Portraiture Studio, ca. early 1960s   *145*
18. Photo from *Auntie Linda's Front Room* series, 1987   *151*
19. *The West Indian Front Room*, Geffrye Museum of the Home, 2005   *153*

ACKNOWLEDGMENTS

This book is the culmination of many years' work. It is the product of scores of interviews in cafés, libraries, and front rooms; of early-morning writing routines in bedrooms, in offices, and at kitchen tables; of conversations with friends, loved ones, and colleagues; and of an infinite number of cups of very strong coffee. Because of this, there are a great many people without whom a book of this kind would never have been possible. First of all, a huge thank-you to all those people who took the time to talk to a young student about their memories of 1980s Handsworth. All of them shaped this book in indispensable ways, though special thanks are due to Vanley Burke, Pogus Caesar, and Brian Homer, who gave up far more of their time than they had to and have subsequently become much-valued collaborators and friends. Thanks also to all those photographers who granted me permission to use their work in this book and to the Arts and Humanities Research Council, which at various points provided a crucial source of funding that allowed me the time and space to research and write it.

Academically, over the years a large number of colleagues have offered invaluable support, guidance, and friendship. At the University of Birmingham, I am grateful to the late Michael Green for the coffees, cakes, and crucial cultural studies connection. Thanks to Dave Gunning, who cosupervised my PhD; Tony Kushner, who examined it and helped me to think about how I could develop it; and Richard Clay, for too many pints to mention. Thanks also to Chris Moores and Gavin Schaffer, for the advice and, just as important, the football chat. The History Department at Queen's has provided an incredibly supportive environment in which to finish this project, and thanks particularly to Sean O'Connell, who kindly read sections of the final manuscript. I would also like to thank the anonymous reviewers of that manuscript and James Vernon, the editor of the Berkeley Series in British Studies at University of California Press, who bought into the project from the beginning and offered input and feedback that went far beyond the call of duty. What follows is an infinitely better book because of it. Finally, it is difficult to quantify the debt of gratitude I owe to Matthew Hilton for believing in an enthusiastic MA student and for subsequently becoming a much-valued PhD supervisor, collaborator, mentor, and friend. Thank you.

I would also like to thank my friends and family. Thanks to Josie Kelly, who employed me as a postgrad on the basis of a Specials badge and to whom I will eventually return her voice recorder. Thanks to the Hall Green and Badock crews for the endless nights of escapism, and to my brother Laurence Connell for always being there. Finally, I would like to thank my parents. My mother, Myra Connell, has read almost every draft of everything I have ever written. She has been a constant source of emotional and intellectual support and remains a complete inspiration. My father, John Dalton, provided the initial spark for many of this book's key themes through his involvement in Birmingham's community arts scene. He died in March 2013 and left a big gap behind. Without either mum or dad, none of this would be possible.

ABBREVIATIONS

AAM	Anti-Apartheid Movement
ACDL	Anglo-Caribbean Dominoes League
ACSHO	African-Caribbean Self-Help Organisation
AFFOR	All Faiths for One Race
ANL	Anti-Nazi League
ARC	Asian Resource Centre
AYM	Asian Youth Movement
BAFC	Black Audio Film Collective
BBS	Birmingham Black Sisters
CCCS	Centre for Contemporary Cultural Studies
ESN	educationally subnormal
EU	European Union
FCF	Faith and Confidence Finance
GLC	Greater London Council
HCTP	Handsworth Community Theatre Project
IRR	Institute of Race Relations
IT	*International Times*
IWA	Indian Workers' Association
NF	National Front
RAAS	Racial Adjustment Action Society
RAR	Rock Against Racism
UCPA	Universal Coloured People's Association
UKIP	UK Independence Party
WASU	West African Students Union
WELD	Westminster Endeavour for Liaison and Development
WMCC	West Midlands County Council

Introduction
Black Handsworth

In 1981 a vision of Africa arrived in a district of Birmingham, Great Britain's second largest city. In the small garden behind its premises in Handsworth, an inner area to the north of the city, a community center unveiled what it called its "African village." Replete with thatched huts, climbing plants, and a pond containing a crocodile crafted out of a chain of elm logs, its aim was to disrupt the well-worn stereotypes surrounding those formerly slum neighborhoods that, like Handsworth, had become home to immigrants from Britain's colonies and former colonies in the postwar years. Pitched as an "African oasis" less than two miles from Birmingham's central hub of modernist shopping malls and concrete subways, the village was certainly an unusual addition to the city's postindustrial landscape. But it was in keeping with an internationalist line of vision the community center had adopted since opening in 1978 as the Handsworth Cultural Centre. At the heart of this was an emphasis on an exploration of the transnational networks and movements that made up what has been termed the "black globality."[1] Inside the center, for example, well-worn posters of Bob Marley and Angela Davis framed a rehearsal space used by a troupe made up of local teenagers who were developing specialisms in Nigerian and Azanian dance. In January 1980 the center raised funds for sixteen young people to visit Jamaica to learn about the island's culture and meet with grandparents, siblings, and other relatives; three years later, to a predictable outcry about the prospect of a "rain dance on the rates," more funds were raised, this time to send a group to Ghana to research West African dancing and drumming techniques.[2]

The center's primary users were the children of the generation of Caribbean migrants who had journeyed to the British metropole in the 1950s and early 1960s, often drawn to Birmingham because of the labor shortages in the region's manufacturing and vehicle industries.[3] By the time the Handsworth Centre opened its doors in 1978, this generation had become formerly colonial peoples, with the last vestiges of Britain's formal empire having largely been swept away.[4] Yet this was an ambiguous moment, something made apparent when, in April 1982, Margaret Thatcher's first Conservative government embarked on a military conflict with Argentina over the Falkland Islands, a British Overseas Territory in the South Atlantic Ocean with a predominantly white population of some eighteen hundred people. The eventual defeat of Argentina helped to stir up a patriotic fervor in Britain that, according to one Conservative minister, "'finally laid the ghost'" of Britain's 1956 humiliation over the Suez Canal.[5]

Located on Hamstead Road, a busy thoroughfare connecting Handsworth with the city center to the south and the affluent Handsworth Wood district to the north, the center's African village was indicative of a different sensibility. It was shaped not only by the black globality but also—as the trips the center arranged to the Caribbean and West Africa suggest—by the lived presence of what might be understood as a "diasporan consciousness."[6] These parallel developments, fueled as they were by contrasting transatlantic perspectives, help introduce a particular set of questions. What, for example, was the significance of a community center opening a mock African village as Britain was about to embark on a conflict so intimately connected with its imperial past? In what other ways was this diasporan consciousness manifest in Handsworth, and what does its presence tell us about the experience of being black in 1980s Britain? How did this consciousness impact Britain's key sites of postwar black settlement, of which Handsworth was only one prominent example? And what can an exploration of the specifics of such a locale tell us about the nature of postcolonial Britain? In this book's reconstruction of 1980s "black Handsworth," these are the questions that provide its guiding focus.

Black Handsworth emerged in the context of what has become the familiar story of postwar migration. The 1948 British Nationality Act was a key legislative marker that in theory granted equal citizenship to all subjects across the empire, even if the act was a politically expedient attempt to respond, following the 1947 partition of India, to the growing specter of imperial decline. Prewar black activists in Britain and specifically London often based their campaigns for racial equality on a demand for citizenship rights that materially advanced the status of black populations across the empire. The passage of the 1948 act meant that when the postwar generation became only the latest example of a long-standing tradition of black subjects settling in the imperial "mother country," they did so as British citizens who could make assertive claims about their right to be there on an equal footing with longtime residents of the metropole.[7] By 1961, 10 percent of the Handsworth population, or some 2,656 residents, had been born in the "New Commonwealth," with the vast majority coming from the Anglophone Caribbean.

Within a decade, largely as a result of the arrival of migrants from the Indian subcontinent and those Asian communities that had been expelled from East Africa in the late 1960s, this number had almost doubled, to 5,407, or almost 20 percent of the local population.[8] Taking into account their British-born children, in 1985 close to 60 percent of the Handsworth population was of African Caribbean or South Asian descent.[9]

By this time, Handsworth had become well established in the popular imaginary as one of Britain's "race relations capitals."[10] This occurred in the context of the growing notoriety of the British midlands more generally and was closely aligned to an acute sense of disorientation among Britain's body politic as those who had previously been heavily invested in the status of empire struggled to come to terms with its loss and the simultaneous presence of one-time colonial subjects "at home."[11] An early forerunner was the 1958 riots in Nottingham in the east midlands, during which gangs of white youths attacked members of the growing black community in the St. Ann's district of the city (events that were quickly followed by similar disturbances in the Notting Hill area of London).[12] Six years later, in the 1964 general election, the Conservative candidate Peter Griffiths won a shock victory over shadow foreign secretary Patrick Gordon Walker in Smethwick, a racially mixed constituency a short drive from the center of Handsworth. Griffith's overtly racist campaign unsettled the political establishment and for a time helped make Smethwick a watchword for what had apparently become Britain's heightened climate of racial tension.[13] This was magnified when in April 1968 Enoch Powell made his often-cited race relations speech at a central Birmingham hotel, using the complaints of his white constituents in nearby Wolverhampton as the basis for a near-apocalyptic vision of racial violence played out on the streets of Britain's inner cities. His Birmingham speech cemented Powell's position as one of the country's most prominent, self-anointed spokespeople on race. By the end of the 1960s, to a backdrop of strikes in protest against his sacking from the shadow cabinet, Powell was advocating the establishment of a new ministry for the repatriation of immigrants.[14]

Handsworth itself was properly transposed into the national imaginary with the moral panic over black street crime or "mugging" that, with the enduring influence of Powell and a marked growth in electoral support for the neo-Nazi National Front (NF), followed a particularly violent attack in the Villa Road area in November 1972. Through the close involvement of one of its students in Handsworth, the case captured the attention of the Centre for Contemporary Cultural Studies (CCCS), the influential research unit that had been established in 1964 by the literary critic Richard Hoggart as a space—attached to Birmingham University in the south of the city—for the scholarly research of popular culture.[15] Spearheaded by the Jamaican intellectual Stuart Hall, who in 1951 had made his own journey across the Atlantic to study at Oxford and by the early 1970s had replaced Hoggart as the CCCS director, a team of researchers argued that street crime in areas like Handsworth was functioning as a lightning rod for much more fundamental anxieties about the fracturing of the postwar consensus, the end of empire, and a more general sense of British "declinism." The understanding of mugging as a supposedly "black," specifically male crime built on earlier anxieties around black masculinity and, it was argued, was a signal that race had become the prism through which the engulfing sense of crisis was mediated.[16] This was increasingly marshaled by a nationalistic "new" right, which presented its law and order agenda as the solution to the nation's ills.[17] In an essay published in the run-up to the 1979 general election, Hall outlined what he saw as the connections between the mugging panic and the rise of what he called Thatcherism, and suggested that many of the themes articulated in their most extreme form by Powell and the NF had become a key element of the Conservative Party's new authoritarian agenda.[18] With the passing of the 1981 British Nationality Act, which effectively abandoned the core principles enshrined by its predecessor some three decades earlier, and with the 1982 conflict with Argentina, the extent to which Thatcher was able to disavow Britain's imperial past while simultaneously stirring up patriotic, proto-imperialistic sentiment became clear.[19]

The status of the black inner city as a violent and near-pathological threat to "British ways of life" was secured following two outbreaks of major rioting at the beginning of the 1980s and again in 1985. Although the unrest in 1981 included Handsworth, the most serious events were in Brixton in south London, which prompted a public inquiry led by Lord Scarman, the former head of the Law Commission.[20] But the outbreak of further unrest four years later seemingly confirmed the idea that Britain's inner cities were in a profound state of crisis, and that race was the primary interpretive mechanism for what was thought to be at stake. The rioting in Handsworth—which took place in September 1985 and was concentrated around the Lozells Road, less than a mile away from the Handsworth Cultural Centre on Hamstead Road—left an estimated £15million worth of damage to property, scores of injuries, and the deaths of the two Asian proprietors of the Lozells Road Post Office. For Margaret Thatcher, reflecting on the events some weeks later, any suggestion that the social conditions of such areas were a contributing factor in the rioting was misleading. Unemployment may "breed frustration," she declared, but it was "an insult to the unemployed to suggest that a man who doesn't have a job is likely to break the law."[21] Instead, West Midlands Police constable Geoffrey Dear suggested Handsworth's rioters had been "driven on by bloodlust," while to the Conservative member of Parliament (MP) Nicholas Fairbairn, the reasons for what had happened were simple: "The West Indians are lazy, the Asians are enterprising.... [T]he West Indians are jealous of the Asians."[22] Others argued that the riots offered further evidence that Britain's inner cities, having already undergone a process of "white flight," were destined to follow an

American trajectory of urban race relations.[23] Handsworth was conceptualized as the "bleeding heart of England," a front line in what had become a "war on the streets." Following subsequent disturbances on London's Broadwater Farm estate and again in Brixton, in the view of another police chief the 1985 unrest constituted "'the worst rioting ever seen on the mainland.'"[24]

Inevitably such narratives ignored black perspectives in areas like Handsworth and what it meant to live race at the level of the community and the locale. As historians have come to assess this period, moreover, the emergent historiography has been shaped by a concurrent emphasis on ideological and political developments and the series of social and economic crises that increasingly dominated British political life. In many ways, as has been argued, the enduring emphasis on the implications of Thatcher's election as Conservative Party leader in 1975, and her three successive general election victories beginning in May 1979, has contributed to a characterization of the period often confined to Thatcher's own political terrain.[25] *Black Handsworth: Race in 1980s Britain* is engaged with a parallel milieu. In shifting the focus onto a specific urban space, the aim is to foreground the significance of those whom Michel de Certeau described as the "ordinary practitioners of the city."[26] In part, this is a story of how the black practitioners of Handsworth sought to negotiate the practical consequences of the racialized anxieties of a particular postcolonial moment. It is also a study that encapsulates the political campaigns that were fought within black Handsworth to redress the damaging inequalities that existed in areas such as housing and education, as well as the emergence of reappropriated versions of "blackness" that were used as the basis for cultural and political movements. Finally, it represents an examination of a more opaque habitus, of what Raymond Williams characterized as the "impulses, restraints [and] tones" of everyday life.[27] This book is about the experience of both living and articulating race in a particular locale: politically, culturally, and in everyday practices and patterns of sociability. In black Handsworth, I argue, this was structured by the routes, ideas, and "open horizons" that constituted the diasporic imaginary. And most significant of all was that this sensibility was being played out on Hamstead Road, Villa Road, Lozells Road, and countless other nondescript, often impoverished inner-city topographies across the country. Away from the political mobilization of what has been termed the "Powellian legacy of guilt-free British nationalism," and contrary to Britain's enduring inability to come to terms with the legacies of its imperial past, the black globality was restructuring Handsworth and similar localities across the country. In so doing, the diasporan consciousness was being established as a core presence in the landscapes of postcolonial Britain.[28]

The period under consideration constitutes what might be understood as a "long" 1980s that reaches back to encompass much of the previous decade. Certainly the mugging panic that erupted in late 1972 not only contributed to a climate in which the politics of Thatcherism was eventually able to thrive. More specifically, it prepared the ground for the heightened anxiety over the black inner city that crystallized around the disturbances of the 1980s. If this discourse had "entirely real" consequences for Britain's black population in terms of the establishment of a terrain that black people had to occupy, black communities were in this period also able to draw on an expanded range of resources with which to negotiate it.[29] This was symbolized most spectacularly by the arrival from Jamaica of Rastafarian reggae music, which had begun to make serious inroads into international markets in the early 1970s. In Britain this helped stimulate the birth of a domestic reggae scene and a cultural revival of a Pan-Africanist imaginary that popularized, often in loose, discursive terms, the political platforms and ideologies that during the interwar period had established London as a locus of Pan-African organization. And there are other factors that mark the period from the early 1970s to the later 1980s as a distinctive conjuncture. By this time, for example, many of the social clubs, churches, and other spaces that had often initially been set up as a first line of defense against the aggressive workings of the British color bar had begun to function as increasingly well-embedded institutions in areas like Handsworth, and as important facilitators of everyday sociability. By 1978 more than half of the black population of Handsworth owned their own homes, and a discernible cohort of young people—who had often been moved to Britain as infants in order to preempt the 1962 introduction of strict immigration controls—were beginning to reach school-leaving age.[30] In many ways, these themes are testaments to a significant shift having taken place among the black population, as those who had arrived in Britain as immigrants increasingly recognized themselves as settlers, rather than sojourners, and their children began to reach political maturity. With the passing of the 1976 Race Relations Act, which finally outlawed indirect discrimination in employment, education, and elsewhere, even the government had seemingly recognized the dramatic changes taking place within the "colored population," a growing proportion of which now constituted people born in Britain.[31] The consequences of these changes were only beginning to become clear in the context of the long 1980s.

By the 1990s a different atmosphere had seemingly emerged. The racialized moral panics continued, along with the police harassment of black communities and racial violence, of which the 1993 murder of the black teenager Stephen Lawrence in London is just one shocking example. But this was played out in the wider context of Britain's multicultural drift: the increasing prominence, particularly in the sphere of popular culture, of black public figures such as the newscaster Trevor McDonald and the footballer Paul Ince, who in the same year as Lawrence's murder became the first black player to captain the English national team. These examples had little to do with government policy, but they were indicative of an increasing, organic sense of familiarity with diversity in Britain and a recognition—in many cases a begrudging one—that this constituted a "natural and inevitable part of the 'scene.'"[32] By the end of the twentieth century, the official inquiry into the police's handling of the Lawrence murder had forced civil society into a belated recognition of the endemic problem of institutional racism, while the cultural reach of reggae and Rastafarianism in black communities had long since been overtaken by African American hip-hop and contemporary rhythm and blues (R & B).[33] It is an earlier diasporic formation that concerns this study, as well as its concurrent emphasis on the activities of the Friday night drinker, attendees at a Saturday evening reggae event, and the Sunday morning worshipper. In focusing on the long 1980s, this book takes the story of the black globality in Britain beyond the context of high imperialism that has hitherto largely preoccupied historians.[34] In so doing, it unearths a lived experience that testifies to the shifting landscapes of postcolonial Britain.

The African village that in 1981 became a feature of the Handsworth landscape was the brainchild of Bob Ramdhanie, a Trinidad-born probation worker who had run the Handsworth Cultural Centre, to which the village was attached, since its opening three years earlier. Based on one of the area's busy thoroughfares, which was made up of an increasingly dilapidated Victorian housing stock, to Ramdhanie was a space that could offer creative channels for black youth to navigate their experiences in inner-city Birmingham by locating them within a historical, transnational framework that encompassed the black globality. His "village" was in some ways an inversion of the exhibitions that were commonly held in Britain and elsewhere in the late nineteenth century, in which the ethnological ideologies of empire were communicated to Western audiences through displays of colonial subjects and installations offering supposedly authentic re-creations of native villages and exotic landscapes.[35] Ramdhanie's Handsworth village, in contrast, was aimed at the children of colonial immigrants and envisaged as just one element in a wider initiative that would enable his constituents to express themselves through a Pan-Africanist emphasis on "roots" culture, whether through music, dance, or other art forms. It was to be a space, Ramdhanie explained, where the "people who come and use our Centre, who may be in search of a cultural identity" would have something "more tangible": a physical nexus within Handsworth's urban geography.[36]

With its thatched huts and faux crocodile, the village was undoubtedly unconventional. But it spoke to a much more pervasive ethos in Handsworth, one that resonated on its streets, in the work of its artists and musicians, in the ideologies of its political organizations, and inside its pubs and social clubs. When in February 1965 Malcolm X visited the region, for example, a matter of weeks before his assassination in New York City, his presence acted as a boon to moves already afoot to develop British and regional iterations of Black Power. When eight years later Bob Marley and the Wailers released *Catch a Fire*, the album's Rastafarianism-inspired oeuvre helped make African iconography and styles an unmistakable feature of the Handsworth locale.[37] By the mid-1980s, the extent to which black Handsworth was shaped by a particular reading of the black globality was, one observer reflected of a visit to the area, emphasized by the colors of the flags and pendants that hung among the cafés and takeout joints on Lozells Road and Soho Road, Handsworth's main shopping streets, and from the rearview mirrors of its cars. These colors were the Jamaican yellow, green, and black, alongside the national colors of Trinidad and other Caribbean islands; the red, gold, and green of Ethiopia, the focus of Rastafarian and Pan-Africanist thought; and the red, green, and black associated with Marcus Garvey's historic brand of black nationalism.[38] It is this specifically African Caribbean formation that this book seeks to address.

There are important parallels here with the experiences of Britain's growing South Asian population. In contrast to what has become conventional usage in current popular British discourse, in the long 1980s *black* often functioned as a label claimed by South Asian as well as African Caribbean communities, as a way of reappropriating the monolithic stereotypes that immigrants encountered in Britain and emphasizing solidarity and mutual sites of political struggle.[39] There undoubtedly were numerous issues that transcended both populations, not least the effects of racial discrimination, physical violence, and a worsening economic climate that was felt particularly acutely in Britain's ethnically diverse inner cities. Moreover, the South Asian formation was also shaped by diasporic perspectives, as Asian communities invoked their own international linkages and made them a feature of the local geography.[40] However, as I show in chapter 1, the 1980s was actually the period in which a unified black politics was proving to be increasingly unsustainable. The explicitly narrow agenda of Handsworth's Black Power groups had meshed with the arrival of a Rastafarian moment energized by a particular African Caribbean trajectory. This functioned alongside spaces such as churches and pubs, which were often used to re-create what were understood to be distinctively Caribbean patterns of sociability, with corresponding locations also having been established by the Asian population. This is not to downplay the critical importance of the South Asian experience or the various forms of everyday multiculture that often functioned as a remarkable source of creativity within Britain's inner cities. But that, alongside the highly complex subject of South Asian ethnicity and the way in which Asian languages and religions functioned in the 1980s, is the subject of an altogether different study. Apart from chapter 1, which deals with black as a "political color," and unless otherwise stated, for the purposes of this book *black* is used to refer to a distinctive African Caribbean milieu.[41]

Black Handsworth attempts to excavate a particular black "structure of feeling." Raymond Williams coined the concept to refer to a whole way of living: a set of common experiences actively lived through shared outlooks, identities, and associations, and in forms of politics and everyday cultures.[42] As Williams reflected, the conjunction between structure and feeling was a deliberate attempt to capture a slippery and apparently contradictory social phenomenon. The notion of felt consciousness gets at a sense of intangibility, leaving room for a significant degree of variation and diversity. In Handsworth, as I demonstrate, the black structure of feeling was manifest variously as political ideology, art, leisure, and everyday practice. In places it was felt most acutely in terms of an increasing emotional nostalgia for the Caribbean and simultaneously a related aspirational desire to be seen to be "getting on" in Britain. Elsewhere, particularly for the black generation that had been born in Britain and was increasingly influenced by the interpretations of Rastafarianism found in the lyrics and on the album sleeves of Jamaican roots reggae, it was Africa and particularly Ethiopia that came to function as the symbolic, "imagined" basis for a modified black cultural and political identity. In Handsworth, therefore, the black structure of feeling was felt in distinct ways within particular locations. It constituted a diverse, though connected, patchwork of communities within which a particular combination of emotions, imaginaries, traditions, and political ideologies operated as the primary guiding force.

Yet on the other hand, this milieu was also structured. It constituted a pattern, a set with "specific, internal relations" that it is possible to "perceive operating."[43] First, inevitably, it was raced. Although there were white activists, artists, and others who identified themselves as allies of Handsworth's black population, and who are encountered at various stages throughout this book, being black in 1980s Britain meant having to come to terms with what Frantz Fanon encapsulated as the pervasive "fact of blackness" and the profoundly damaging effects of the white gaze: of having to inhabit subject positions generally coded by white society and attempting to both navigate and challenge the material consequences of racial discrimination. "I became black in London, not Kingston," Stuart Hall reflected, and it was with his move to provincial Birmingham in the mid-1960s that, for Hall, a particularly acute brand of racism came into view.[44] The climate of the 1980s had in various ways shifted, but with no less serious consequences, particularly for those black people who inhabited what many now conceptualized as Britain's overtly violent, riotous inner cities.

Second, this was a formation that was also often highly gendered. If the moral panics of the 1980s focused primarily on the image of the young black man as a perennial mugger or rioter, stereotypes about the supposed over-fecundity of black women, coupled with their status as migrant laborers, often meant that they were represented in relation to an almost pathological emphasis—commonly articulated in the postwar sociological literature on race relations—on what was seen to be the fundamental inadequacies of black familial structures.[45] As I show, women were often able to subvert such narratives through the articulation of assertive versions of black femininity that emphasized respectability, religious spirituality, and the importance of cultural capital in spaces such as the church and the home. This came in the context of the manifestation of the more masculine Caribbean street and reggae cultures as they emerged and were reappropriated in Handsworth, and a political culture in which women activists often found themselves fighting on a number of different fronts. Here, this was not only a project to challenge and attempt to alleviate the damaging effects of societal racism. It also meant having to deal with a male gaze within black organizations and what could often be an unwillingness among some male activists to seriously engage with the highly specific inequalities that black women faced.[46]

Above all, however, the black structure of feeling was shaped by a diasporan consciousness and perspectives that traversed what Paul Gilroy encapsulated as the "black Atlantic."[47] This was present in the ideologies of Handsworth's political organizations, in which the struggles that were waged against domestic racism were understood in relation to global equality movements, both the contemporaneous anticolonial campaigns that were taking place in countries such Angola, Mozambique, and South Africa and a historic frame of reference that took inspiration from the fight against British colonialism and ongoing movements for race equality in the United States. It was there in the work of its artists, who saw themselves as engaged in a process of mapping black Handsworth in a manner that could contribute to the establishment of a visual archive that captured, at street level, the development and contradictions of postcolonial Britain. Finally, it was there in black Handsworth's lived cultures and patterns of sociability: in the African symbolism at the heart of its reggae cultures and styles, and in the practices that took place inside its pubs, churches, cricket clubs, and domestic interiors that helped establish the diverse and often ambiguous elements of the Caribbean inheritance as a forceful presence in the Handsworth locale.

Cast in this light, the experience of being black in 1980s Britain was a shared one. Running counter to another prevailing historical narrative of the period that sees the political ascendancy of Thatcherism as having corresponded with a growing individualism manifest across myriad locations and settings, in Handsworth, I argue, race was felt collectively as a structure of feeling.[48] Differently viewed, but avowedly black, it was a social process that had important effects on the contemporary conjuncture. First, the emphasis on diaspora and the black globality provided black Handsworth with a means of navigating and attempting to come to terms with the many inequalities of Thatcher's Britain. Second, this also posed challenges to popular and political attitudes toward Britain's imperial past: the enduring inability to come to terms with the black presence as a domestic transformation that was the direct result of Britain's one-time status as a colonial power, coupled with a widespread nostalgia for that status that was increasingly tapped into by the politics of Thatcherism and illustrated by the popular jingoism that greeted the 1982 conflict with Argentina. In spite of this, as Handsworth's black community developed its political programs, art forms, leisure spaces, and patterns of sociability, it was establishing a black, transnational sensibility as a powerful feature of the fabric of urban Britain.[49] It is in this sense that the story of Handsworth's African village was an apt metaphor for what was taking place around it. As perspectives oscillated between the global and the local, the routes that had once underpinned the empire were coming home. In Handsworth, what this in many ways amounted to was a postcolonial reordering from within. Ultimately, in the specific context of the enduring impression left behind by Britain's imperial past, this was heralding the unequivocal arrival of *black* Handsworth.[50]

. . .

This book is about a particular inner-city area of Birmingham and its black population, one that, reflecting more general migratory patterns from the Caribbean, was particularly dominated by people of Jamaican origin or descent.[51] The focus on Birmingham represents a pivot away from the dominant presence of London in the historiography, both in histories of race and immigration and across thematic areas and time frames.[52] The range of archival material relating to the capital means that its continuing allure for historians is in many ways understandable. Yet given London's size; specific geographic divisions; nature as a political, financial, and transportation hub; demographic mutability; and mythological status in popular and literary imaginaries, it is—as scholars of London generally concede—difficult to avoid the fact that it generally constitutes an atypical case study.[53] At the most basic level, the experience of navigating a city that by the early 1980s had a population more than six times greater than the next most populous cities of Birmingham and Manchester was qualitatively distinctive in ways that presented—with respect to the greater degree of anonymity a metropolis as big as London allows, for example—both challenges and opportunities.[54] Certainly histories of London commonly have little to say about the experience of inhabiting Britain's large and medium-sized cities. This is not to claim Handsworth as a district paradigmatic of black Britain. But it was at least broadly comparable in size to what had become identified, outside London, as Britain's other "race relations capitals": Moss Side in Manchester, Toxteth in Liverpool, and St. Paul's in Bristol. As long-standing port cities, Liverpool and Bristol played significant roles in the transatlantic slave trade and, like Cardiff in Wales, have a history of ethnic diversity stretching back at least to the late nineteenth century, when a transient population of black merchant seamen began to have a significant presence. Birmingham, by contrast, had no comparable prewar black presence and moreover is one of the most landlocked cities in the United Kingdom.[55] Yet this further emphasizes the significance of the transatlantic dialogues that, in the context of the long 1980s, sustained the lived cultures of one of its foremost black districts.

In many respects, Handsworth was unusual too. From the 1960s onward, for instance, as the midlands grew increasingly notorious as a supposed hotbed of racial discord, Handsworth captured the attention of a remarkable range of stakeholders.

This included academic researchers at Stuart Hall's CCCS and, later, a race relations institute at Warwick University headed by the South African sociologist John Rex, who was invested in a project to develop a modified sociology of race that moved away from the studies of the late 1940s and 1950s, which, as Chris Waters has shown, were often both highly racialized and intimately bound up with growing uncertainties about "Britishness" in the context of decolonization.[56] It also included charitable bodies, local and national journalists, writers, television producers, and filmmakers. Indeed, with every passing local incident interest in Handsworth grew, to the point at which one local minister felt moved to place a sign outside his church reminding passersby that "Handsworth is not a zoo."[57] Apart from the sociological investigations, sensationalist newspaper stories, and television news bulletins, by the long 1980s Handsworth had also become home to an extraordinary range of creative black talent. This included the reggae band Steel Pulse, formed in 1975 and whose debut album, *Handsworth Revolution* (1978), became an immediate UK hit; the poet Benjamin Zephaniah, who in the late 1970s honed his trade as a master of ceremonies (MC) on local reggae sound systems or hi-fis and in 2009 came in third in a poll to find Britain's favorite poet; the documentary photographer Vanley Burke, one of the most prominent chroniclers of postwar black settlement; and numerous other photographers, sound system performers, reggae bands, amateur memoirists, and dance troupes that achieved varying degrees of prominence. This talent ranged from Steel Pulse, who in 1987 became the first non-Jamaican act to receive a Grammy award for best reggae album, to the unheralded Jamaican writer whose memoirs of his life in Handsworth never made it into print, and included everything else in between.

It is this body of material that—alongside the literature of local political organizations and scores of interviews with a cast of characters who occupied various positions within the social fabric of black Handsworth—provides this book with its archival base. The limitations of such sources are well known. Certainly the material drawn upon here is by no means exhaustive. Many of the case studies under consideration—for example, pubs, cricket clubs, and reggae bands—functioned at least in part as sites for performances of masculinity, meaning the voices of women could in these instances often be more difficult to access. At the same time, the diversity of the sources that have been assembled does represent an attempt to get at a sense of lived consciousness that for Williams was encapsulated by the notion of a structure of feeling.[58] And it also indicates the extent to which this study sits at the intersections between social and cultural history and the related field of cultural studies. As Geoff Eley has pointed out, some of the earliest work on the legacies of empire and its place within the domestic British milieu emanated not from within the discipline of history, but from scholars operating within the often-marginalized field of cultural studies in the late 1970s and 1980s.[59] In what became seminal interventions, *Policing the Crisis* (the CCCS study of the moral panic around mugging), the jointly authored *The Empire Strikes Back*, and Paul Gilroy's *There Ain't No Black in the Union Jack* (which began life as his doctoral dissertation at the CCCS) aimed to bring race to bear on cultural studies and its by now familiar ways of operating: the use of Williams and continental Marxism as theoretical paradigms; the rigorous appraisal of the spectrum of popular cultural forms; and the anthropological understanding of culture that saw it as embedded in people's everyday behaviors and patterns of living. While a subsequent historiography began to engage with the project of unpicking the ambivalent presence of the imperial legacy in postcolonial Britain, with respect to the latter decades of the twentieth century, works emanating from the cultural studies tradition have largely been left to dominate the field.[60]

My own work builds on this approach in order excavate and foreground the significance of black cultural forms, political movements, art, leisure, and sociability. The arguments made by Hall, Gilroy, and others are engaged with throughout this book, but these scholars also often appear as historical characters who were in different ways shaped by the social and political climates they were each attempting to understand. Hall in particular is a pervasive figure. As the recipient of a Rhodes scholarship to study at Oxford, his was undoubtedly a highly specific trajectory. But his middle-class upbringing in Jamaica would to some extent have been a familiar habitus to many postwar Caribbean immigrants.[61] Moreover, he shared with them the disorientation that came with the realization that the move to the metropole often corresponded with the effective dissolution of both the Caribbean "pigmentocracy," in which class and social position were closely aligned to the particularities of skin tone, as well as the specificities of island-based national identities.[62] The parallel arrival of that early generation of Caribbean migrants on boats such as the SS *Windrush*, "dressed to the nines" in suits and frocks indicative of a determination to make an impression in Britain, constituted for Hall—as he recounted in his posthumously published memoir *Familiar Stranger*—a highly emotive moment. In 1979, having followed many of this generation to Birmingham, Hall left the CCCS to take up a professorship at the Open University. It was during this period that he became an important sounding board for a cohort of British-born black artists who were, from their own particular vantage points, attempting to use their work to grapple with many of the subjects that energized Hall throughout his life, including a number of artists emanating from, or engaging with, Handsworth specifically. Hall was at different times part of the academic surveillance of Handsworth, not only in the context of his work on the mugging panic, but also with respect to his later role as a member of the independent inquiry into the 1985 riots. He was in a whole host of ways at more than one remove from black Handsworth. But he was also in dialogue with it and, more generally, both a chronicler and a product of a diasporic trajectory between two islands, the legacies of which, at a specific time and space, this book seeks to understand.[63]

Honing in on black Handsworth is an approach that, in also drawing on the field of microhistory, allows us to see the complexities of community formation in the long 1980s in "microscopic detail," foreground the activities of a range of previously marginalized actors, and place them alongside prominent figures such as Hall at the center of the historical narrative.[64] If Handsworth was in many ways exceptional, it also existed as part of what had by the 1980s become a well-established, interlinked network of black localities throughout Britain. For example, its sound systems and cricket teams competed against similar outfits from Leicester, London, Nottingham, and elsewhere; its political organizations shared platforms with like-minded groups from across the country and took part in many of the same campaigns; and its artists attended each other's exhibition openings and film screenings and often sought to use their work to address many of the same issues. If the focus on black Handsworth casts light on these translocal dynamics, a microhistorical approach can, as Lara Putnam has suggested, paradoxically also contribute to a better understanding of how transnationalism and diasporas operate in practice: of how ideas and social networks move across oceans and national borders; the diverse ways in which they are utilized and experienced by people in their day-to-day lives; and how they impact life in a particular locale as new political programs are implemented, artwork is created, and social institutions are established.[65] This book testifies to the enduring significance of the black globality in the ambiguous context of postcolonial Britain. In this respect, as the effects of immigration were playing out in Britain in a radically altered geopolitical climate, what follows might also be seen as part of an emergent, far larger historical project to understand how late twentieth-century globalization was experienced, but also shaped, at the national, regional, and micro levels.[66]

Black Handsworth begins by demonstrating the ways in which the black globality was used by Handsworth's political organizations as a means of framing the struggles they waged locally over issues such as a culturally insensitive education system, a lack of adequate housing, and the passing of ever-more-restrictive immigration controls. This perspective, "lodged between the local and the global," for some organizations formed the basis of a strategically inclusive politics that emphasized the shared trajectories of Handsworth's African Caribbean and South Asian populations: both a historic relationship to British colonialism and the mutual attempts at navigating the effects of what was understood as a form of neocolonialism in contemporary Britain.[67] But as these global perspectives played out in the locale, chapter 1 suggests, this notionally inclusive "black" political platform was beginning to break down. Activists increasingly saw their role in Handsworth as committed social workers, as well as, more conventionally, lobbyists and political campaigners. In wanting to develop practical responses to the many inequalities that were faced by their constituents, however, many often found this necessitated ethnically tailored responses. To some extent, as women activists fought to gain recognition of the particular position black and Asian women were in, this is in keeping with the familiar narrative of the fragmentation of new social movements and the concurrent rise of identity politics. However, as subsequent chapters make clear, this is also a story about the growing importance within African Caribbean communities of a specific reading of the black globality and the reemergence—culturally, as well as politically—of a Pan-Africanist frame of reference.

Chapter 2 moves from the domain of formal politics to the politics of representation in the context of the ongoing moral panic around the supposedly violent, insurrectional threat posed by the black inner city and the parallel emergence of a nationwide black arts scene developed by practitioners from within neighborhoods like Handsworth. Focusing specifically on the visual arts, the chapter shows how local artists were engaged in a dual project to, on the one hand, undermine the images of rioting, violence, and conflict that had come to define the black inner city in the popular imaginary, and, on the other hand, contribute to an expanded archive of the development of postcolonial Britain. For some practitioners—such as the London-based filmmakers the Black Audio Film Collective (BAFC), whose 1986 documentary *Handsworth Songs* marked a key intervention in Handsworth's visual cultures—this meant seeking to connect contemporary race relations discourse with the legacies of colonialism in order to disrupt the widespread social and political disavowal of Britain's imperial past. For others, such as the documentary photographer Vanley Burke, it meant a quasi-anthropological ambition to record a more community-oriented formation and the political marches, reggae concerts, street styles, pubs, churches, and other institutions that testified to the establishment and evolution of black Handsworth. In both cases, there could often be a tension between the desire to present an ostensibly authentic image of postcolonial Britain and the perennial appearance in artists' work of images that could conform to the stereotypes commonly found in the pages of tabloid newspapers. Nevertheless, taken together, this body of work is seen as forming part of a shared political project, one that constitutes an alternative, if at times problematic, visual cartography of a black locality—one that in many ways the remainder of this book sets out to understand.[68]

The final two chapters interrogate Handsworth's everyday social life and the presence of the diasporan consciousness within it. They traverse contrasting diasporic routes, in which the emphasis shifts from the figure of Africa and specifically Ethiopia in chapter 3 to, in the final chapter, the invocation of Caribbean symbolism and patterns of sociability. Chapter 3 charts the reemergence—more than four decades after London had become a hotbed of Pan-African political organization—of more general, cultural, and social iterations of a Pan-Africanist outlook. Prompted by the transatlantic crossing of Rastafarianism via Jamaican reggae music, this was manifest in a diverse range of settings, from theater and dance groups and the work of reggae bands and "dub poets," to the prominence of a Rastafarian style and a related subculture that revolved around sound system events. In this often masculine milieu, African and Ethiopian imagery contributed to an imagined transnational community that helped a young black generation in particular to enact a powerful reappropriation of blackness and, in so doing, negotiate the inequalities they encountered in the context of 1980s Britain. Chapter 4, with its emphasis on the case studies of a cricket club, pubs, churches, and the home, enters into the most quotidian elements of everyday life. It finds that for the older generations that largely occupied these spaces, the practices that took place inside were a means of evoking their previous lives in the Caribbean: for example, the adoption of what was seen as a specifically West Indian style of cricket; the centrality of the pub game dominoes; the importance attached to a specific style of religious worship; and, entering into the domestic sphere, a particular aesthetic in which the front room functioned, for women in particular, as a key signifier of status and cultural capital. The sociability inside these spaces gets at the enduring ambiguities of the Caribbean inheritance: the lingering, lived presence of a Victorian colonial ethos, an aspirational desire for respectability in Britain, and—signaling a move from an imagined community to an emotional one—an affective attachment to life in the Caribbean. Having unequivocally moved from the status of sojourners to settlers, Britain's black population continued to look out across the black globality. In so doing, they were establishing this particular diasporic formation as an assertive presence in the one-time mother country.

There are certainly absences in this story and areas that warrant a more detailed exploration than *Black Handsworth* can provide. For example, while chapter 1 deals with the alternative, "supplementary" schools that were set up by black activists in response to the ethnocentricity of the mainstream curriculum, more historical work is required to trace the long-term effects of inequalities in schooling and the impact of the "multicultural" reforms that were gradually introduced from the mid-1970s onward.[69] Likewise, the issue of employment—so central to narratives of postwar migration and, in a different way, to understandings of the effects of the fracturing of the postwar political consensus in Britain—needs to be more fully examined in relation to black communities. This not only includes the ongoing demands for trade unions to seriously mobilize to counteract racial discrimination in the workplace, but also the ways in which the particularities of class, age, and gender within black communities influenced experiences of a rapidly changing economic climate. Education, work, and trade unionism each held prominent positions in what would become the classic social histories of working-class life in Britain that were published in the 1970s and 1980s.[70] If these themes are relatively absent here, in other respects the spatial settings I do examine—for example, social clubs, pubs, churches, and domestic interiors—echo the other case studies drawn upon by historians in their explorations of late nineteenth- and early twentieth-century working-class formations.[71] These works were often indebted to *The Uses of Literacy* (1957)—Richard

Hoggart's classic, semiautobiographical study of class and community in the Hunslet district of Leeds—and were published just as Hoggart's cultural studies project was developing out of his Birmingham Centre into a dramatically expanded examination of the politics of representation.[72] In different ways, both traditions have guided the rationale for the choice of case studies in this book.

The later chapters, in their focus on black Handsworth's musical forms and sites of leisure, perhaps stand out as having the most obvious parallels with an earlier brand of social history. The opening chapters, in contrast, are concerned less with how the black structure of feeling was lived on a day-to-day basis in Handsworth than with the ways in which it was articulated and represented: first ideologically, through forms of community politics, and then artistically, primarily through photography and film. It is chapter 2, "Visualizing Handsworth," that draws most explicitly on work emanating from cultural studies. This chapter not only acts as a bridge connecting the study of Handsworth's formal political activity with the later chapters that examine music, leisure, and everyday life. It also emphasizes the central role of representation in community formation. As I show, this was often aimed at external audiences, as part of an attempt by Handsworth artists to both neutralize and challenge the potency of racialized stereotypes regarding the black inner city. But it also had important internal functions, as a means of recording key moments in the development of a particular black locality: marriages, funerals, and political marches. It was thus simultaneously part of an ongoing process of reimagining a black sensibility that was, it was becoming clear, increasingly grounded both in Handsworth and in Britain.

Like all historians, I am an outsider to my subject. Moreover, although the germination of *Black Handsworth* came with my own formation in inner-city Britain in a different time and space, I have never had firsthand experience of what bell hooks famously described as the "killing rage" that the prevalence of racial discrimination can induce.[73] If a key aim of this book is to emphasize the importance of everyday cultures and ordinary experiences, this is not—as Raymond Williams reminded us—to vacate the arena of politics.[74] The black structure of feeling had far-reaching implications. In the context of the long 1980s and the resolute presence of Britain's postcolonial amnesia, it was part of a process of confronting Britain with the implications of its imperial past and, in so doing, of moving toward the belated decolonization of the metropole itself.[75] But the importance of race in 1980s Britain should also be understood on its own terms. What I describe in the pages that follow represents just one manifestation of what might be conceptualized as the "diaspora-ization" of urban Britain.[76] Propelled by the transatlantic energies of the black globality, this was a process that, paradoxically, was enabling a black community to arrive at a sense of rootedness in the one-time mother country. Black Handsworth in the long 1980s is just one chapter in the continuing story of the making of black Britain.

1

Shades of Black

Political and Community Groups

INTRODUCTION

On 4 and 5 June 1977, as Britain was readying its street parties, processions, and Union Jack bunting for the queen's forthcoming Silver Jubilee, the Handsworth-based African-Caribbean Self-Help Organisation (ACSHO) hosted Birmingham's inaugural African Liberation Day. The idea had first been mooted by newly independent African states in the late 1950s, and the date had been set as 25 May to mark the anniversary of the formation of the Organisation of African Unity, a coalition committed to ending all colonial influence across the continent.[1] A decade later, African Liberation Day began to be picked up across the black globality. In the United States the Black Power activist Owusu Sadaukai envisaged that it would be a means of drawing public attention to events in apartheid South Africa, as well as emphasizing "'the relationship between what is happening to our people in Africa and what is happening to us in the United States and other places.'" Drawing on a network of support that included prominent civil rights and Black Power groups, Sadaukai's 1972 Liberation Day comprised a demonstration in Washington, D.C., of thirty thousand participants and protests outside the Portuguese and South African embassies.[2] In Handsworth five years later, events consisted of poetry readings, music, drama, and workshops, and culminated in a march of one thousand people from a local school to Handsworth Park. The ACSHO shared Sadaukai's rationale for a Liberation Day as a means of emphasizing the transatlantic connections between liberation movements in Africa and political struggles across the diaspora and, given the historic role of jubilee events as a means of generating loyalty to the British Empire, no doubt recognized the political symbolism of staging the event over jubilee weekend. In the context of recent declarations of sovereignty in Angola and Mozambique, the group pitched its Liberation Day as a simultaneous celebration of victories in the struggle against colonialism and an expression of a commitment to defeating "'the last colonial outposts'" overseas, as well as what was understood as domestic neocolonialism in contemporary Britain. The overarching theme of the event was "'Africans in struggle at home and abroad.'"[3]

Similar events were subsequently held in London and Manchester, though by the 1980s the ACSHO had become the main organizational driver behind African Liberation Day in Britain.[4] The group had been established in the mid-1960s to attempt to combat the racism black communities faced across British society, but it maintained a line of analysis that placed these struggles in the context of worldwide anticolonial and antiracist movements past and present. It was therefore part of a long-standing tradition of black political organization in Britain stretching back at least to the 1930s, when London in particular had become a focal point for Pan-Africanist mobilization thanks to the activities of black students, intellectuals, and other sojourners, who used the city as a base for the development of campaigns against empire and demands for the advancement of the rights of black populations within it.[5] A more immediate influence on the ACSHO was the political associations and pressure groups that were set up to advocate on behalf of the growing black population in the 1950s and 1960s. Although the battles fought in this period were largely stimulated by domestic flashpoints, activists again emphasized a perspective that encompassed the black Atlantic. Activists such as the Trinidadian journalist Claudia Jones drew parallels between the struggles of "'Afro-American freedom fighters'" and domestic campaigns against racist violence, the British color bar, and the onset of increasingly discriminatory immigration legislation.[6] The transatlantic nature of these currents was signified in 1965 when, following the Conservative candidate Peter Griffiths's shock election victory in Smethwick, the Indian Workers' Association (IWA) extended an invitation to Malcolm X to pay a visit to Griffiths's new constituency, two miles from the IWA's base in Handsworth. If his earlier spells in London and Oxford had contributed to his characterization of the sun finally setting on the "'monocled, pith-helmeted'" British colonialist, Malcolm X's stint in the midlands prompted him to reach for another analogy: black people in Smethwick were, he told reporters, being treated "'in the same way as the Negroes ... in Alabama—like Hitler and the Jews.'"[7]

Focusing on the ACSHO, the IWA, and other local organizations, this chapter unpicks the nature of black politics in Handsworth over the long 1980s. As the ACSHO's rhetoric around African Liberation Day suggests, what Kennetta Hammond Perry has underlined as the "overlapping imperial, diasporic and global valences" of black politics in the 1950s and 1960s continued to resonate in the politics of Handsworth-based organizations in the later period.[8] What was distinctive, however, was the extent to which this perspective was able to contribute to mobilizations across ethnic lines, as a growing South Asian population took up residence alongside African Caribbean communities in Britain's inner cities. To varying degrees, it has been argued, groups in the 1960s emphasized the importance of an inclusive politics based on mutual experiences of discrimination and a shared relationship to empire. In February 1962, for example, the newly established Afro-Asian-Caribbean Conference urged all "'Afro-Asian-Caribbean citizens'" of Britain to march on the House of Commons to protest against the imminent passing of the Commonwealth Immigrants Act. Other groups likewise adopted an inclusive outlook that was at once "transracial, multiethnic and universal," something anticipated by Claudia Jones in 1959 when she renamed her campaigning organ *The West Indian Gazette* so that it included the epigraph *And Afro-Asian Caribbean News*.[9] By the later 1960s, influenced by the spread of Black Power across the Atlantic following the visits of Malcolm X, Stokely Carmichael, and other American-based activists and the formation of groups such as the Universal Coloured People's Association (UCPA), this unity began to manifest itself among immigrant communities with a shared embrace of the semiotic power of "black."[10] Just as Carmichael had emphasized the importance of the "Third World" jointly mobilizing under the Black Power program, so in this milieu a "peculiarly British notion of 'blackness'" was said to have emerged in which the generalizations and stereotypes immigrants faced upon their arrival in Britain were reappropriated into an internationalist tool of political unity. According to Ambalavener Sivanandan, the Sri Lankan activist and one-time affiliate of the reconstituted UCPA, black had begun to be understood as a "political colour" to which Africans, Caribbeans, and Asians could each lay claim.[11]

This is an important reminder of the malleability of *black* in postwar British discourse. In order to examine the nature of black politics in Handsworth, in this chapter it is necessary to include an interrogation of those South Asian organizations that also sought to mobilize under the same inclusive banner. Indeed, the long 1980s have been identified as the period during which the encompassing notion of *black* fragmented, giving rise to a "community of communities" that focused on cultural differences rather than on sites of mutual solidarity.[12] This has commonly been attributed to the state's embrace of a policy of multiculturalism in the early 1980s, in particular its monetary arm, which increasingly allocated funds to minority groups on the basis of ethnicity.[13] Following the recommendations of the Scarman report on the 1981 Brixton riots and the lead of Ken Livingstone's Greater London Council (GLC), local authorities in Birmingham and across the country began to roll out comprehensive multicultural programs that made funds available on the basis of increasingly narrow definitions of ethnicity. The result, it has been claimed, was the breaking down of black as a political color. The cohesion that had previously characterized black politics was eroded as the state began to absorb a generation of ethnically distinct, self-professed "community leaders" into its machinery. Black politics had been taken off the streets and into the council chamber, where, divided and then subdivided along ethnic lines, it became a scramble for state resources to fund what was now understood to be primarily a salaried exercise.[14]

This chapter offers an alternative story. While the specter of public funding has been presented as a marker signaling a shift from one form of politics to another, the relationship between a group's decision to accept state monies and its political ideology was in practice complex. In the first instance, as the opening section of the chapter demonstrates, the state had already begun to develop a pluralist conception of multiculture in the context of mid-century anxieties about decolonization and the viability of the Commonwealth, which coincided with moves to direct funds toward inner-city areas with large black and Asian populations. By the high point of multiculturalism of the 1980s, moreover, groups such as the IWA emphasized the importance of a unified definition of *black* and ongoing connections to global anticolonial struggles, yet simultaneously accepted state funds. The ACSHO argued vociferously against the practice of political organizations accepting state monies but subscribed to a version of Black Power as a global, yet explicitly narrow, African Caribbean identity. As shown here, the funding system undoubtedly favored those predominantly white, antiracist organizations born out of the New Left, which were often better placed to speak the state's language of multiculturalism. But there was no straightforward relationship between the proximity of a group to the state and its political agenda. Much more relevant was the expanded role local organizations increasingly sought to play. In the context of demographic shifts that saw the majority of the population of areas such as Handsworth become either immigrants or the descendants of immigrants, by the long 1980s the inadequacies of the state in addressing the issues faced by these communities had become apparent. The dedication of local organizations was such that many increasingly sought to simultaneously perform the roles of social agencies and campaigners, in an attempt to develop practical solutions to the inequalities that were experienced by their constituents. The problem for those subscribers to black as a political color, however, was that at the local level these issues were often manifested in ethnically specific ways.

For example, the IWA and the Asian Youth Movement (AYM), another group made up of South Asian activists, increasingly found that their time was spent attempting to help Handsworth residents deal with the threat of deportation—something that, following changes to the law in the 1980s, particularly affected South Asian communities. The ACSHO, in contrast, focused on the provision of alternative education for African Caribbean youth in the context of a growing awareness of the acute disadvantages this section of the community experienced in mainstream schooling. This was undoubtedly part of a wider story of the fragmentation of political identities in Britain. In Handsworth, women activists were also positing their own demands for a modification of black politics that would recognize—in opposition to what could often be the masculine organizational structures of many groups—the critical importance of issues such as domestic violence and the gendered, as well as raced, inequalities that black and Asian women faced. For all groups, it was the practical experience of black Handsworth—conflict with the police, racism in schools, a lack of suitable housing, the threat of deportation—that rendered the black globality both intelligible and, in the eyes of many, a political necessity. In Handsworth, the local facilitated the global. But it was also at the level of the local that ideas about an encompassing black political color weakened, particularly as the provision of ethnically tailored services increasingly took center stage. The issue was not so much the rise of the community leader, but rather the extent to which by the long 1980s the political activist was in many ways also compelled to perform the role of the dedicated social worker. Whether groups accepted state funding or not, in the context of the long 1980s a unified notion of blackness was becoming difficult to maintain.

STATE INTERVENTION

Both local and national governments had played a limited role in black and Asian community relations prior to the turning point of the 1981 urban unrest. In Birmingham the local authorities took the lead. In 1950, for example, Birmingham City Council established the Co-ordinating Committee for Coloured People, which consisted of representatives from local religious and voluntary organizations, and four years later it was the first authority to create the post of liaison officer for colored people, with the aim of acting as a bridge between the council and black community representatives.[15] Such initiatives were undoubtedly modest, and they also demonstrate the extent to which this fledgling approach to race relations was shaped by the legacies of empire; there were no black representatives on the Co-ordinating Committee, for example, and the post of liaison officer was initially held by a white former colonial officer who had served in Africa.[16] Nationally, the gathering pace of decolonization saw community relations manifested in other ways. In the early 1960s, influenced by the ongoing shock caused by the Suez Canal crisis as well as concerns about the viability of the Commonwealth in light of racial atrocities in South Africa, the British government agreed to sponsor an arts festival as a means of articulating a renewed vision for the Commonwealth. The festival took place in 1965. The aim, as Radhika Natarajan has shown, was to curate it in pluralist terms, as a means of generating cross-Commonwealth respect for diversity and difference. Planners often presented a nostalgic representation of Britain's imperial past, however, and virtually ignored the by now substantial Commonwealth populations actually residing in Britain. Moreover, the contrast between the festival's emphasis on equality and the government's concurrent, discriminatory attempts to restrict immigration was widely noted.[17] It was indicative of the then Labour government's ambivalence on the issue of race that the festival also coincided with what might be seen as the genesis of the multicultural policies that would be adopted on a much larger scale in later decades.

Nationally, the key marker was the 1965 Race Relations Act, which although limited in practice nevertheless for the first time formally outlawed racial discrimination in public places.[18] The Local Government Act of the following year also represented the moment the state began to play a significant monetary role in intercommunity relations. The act included a funding package for local authorities with large numbers of immigrants, which was primarily used to employ teachers with the relevant skills to teach English to Asian pupils in schools.[19] By 1969 the central government was contributing £15 million under the terms of the act, and there was a more general recognition among policy makers that inner cities—with their vastly disproportionate levels of unemployment, poverty, and immigration—were in a state of acute crisis.[20] Initially, wider policy responses were ostensibly concerned with structural issues such as unemployment and housing, though local authorities in particular often used these issues as a de facto way of dealing with race. The Urban Programme, influenced by Lyndon Johnson's Great Society programs in the United States and introduced in October 1968, signaled a more explicit focus, with the channeling of resources to areas where more than 6 percent of the school population was pupils from immigrant backgrounds. By the mid-1970s and the passing of the 1976 Race Relations Act, which made it a statutory duty for local authorities to legislate to end racial disadvantage and encourage equality of opportunity, the program was explicitly being aimed at ethnic minority organizations.[21] However problematically and incoherently, then, the vision of pluralism and equality ostensibly articulated at the 1965 Commonwealth Arts Festival had also begun to inform both local and national government in the shaping of a domestic multiculturalist agenda—increasingly in monetary terms.

Because of a lack of clear direction from the central government, the period following the passage of the 1976 act was characterized by diverse and sometimes confused responses from local authorities. In Birmingham, this largely continued into the 1980s. If the GLC took the lead in establishing the multicultural model, the Birmingham council embarked on a more cautious path. In 1984 the Labour administration created the Race Relations and Equal Opportunities Committee, but rather than implement the GLC blueprint it made a conscious effort to avoid being identified with the "looney Left."[22] The committee focused on the process of defining the council's equal opportunities policy; even as late as 1985, it claimed it did "not have a specific fund for supporting organisations of ethnic minority people." Two years later, because of concerns that its work could harm support among Labour's electoral base, the committee was abolished and replaced by the Personnel and Equal Opportunities Committee.[23]

In spite of this reticence, throughout the 1980s more funds were being directed by the council toward black and Asian groups and projects, usually under the euphemism "inner-city aid." In March 1985, for example, the Birmingham City Council's Economic Development Committee reported that it had made £400,000 available to projects that aimed to improve the employment opportunities of those living in inner areas of the city, where 75 percent of the city's "ethnic population" lived.[24] The West Midlands County Council (WMCC) explicitly set out to fund better community relations and most obviously adopted the language of multiculturalism. The race relations subcommittee of the council was established in 1981 with a remit to "consider matters affecting ethnic minorities" and allocate monies to "voluntary sector organisations involved with ethnic relations matters." The subcommittee's response to the rioting certainly illustrates the tendency of the state to assume that if there was a problem in black areas, the remedy could straightforwardly be found with the distribution of funds. In the aftermath of the 1985 rioting in Handsworth, the immediate response of the committee was to express concern about whether black and Asian organizations had been able to gain equal access to the funding that was available. To address this problem the council assigned a community liaison officer to "advise, support and consult voluntary organisations on various issues affecting themselves and the county council." The subcommittee then set up an emergency "Handsworth Disturbance fund" of £11,000, which was signed off on just days after the riots and was made available specifically to black and Asian groups in the area.[25]

The county council system was abolished following passage of the Conservative government's Local Government Act of 1985 in the context of its ongoing battles with the GLC and attempts made by authorities in the north of England to implement "local socialism."[26] Other bodies began to play a greater role, including the charitable Cadbury Trust, which between 1985 and 1986 allocated a total of £186,933 to "race relations" projects in Birmingham in an attempt to help fill the gap left by the county council.[27] And the mid-1980s also witnessed national government becoming increasingly active. According to David Waddington, the Home Office minister responsible for racial minorities between 1983 and 1987, the strategy was to "try and identify the leaders of the various communities with whom the government could deal" with a view to the allocation of monies.[28] Following the 1985 riots, Kenneth Clarke, then minister for employment, identified Handsworth as the pilot area that would receive the attention of an inner-city task force, a scheme conceived by the government for areas that were "showing acute signs of economic and social distress." Almost £5 million of central government money was made available to various projects in Handsworth with the primary object of increasing the employability of people in black and Asian communities. This was to be a "proactive" project, developed alongside community representatives to target particular ethnic minority groups. The task force was regarded as a success, with

73 percent of projects funded regarded as meeting targeted audiences. In 1987 further funds were made available for task forces in sixteen inner-city areas across the country.[29]

Policies such as these show how in spite of Thatcher's rolling back of the state, there was also a parallel willingness on behalf of the government to sanction the kind of focused investment that is rarely associated with the politics of Thatcherism.[30] This is not to say that the idea of an inner-city task force did not cause unease within the Thatcher administration. In response to earlier proposals from Home Secretary Douglas Hurd that a program of positive action was required to remedy what he diagnosed as a "thoroughly dangerous situation" in Britain's inner cities, Oliver Letwin and Hartley Booth, then junior policy advisers to Margaret Thatcher, warned against any further distribution of funds. In overtly racialized terms they suggested that it was unlikely that any increased investment would have a positive effect, given that "lower-class unemployed white people had lived for years in appalling slums without a breakdown of public order on anything like the present scale." The inner-city unrest, Letwin and Booth made clear, had been caused "solely by [the] individual characters and attitudes" of those involved. As long as this persisted, "all efforts to improve the inner cities [would] founder." Any funds that were allocated, it was suggested, would merely end up subsidizing the "disco and drug trade" or "Rastafarian arts and crafts workshops."[31]

Such comments offer an insight into the inability of some in government to comprehend the black inner city as anything other than profoundly alien. In spite of this, the projects and organizations that were supported by local and national funds—many of which were small grants that covered the cost of new equipment or the employment of temporary project workers—do illustrate the extent to which the inner areas of Britain's major cities had by the 1980s become sites of a remarkable tapestry of diversity. In Birmingham, organizations supported by the city council included the Bangladeshi Women's Association, the British Association of Muslims, and the Midlands Vietnamese Association; among the many others the county council supported were the Bethel Church of Jesus Christ, the Selly Oak Punjabi School, the Birmingham Jewish Council, the Sikh Youth Service, the St. Kitts, Nevis and Anguilla Society, and a project to develop resources for teaching black history in schools.[32] Thus what Bill Schwarz has described as the haphazard "black locality" of an earlier period, traceable through the presence from the 1950s onward of new black businesses and shops in areas of immigrant settlement, had by the 1980s become a global sensibility that corresponded with a voluntary and local political sector that attempted to advocate on behalf of the particular community it claimed to represent.[33]

Criticisms of this process have been twofold. First, the extent to which groups were actually representative of the constituents on whose behalf they claimed to speak was not always apparent. Certainly groups that were successful in their funding applications possessed no democratic mandate. The 1980s witnessed the rise of the community leaders, generally men from comparatively middle-class backgrounds who, because of their ability to speak the language of the state, were often presumed to be the authentic gatekeepers to the particular ethnic group they claimed to represent. Reflecting on his own ministerial responsibilities, David Waddington admitted that the government was regularly mistaken about "who the real community leaders were" and was too often seduced by "noisy chaps" whose claims of influence within a particular community often did not match reality.[34] More than the unaccountability of these processes, however, for Sivanandan and others it was the way in which the state's embrace of multiculturalism in the 1980s was seen to provoke ethnic divisions that was the program's most damaging legacy. People began to see their ethnic identity—as opposed to the more inclusive identity of *black*—as the only way of obtaining either influence or money. The state's policies "did not respond to the needs of communities," the writer Kenan Malik has argued, "but to a large degree *created* those communities by imposing identities on people."[35] If the emphasis on plurality and diversity in the 1965 Commonwealth Arts Festival occurred in the context of the disorientation experienced by Britain at the moment of decolonization, to Sivanandan the program of multiculturalism that was aimed at black Commonwealth citizens and their descendants in Britain was—echoing the language used by the ACSHO at its African Liberation Day—nothing less than a form of "domestic neocolonialism."[36]

It is certainly striking that the groups who were awarded funding in Birmingham in the 1980s often defined themselves in narrow terms—for example, as the St. Kitts, Nevis, and Anguilla Society, as opposed to the black or even Caribbean society. Allegations of corruption in the distribution of state resources were also commonplace and were often couched in interethnic terms.[37] With respect to the attitude of the state, however, a confused picture has emerged. The council actually began to liaise with black community groups from the mid-1960s, adopting the language of plurality and equality and beginning to play a monetary role in community relations. When the multicultural moment definitively arrived following the 1981 rioting, the Birmingham Labour authority, at least, adopted it ambivalently in light of concerns about the effects it would have on their white working-class vote. Nationally, following the 1985 unrest the government allocated a considerable sum of money to Handsworth, ostensibly with the aim of job creation, though this was met with vocal opposition from others inside government. As discussed in this chapter, there were divisions along ethnic lines in Handsworth, but it is simplistic to suggest that this was solely because of the way in which state funding had come to be distributed. In fact, within many organizations this was a process that was already under way independently from the often-confused reach of the state.

ANTIRACISM

In 1970 a group of teachers, academics, and campaigners organized a march on Edgbaston cricket ground, a venue in the south of the city that was due to host a match in a series between England and a whites-only South African team. The march was part of a national Stop the Seventy Tour campaign, led by the activist and future Labour cabinet minister Peter Hain with the support of the Anti-Apartheid Movement (AAM). In the event, the protests were a success; the planned matches were abandoned. But the organizers of the Birmingham march—which included local businessman John Plummer; Leslie Mitton, a teacher at a local Methodist College; and John Hick, a prominent lecturer in religious philosophy at Birmingham University—pressed ahead, transforming it into a demand for better community relations. Nine hundred people attended the march, out of which a new organization was born: All Faiths for One Race (AFFOR). From 1974 the group operated out of premises at the corner of Finch Road and Lozells Road in Handsworth, where it continued to be active throughout the 1980s. Initially its members were dismissed as "angry young men intent on stirring up trouble." Not everyone active in AFFOR was either male or young, Hick later recalled in his memoirs. But it was true "that we were angry—about the injustices of racism."[38]

AFFOR had emerged out of a particular conjuncture with respect to the Left's engagement with Britain's black population. As Jodi Burkett has suggested, although an anticolonial stance was at the heart of organizations such as the AAM, this did not mean they stood apart from the wider ambivalence about Britain's imperial past that had emerged in the context of decolonization. In the 1960s, the focus of such organizations on what was understood as the growing imperial status of the United States and the "little empire" that was seen to have developed in South Africa not only displaced the memory of Britain's own imperial past but also meant that the experiences of its formerly colonial subjects living in Britain could often be overlooked.[39] There was a reluctance, as Stuart Hall has reflected with respect to his own experience in the New Left, to explicitly comprehend the black presence as being the product of a colonial formation.[40] By the end of the decade, however, the passing of successive race equality acts, immigration legislation and the arrival of Powellism meant that it was virtually impossible for the largely white membership of groups such as the AAM to ignore the domestic race relations scene. As Hain reflected, the prospect of a deterioration in community relations if the South African tour of England were to be allowed to go ahead had become a central plank of the Stop the Seventy Tour's campaign.[41] In Birmingham the transformation of a protest against a segregated South African cricket team into AFFOR, an agency that would both conduct antiracist campaigning and run services for local black communities in Handsworth, was a signal of this broader direction of travel.

By the mid-1970s, prompted by the increasing visibility and electoral successes of the NF, a national antiracist movement had emerged.[42] Like AFFOR, it was led primarily by white activists. A key driver was Rock Against Racism (RAR), a coalition established by the Socialist Workers' Party that capitalized on the popularity of the punk, reggae, and "two-tone" scenes by staging consciously multiracial festivals featuring both white and black acts. This culminated in a carnival in London in 1978 that was attended by more than seventy thousand people. By this point, RAR had been joined by the Anti-Nazi League (ANL), a group formed in 1977 to give the antiracist movement a formal political voice. Its central aim, through the organization of protests and marches and the distribution of its campaign literature, was to expose and raise awareness of the Nazi sympathies of the NF. Between 1977 and 1979 it was estimated that there were 250 ANL branches across Britain and more than forty thousand members.[43]

The ANL, in particular, has been subject to criticism from those who saw its focus on exposing the "sham patriotism" of the NF as accepting the debate on the nationalist terms of the Far Right. For Paul Gilroy, the ANL closed down what were the broader concerns of RAR and honed in on the Nazism of the NF "to the exclusion of every other consideration," including the NF campaign of street violence and myriad other forms of racial discrimination that black communities faced on a daily basis.[44] Both RAR and the ANL were relatively quiet in Handsworth. In 1978 there had been a failed attempt to stage a "musical march," for example, partly due to the divided nature of the local ANL branch and its inability to attract the support of local black communities.[45] AFFOR, in contrast, continued well into the 1980s. It was undoubtedly at more than one remove from the politics of RAR and the ANL. While AFFOR undertook antiracist campaigning and attempted to uncover the Nazism of local NF members, this was always counterbalanced by a localized politics that was explicitly focused on attempting to meet the varied needs of local black and Asian communities. There could be tensions between these twin ambitions. In 1977 AFFOR summarized its core dilemmas as being "to what extent it should concentrate on casework and to what extent on 'campaigning.'"[46] But it was the focus on local casework that was arguably the critical factor in the group's ability to outlast RAR, the ANL, and other antifascist organizations following the NF's decline as an electoral force from 1979 onward.

In 1976 Clare Short, a local activist who like Hain would go on to become a Labour cabinet minister, became director of AFFOR. She characterized the group as a "hub of anti-racist activity" in which the guiding principles were "respect [for] each other's religious institutions" coupled with an "absolutely uncompromising" position on racism.[47] The group published articles discussing the nature of fascism and an exposé of a local NF leader's comments regarding the supposed "swamping" of Britain by "coloured invaders," comments that echoed those later made by Margaret Thatcher in the run-up to the 1979 general election.[48] As with the ANL, this tactic of exposing the fascism or Nazism of the Far Right often stemmed less from a desire to counter the effects of racism on minority communities and more from a concerted effort to appeal to as broad a white audience as possible. Thus the author of one AFFOR pamphlet, *So What Are You Going to Do About the National Front?*, urged "white society" to recognize that "compared with the hurt and bitterness and anger of many black Britons" the distaste white communities felt at the presence of a neo-Nazi party in Britain was "minute." Other articles published in AFFOR's quarterly newsletter highlighted the legal problems faced by local ethnic minorities and lobbied the Commission for Racial Equality to expand on its remit in relation to the needs of ethnic minorities across the city.[49]

Yet unlike either RAR or the ANL, AFFOR maintained a strong connection to a particular locale. The initial decision to base AFFOR in Handsworth was made because it was felt that this was the area in which the group would best be able to make tangible improvements in the lives of black communities. From the perspective of the university campus, where the group's founding member, John Hick, spent his working life, there was an exoticism to "multi-racial Handsworth" as a place of comparative excitement and turmoil. Situating AFFOR in Handsworth was, one activist wrote in 1979, about "taking sides . . . with the black communities . . . choosing an innercity area and trying to cope with the advantages and disadvantages of such a place."[50] While the initial depiction of the group as angry young men was an easy characterization to make, the group's commitment to developing practical responses to the inequalities experienced by the local population meant that by the 1980s it had undergone a significant transformation from the direct action associated with the Stop the Seventy Tour to being among the most established players on the local race relations scene, regularly obtaining some of the largest funding grants with the most regularity.[51]

Throughout its existence local casework was never off AFFOR's organizational agenda. In the aftermath of the 1971 Immigration Act, for example, the group provided assistance with the act's new requirement that family members obtain work permits before entering the United Kingdom. Following the establishment of the Asian Resource Centre (ARC) in 1976 (discussed in detail in the next section of this chapter), the emphasis shifted to providing social security advice, though in practice AFFOR continued to deal with a wide range of cases. As was made clear in the group's 1977–1978 annual report, "One cannot turn away individuals who turn to you for help. . . . [T]he door remains open and people arrive when they choose to arrive with problems ranging from social security, to immigration, to conflicts with the police, the need for a job, a divorce, a death certificate, etc." AFFOR's community worker described having to represent an elderly Asian man who had been refused reentry into the United Kingdom on the grounds that his face looked too young for his passport photograph; helping a recently widowed black woman who was unable to pay her energy bills following the death of her husband; and enabling a man whose union was on strike to gain access to benefit money. By the 1980s the group was also becoming increasingly active in local education. In the context of belated attempts by local authorities to introduce better provisions for ethnic minority pupils, AFFOR ran workshops for local teachers on "multicultural education" and on the effects an ethnocentric perspective could have in the classroom.[52]

The group's focus on local issues generally chimed with its wider campaigning program, but there were also tensions. A moment of crisis came in the mid-1970s when AFFOR campaigned for an inquiry into the increasingly fraught relationship between police and the black community in Handsworth, with the ambition of bringing the issue to a wider audience. The campaign eventually resulted in John Brown, an academic at the Cranfield Institute of Technology and a supposed expert on police-community relations, receiving sponsorship from both AFFOR and the Barrow-Cadbury Trust to conduct an investigation, whose results were published in 1977 as *Shades of Grey*.[53] In the event, the report exacerbated the already-fraught climate of anxiety around black youth, the inner city, and street crime. It fudged the issue of police harassment, focusing instead on what Brown described as a "hard-core" group of black youths who had "taken on the appearance of followers of the Rastafarian faith" and were notionally responsible for the high crime rates in the area—the victims of which, Brown suggested, were often white elderly women. As Paul Gilroy has argued, *Shades of Grey* often deployed Powellian imagery that painted a pathological picture of the supposed inadequacies of black familial structures as the cause of the growth in crime, a narrative that inevitably captured significant media attention. In the aftermath of the report's publication, for example, the *Birmingham Evening Mail* ran a series of features under the banner "Terror Gangs Shock," and the report also captured the imagination of the national media.[54] The emphasis Brown placed on groups of black youths merely shifted the terms of the debate from a focus on an individual black mugger to what was perceived to be a growing collective threat. In effect, it was a precursor to what would, particularly following the rioting that in September 1985 engulfed the very street on which AFFOR was based, become the dominant narrative around the black inner city.[55]

AFFOR immediately disowned *Shades of Grey* and ordered a new investigation into policing in Handsworth. The group obtained a small grant, sufficient to buy a tape recorder and a transcribing machine, and commissioned Carlton Green, a local bus driver, to interview members of the black community about their relationships with the police. The result was *Talking Blues*, a forty-seven-page pamphlet summarizing local opinion. Twenty-two hundred copies of *Talking Blues* were sold in the first year, and copies were distributed to senior officers in the West Midlands Police. Its aim, Clare Short wrote, was to "attempt to communicate . . . the experiences, frustrations and sense of bitter injustice of black people concerning police behaviour." Five years later, the group produced a follow-up, this time detailing the black community's disillusionment with the education system.[56]

If the *Shades of Grey* episode was an illustration of the pitfalls involved in AFFOR attempting to remedy local issues by bringing them to the attention of wider, often white audiences, locally the group's ability to respond to the needs of both black and Asian communities was its strength. The ANL's brand of antiracist politics hinged on a patriotic reading of Britain as a country with a historic respect for freedom, democracy, and difference. While this may have proven successful in the eventual hampering of the NF's electoral appeal, it was a platform that further demonstrated the extent to which the memory of colonialism had been disavowed in Britain, on the Left as well as the Right. Moreover, it left little room for serious engagement with the diversity of issues faced by Britain's black and Asian communities. AFFOR, in contrast, attempted to respond directly to these issues. For instance, the group ran "language recognition" classes for teachers on Urdu, Punjabi, Hindi, and Patois, as well as an "interpretation and translating service." In light of a local unemployment rate four times the national average in the mid-1980s, the group produced leaflets in four Asian languages to promote awareness about how to claim unemployment support.[57] In many ways, AFFOR's embeddedness in the community and willingness to campaign on a range of social issues meant that it was less a part of the ANL's brand of antiracism than of the radical social work movement that emerged out of the post-1968 era of experimentalism and that emphasized the need for solidarity with clients in defense of the wider community.[58]

Unlike many of the radical black organizations that operated alongside AFFOR in Handsworth, the group's ability to work with clients across ethnic communities did not arise out of any ideological commitment to black as a political color. Rather, local clients perhaps associated AFFOR's whiteness with neutrality and recognized the cultural capital that this well-funded organization had to offer. AFFOR's success in obtaining grants undoubtedly demonstrates the way in which the funding system could often favor groups that were better able to speak the language of state multiculturalism—an issue that was the subject of apparent resentment from other local groups.[59] And as the *Shades of Grey* episode indicated, there were tensions between the group's emphasis on local casework and its wider campaigning stance. Given the moral panic around black street crime and mugging and the fact that Handsworth was already lodged in the national imaginary as a key crucible for such anxieties, AFFOR was undoubtedly naïve in its expectation that an academic who reportedly also had ties to the police would be able to contribute to a meaningful discussion.[60] Yet the group was also evidently valued by its clients, who had "almost always tried the normal channels and have come to the point where they do not know what to do next." As shown in the following discussion, for those groups that maintained an ideological commitment to a unified politics of *black*, tensions could often be much more pronounced.[61]

BLACK AS A POLITICAL COLOR?
SOUTH ASIAN GROUPS IN HANDSWORTH

In postwar Britain, South Asian politics was dominated by the IWA. Initially set up by Indian peddlers in London and Coventry in the 1930s to agitate for Indian independence, in the 1950s IWAs reemerged with a focus on providing welfare support for the increasing number of Punjabi immigrants who were settling in Britain. The groups were often heterogeneous in their ideological approach, however, and even after the establishment in 1958 of a national organizing body they remained susceptible to splits, particularly over loyalties to an Indian Communist Party that had itself divided into Marxist and Marxist-Leninist factions.[62] By the mid-1970s the IWAs had been joined by a newly politicized, younger generation of largely British-born South Asian activists. Although it retained an internationalist perspective, the AYM was much less influenced by the factionalism of far-left politics on the Indian subcontinent. Instead, it was the growth of racist street violence that Asian communities increasingly found themselves subject to that often provided the initial driver. A turning point came on 4 June 1976, when an Asian teenager, Gurdip Singh Chaggar, was stabbed to death in a racist attack in Southall, West London, outside a welfare center run by the Southall IWA. The IWA's response to the murder was perceived by younger generations as hesitant and acted as a lightning rod for wider concerns about IWA democracy and accountability. The formation of the Southall Youth Movement bypassed the IWA and took the lead in organizing the response to the Chaggar case and protests against a perceived lack of police protection. The group's visibility helped inspire a rapid growth in AYMs across the country. In Handsworth, however, where the IWA maintained a greater level of political independence than its Southall counterpart, the newly established AYM took part in many of the same campaigns and shared broadly similar political perspectives with the older organization.

A key plank of the ideology of both organizations was the adoption of a strategically wide political viewpoint that situated their contemporary activities in Britain alongside both historical struggles against empire and present-day global liberation movements. The IWA's constitution included a commitment to waging "militant ... struggle in every possible way against racism and fascism," for example, and to "support the national liberation struggles of the Asian, African and Latin American peoples." Similarly, the AYM pledged to "fight against racism in all its forms" and "to support all anti-imperialist and national liberation struggles."[63] References to historic anticolonial figures featured prominently within each organization. In May 1978, for example, the IWA opened a welfare center at 346 Soho Road, Handsworth's main shopping street, less than two miles from AFFOR's base on the Lozells Road. The center was named after Shaheed Udham Singh, the Indian anticolonialist who in 1940 murdered the lieutenant general of the Punjab in retaliation for his ordering of a massacre of more than three hundred people. Singh also featured in AYM literature, including in a 1986 calendar that attempted to situate the group's activities in Handsworth in relation to historic anticolonial struggles. On one side of the calendar was a photograph of Udham Sing following his arrest for the 1940 murder; on the other was a photograph of a contemporary demonstration that had been organized by the AYM.[64]

Arguably the most significant convergence between the two organizations was their ideological commitment to black as a political color. Like the early ideology of the British Black Panthers, which was influenced by the radical politics of figures such as the Trinidadian writer C. L. R. James, within the IWA this came from a particular reading of Marxism. Avtar Jouhl, a senior member of the IWA in Handsworth who drank with Malcolm X on the latter's 1965 visit to a Smethwick pub, argued that it was important for black and Asian communities in Britain to unite because he understood them to be at the forefront of a wider struggle against capitalism. Immigrant communities were regarded as playing a particularly important role in this struggle, both because of a recognition of the racism of parts of the white working class and from the conviction that black and Asian workers alike could draw directly on their own experiences of struggle against empire and colonialism abroad, as well as against contemporary racism in Britain. Unless black workers "raise their voice the solidarity will not be there. Black people's unity," Jouhl emphasized, "is of utmost importance."[65]

For the AYM, a unified black identity was necessary because, according to one activist, it would allow "a solidarity to develop in the struggle against the racism of the street."[66] The influence of Black Power on the group was emphasized by the decision of the Southall Youth Movement to use the clenched fist as its logo.[67] In the aftermath of the 1985 riots in Handsworth, both the AYM and the IWA were vocal exponents of the need for interethnic unity. Writing in the IWA's journal *Lalkar*, for instance, Jouhl warned of a plot to "set the Asians and the Afro-Caribbeans at each other's throats" and reminded his readers that his organization was "for the unity of the West Indians and Asian communities."[68] Likewise, the AYM's organ *Asian Youth News*—which on its masthead also displayed the Black Power clenched fist—called for its readers to see through portrayals of the unrest that presented it as the result of interethnic tensions. The police, the newsletter warned, were "trying to divide our community by making a pretence of sympathy towards the Asian shopkeeper"; people "should not to let this affect relations between Asian and African communities where they live side-by-side." The AYM denounced the actions of community leaders in the aftermath of the rioting, who they claimed had "strong links within the racist Tory party" and were willing to "sell their communities for the reward of white status and privilege." The AYM instead urged its readers to see what happened in Handsworth through a global lens. The United States and Europe were seen to "hold the world's purse strings while our countries in Asia, Africa and South America are wracked with poverty and starvation." The "black ghettos" of Handsworth, Brixton, and elsewhere, which "our parents and grandparents struggled for years ... to build" and which in the 1980s had become scenes of violence and looting, should be seen from a geopolitical perspective. They were, the AYM concluded, the inevitable result of the continued "racism of white domination."[69]

Unlike the older generations active in the IWA, a significant number of AYM activists were university students and were influenced by political theory—specifically by the writings of Ambalavaner Sivanandan, who, having usurped the white establishment of the London-based Institute of Race Relations in the mid-1970s, set about radicalizing both the institute and its journal so that both adopted class-based, anticolonial campaigning stances. Just as Sivanandan viewed the multiculturalist programs of local and national authorities alike as a tool to "blunt the edge of black struggle," Bhopinder Basi—who was active in the Handsworth AYM throughout the 1980s—understood that "the real purpose behind multiculturalism wasn't to help us all live together better, but to create the necessary divisions in our communities so that an oppressive process could be maintained."[70] Just as Sivanandan—writing in the Institute's newly radicalized journal *Race and Class*—argued that Asian and Afro-Caribbean activists in the 1970s were united over their "parallel histories of common racism," the Handsworth AYM in 1985 pledged to "work for black unity ... against divisions based upon caste, religious, national and cultural prejudices." The writings of Sivanandan were reproduced in AYM journals, and Basi even remembered quoting him directly at AYM meetings.[71]

There was, however, often a schism within these organizations between an ideological commitment to a unified black platform and practical programs that focused on more ethnically specific themes. There was an ambivalence toward ethnicity in the politics of these groups. On the one hand, the appeal of Black Power corresponded with a commitment to secularism that saw many activists consciously refuse religious social codes. Yet on the other hand, both the IWA and the AYM printed much of their campaign literature in South Asian languages and used Punjabi slogans and musical instruments at demonstrations, while religious institutions inevitably continued to exert an influence through family and other ties. This ambivalence was to some extent embodied by Sivanandan himself, who cultivated ties with Black Power but in a celebrated essay simultaneously stressed the political potential of a particular community using its own traditions, cultures, and languages as a tool of opposition to British racism.[72] Certainly by the late 1970s and 1980s, in its practical operations in Handsworth if not in its ideological approach, the IWA in particular had seemingly begun to function primarily as an advocate for the Indian community specifically.

These tensions are apparent in the IWA's internal correspondence. In one 1982 memo, for example, IWA members were reprimanded for their "absolutely disgraceful" behavior in not attending a specifically inclusive conference of all "the various organisations of black people in Britain." But the same memo also called for members to be vigilant with respect to the threat posed by the Punjabi separatist group Akali Dal in British Sikh temples, an issue that could have had little or no resonance beyond the Sikh community.[73] By the 1980s such ethnically distinct themes had begun to dominate the IWA's agenda. Thus, although the Udham Singh Welfare Centre claimed to offer welfare and legal advice on a broad range of issues relating to immigration, police harassment, housing difficulties, and passports, the latter had taken precedence because of the large number of Indian migrants who had arrived in Britain with forged papers, a situation that required bilingual negotiations with both British and Indian officials.[74] The IWA was able to distinguish itself from the services offered by white groups such as AFFOR by drawing on its expertise in issues that specifically affected South Asian and particularly Indian communities, in the native language of Indian immigrants. The group spoke out against other issues of particular significance within the Asian community. It took a leading role in campaigning against domestic violence, for example, issuing a leaflet expressing its concern "about the mounting violence against women" in Asian communities. In March 1986 it organized a public meeting to discuss these issues, with the intention of drawing attention to the presence of "feudal customs" within Asian communities, which, the IWA stressed, "must not be tolerated."[75]

If ethnicity was a source of incongruity, the position of women within the IWA and AYM alike was often overtly problematic. That the IWA, by the mid-1980s, was beginning to address issues such as domestic violence was the achievement of women within such organizations, who fought against what was seen to be their "distinctly masculine" cultures.[76] Historically, in the view of one activist, "if women were incorporated [into the IWA], they were incorporated as the secretaries or the food makers, rather than being represented in their own right in terms of what was best for women." Women often found it difficult to be heard at meetings, and when they did speak often found they were being humored, while the men continued to make decisions behind the scenes without serious consultation.[77] In the 1970s this issue was so acute that it contributed to the formation of separate, breakaway women's bodies such as the Liverpool Black Sisters and Brixton Black Women's Group (both founded in 1973) and, by the end of that decade, the Southall Black Sisters and Birmingham Black Sisters (BBS).[78] Although these organizations had some African Caribbean members, the vast majority were South Asian women. The well-publicized industrial disputes at the Imperial Typewriters factory in Leicester in 1974 and subsequently at a film-processing plant in Grunwick, North London, had already signaled the growing visibility of radical activism among Asian women in Britain, belying the stereotypes often peddled by journalists and social scientists alike regarding the supposed passivity of South Asian women.[79]

Participants in Black Sisters groups were generally younger, were often university educated, and largely came not as a result of disillusionment with conditions in the workplace but in response to the masculine cultures of groups such the AYM and the IWA, as well as the ethnocentricity of existing feminist organizations.[80]

The BBS consciously decided to avoid any contact with the state—whether monetary or otherwise—because of fears that this would jeopardize its independence. Like the IWA and the AYM, the BBS was also drawn to the political power invested in "black" following Black Power's crossing of the Atlantic a decade earlier.[81] For Surinder Guru, who was active in the BBS throughout the period, this was because of an appreciation of the shared legacies of colonialism, on the one hand, and their mutual experiences of racism in Britain on the other. "We came under the banner of 'black,'" she recalled,

> because our responses were to white racist society, we were organising around the histories of our people. There was a commonality of experiences with racism.... [W]e recognised that if there was a trajectory to organise separately, with different groups for Africans, Caribbeans, Asians.... [W]e weren't going to get anywhere. It was that recognition that brought us together to make us strong.[82]

The first BBS newsletters appeared in 1988 and were distributed only to black women. In the second issue, the newsletter encouraged contributions in languages other than English and stated that it was important for "black women of Asian and African-Caribbean descent to come together and express the sort of oppression which we as black women face in this racist, patriarchal, capitalist society."[83]

What increasingly occupied the focus of the BBS, the IWA, and the AYM was the growing precariousness of black and Asian communities following the passing of the 1981 British Nationality Act, which introduced a streamlined definition of British citizenship along crudely racialized lines, and the 1988 Immigration Act, which gave the state increased powers of deportation by limiting potential avenues for appeal. Between 1986 and 1989 the number of people being deported from the United Kingdom more than doubled, to over four thousand per year.[84] It was this precariousness that increasingly took up the attention of each organization. The AYM provided regular legal advice in its newsletter, explaining the difference between deportation and removal orders and encouraging readers to organize demonstrations, meetings, and social events to increase the publicity for their campaigns. A critical strategy was to focus on individual cases as a way of demonstrating the perceived inhumanity of the state.[85] AYM drew on its professional expertise to highlight inconsistencies in the law. In the mid-1980s the group helped win an important victory in the case of Baba Bakhtaura—a Punjabi folk singer in Handsworth who was threatened with deportation for overstaying his visitor's permit—by pointing to a legal loophole that meant that any Commonwealth citizen was able to stand as a UK electoral candidate even if his or her right to reside in Britain had been removed. The AYM's focus on campaigning against deportation was epitomized by what would become the group's key political slogan: "Here to stay, here to fight."[86]

It is significant that the causes the BBS primarily focused on concerned women, particularly given that the changes to immigration laws were often experienced in highly specific ways by women—symbolized most acutely by the revelation in 1978 that prospective female immigrants from the Indian subcontinent could be subject to vaginal examinations in order to "prove" their marital status.[87] Increasingly, the BBS also mobilized on behalf of women in Britain who were the victims of domestic abuse. A key moment was the campaign the group fought on behalf of Iqbal Begum, a Kashmiri woman who in October 1981 was convicted of murdering her abusive husband. Begum's dealings with the police had been prejudiced by the fact that she spoke little English and by the consistent failure of the police to find an interpreter who spoke in her native Mirpuri dialect. At her trial, when asked to enter a plea, Begum was reported to have responded with *gulti*, which in Mirpuri Punjabi translates as "I made a mistake," but at the trial was recorded as *guilty*.[88] The BBS "fought a campaign for her within our own communities," drawing attention to comparable cases involving white women in which the defendant was acquitted on the basis that she was acting in self-defense.[89] The group was eventually successful in persuading a judge to overturn Begum's conviction on the grounds that she was not granted access to an adequate translator.[90]

Such campaigns had some impact on the outlook of male-dominated organizations. Anandi Ramamurthy has shown how both the Bradford and Manchester AYMs supported the BBS with respect to the Begum case and also took part in the concurrent Black Wages for Housework campaign. The Birmingham AYM, in contrast, was perceived as being particularly macho and often attacked the BBS on the basis that its membership was supposedly too middle class and out of touch with the experiences of black and Asian workers.[91] But by the mid-1980s the Birmingham AYM was at least paying lip service to the importance of gender politics, devoting a section of its *Asian Youth News* to exploring the status of women both in Britain and across the Indian subcontinent to mark International Women's Day.[92] The campaigns by women activists to persuade larger, male-dominated organizations to recognize the specific inequalities that women faced might be seen as part of a continuum that took in the demands made by women workers at Grunwick and elsewhere for adequate trade union recognition. If the class-based attacks on the BBS from without were eminently familiar to the spectrum of feminist activities in this period, internally it was the issue of ethnicity that was rendering these activities increasingly fraught. The focus on campaigning against deportations had contributed to tensions, particularly given that unlike other organizations the BBS did have a number of African Caribbean members. As has been pointed out, although there were cases that affected Afro-Caribbeans, this was a demographic that even in the 1960s made up a minority of actual deportee cases. By the 1980s, the fact that Asian communities were most at risk of deportation—coupled with the traumatic experiences of Asian women in particular when attempting to navigate Britain's increasingly racist and sexist immigration laws—meant that this issue resonated most clearly among the South Asian members of the BBS.[93] There was reportedly increasing disillusionment among the few African Caribbean members that other issues were not being taken seriously. There was a perception, Guru admitted, that the group was only about "tackling south Asian women's issues." Increasingly, rifts had developed within the BBS, and its few African Caribbean members left the group. Shortly afterward, the BBS folded.[94]

In 1976 an organization was established in Handsworth explicitly to provide ethnically specific services to Asian communities. In contrast to the stress Sivanandan and others would place on black unity, according to Ranjit Sondhi, one of its cofounders, the ARC was established because of a commitment to the importance of an "autonomous and physically distinct base" for Asian community activity.[95] As Anil Bhalla, who worked at the ARC during the 1980s, explained, organizations like AFFOR often lacked either language skills or cultural awareness and therefore had only a limited attraction in the context of the heterogeneous cultural and linguistic frameworks within Asian communities.[96] Sondhi described what he saw as the ARC's typical client:

> Just imagine a villager coming from India, who had not even been to the big cities in India like Delhi, and comes straight out of a rural way of life to a big city in England . . . finding themselves [living] next door to people they had never before seen in their lives. Not just the English, but the Caribbeans and the Chinese and the Vietnamese, and the Pakistanis if you were Indian, and visa versa. People never really developed an in-depth understanding of [the significance] of different cultures.[97]

The ARC attempted to fill this perceived gap by providing services that were specifically tailored to the needs of different Asian communities "through the use of their own mother-tongues, with a deep understanding of the religious, cultural and national aspirations of the people it serves."[98] On the first day the ARC opened, Sondhi recalled, "forty people lined up outside. Soon we had 500 visitors a week. Suddenly we had created a little cocoon, a little oasis in which people could move around with ease. We had opened the floodgates."[99]

The ARC offered advice and assistance on issues relating to social security, debt, immigration, nationality, asylum, and housing, and provided practical help with letter reading and form filling. It also responded to broader issues within Asian communities and, perhaps indicating the success of the campaigns waged by the BBS, ran a hostel in Handsworth for female victims of domestic abuse. In the early 1980s the ARC also began to respond to the increasingly important issue of elderly homelessness within South Asian communities. Running counter to assumptions often made by local authorities about the durability of Asian family care networks, the problem had grown partly due to the perennial lack of adequate housing. The ARC responded by collaborating with a housing association to set up an eleven-bed, self-contained hostel specifically for the Asian elderly on St. Peter's Road, Handsworth. The ARC was the subject of significant criticism from within Asian communities for "bringing shame on the community" by revealing the problem, though for the ARC such concerns were superseded by a commitment to responding to the practical issues that faced Asian communities. Although the claims made by one caseworker that the group's approach was simply to "respond to what is required" downplayed the radicalism of attempting to tackle such potentially controversial issues, it is undoubtedly striking that in comparison with other organizations, the ARC lacked an explicitly ideological agenda.[100] In Handsworth, the AYM and the BBS consciously refused to accept any form of state funding or involvement in their activities. The ARC, in contrast, from the outset survived on grants from the state and various charitable bodies. Although the ARC "celebrated the ethos of self-help," its commitment to providing services for the Asian population led it to the conviction that funding was essential.[101] In 1979 the ARC received funds from, among others, the City of Birmingham Social Services Department, the Inner-City Partnership, and the Barrow-Cadbury Trust. By the early 1990s the group was receiving grants of over £100,000 from Birmingham City Council.[102]

There was, however, no clear correlation between the decision of a group to accept state funding and the emergence of ethnicity in its politics. The AYM and the BBS refused to accept any form of state funding and subscribed to the ideology of black as a political color. Yet practically, these groups often engaged in the provision of services and campaigns that were primarily about responding to a particular set of issues as they were experienced by a particular community. From the perspective of the ARC, there was a recognition that reliance on state funding made it vulnerable. In a memo from the early 1980s, for example, it was noted that the "grants are barely paying [the staff] salaries" and that there was a need to expand its income source by approaching other charitable organizations.[103] Yet this reliance did not make the ARC weaker than any other organization operating in Handsworth. In one sense, perhaps, this is a story of a convergence between groups who saw their primary remit as campaigning and those who focused on service provision. By the 1980s such distinctions had become difficult to maintain. When in the late 1970s the IWA embarked on its project to build the Udham Singh Welfare Centre, it made the decision to do so with the benefit of state monies. This was perhaps a recognition of the direction of travel in which the group was already moving. By the later 1970s the IWA was beginning to leave the Marxism-Leninism of its past behind as it gravitated more closely to the Labour Party.[104] In the same way that AFFOR was able to marry its practical services with a wider antiracist agenda, the IWA's political commitments began to match more closely the services it now provided. It increasingly became preoccupied—both practically and ideologically—with ethnically distinct issues. Like the ARC, the IWA and its Udham Singh Welfare Centre remained active in the first decades of the twenty-first century. The AYM and the BBS, by contrast, where tensions between ideology and practice were much more pronounced, had by the end of the 1980s ceased to exist.

AFRICAN CARIBBEAN POLITICS

Alongside its African Liberation Day, which it held annually from 1977, the ACSHO maintained an internationalist line of vision that attempted to draw events from across the black diaspora into the everyday lives of the group's constituents. The group was based at 104 Heathfield Road, a short walk from the Villa Cross pub at the junction with Lozells Road and the nearby Acapulco café (outside which the incident that sparked the 1985 riots took place), an area known locally as black Handsworth's front line. In December 1972, in the context of rising anxieties about the presence of radical black activism in Britain, a *Sunday Telegraph* correspondent attempted to visit the ACSHO headquarters. The journalist characterized the ACSHO as Black Power emanating from a terraced house and had obtained a copy of the group's newspaper, which, it was reported, married allegations of discrimination locally with updates on the progress of anticolonial movements in Mozambique, Angola, Namibia, and Zimbabwe.[105] By the end of the decade, in the context of anticolonial victories in Portuguese Africa, the ACSHO turned its attention to events in the south of the continent. It received visits from representatives of the South African Black Nationalist group the Pan African Congress as well as the Zimbabwe African National Union, the future ruling party of independent Zimbabwe.[106] There was also a humanitarian strand to the ACSHO agenda. Under the banner of the Marcus Garvey Foundation, a subsidiary charity run by the ACSHO, the group raised funds to help the victims of Hurricane Gilbert, which in 1988 had killed more than forty people in Jamaica. It also sent fifty tons of medical supplies to help in the response to the Ethiopian famine and made a gift of twenty-five hundred pencils and exercise books to schools in Burkina Faso, where the ACSHO also directed funds toward a new orphanage and hospital. This was a vision of Pan-Africanism rooted in Handsworth through the familiar humanitarian call for charity: "Spare a thought for the starving and the needy," the ACSHO urged its followers. When "you see our street collectors in Britain's city centres, pubs, parks and on your doorstep . . . give whatever you can."[107]

As a means of generating solidarity across the Atlantic and throughout the diaspora, these tactics were almost as old as Pan-Africanism itself. For example, the London-based League of Coloured Peoples, established in 1931, encouraged its members to make a practical difference in the lives of those elsewhere in the black globality by raising money for the victims of natural disasters, including a major hurricane strike in British Honduras in 1938. And just as Heathfield Road was used by the ACSHO as a base for cultural activity as well as political mobilization, in 1931 the West African Students Union (WASU) opened a hostel on Camden Road, north London, which not only acted as a destination for sojourners looking for accommodation but also became a meeting point where residents of black London could enact "black internationalist solidarity . . . as much over a spicy rice dish and on the dance floor as through political organising."[108] The global outlook of such organizations went hand in hand with a concern to remedy the daily discrimination their constituents faced in the metropolis. The need for a hostel of the kind set up by the WASU was crystallized when in 1929 Paul Robeson was refused service at a prominent London hotel, causing a significant public scandal.[109] The incident rang true for the black residents of 1930s London, just as it would have for Handsworth's black population in the postwar period. As black Britain grew, the pervasiveness of the inequity that faced it became apparent. Like other groups, black organizations such as the ACSHO matched their globalist ideologies with practical attempts to respond to what had become obvious was British institutionalized racism on an industrial scale. And as the ARC recognized with the establishment of its hostel for the Asian elderly, housing proved to be one of the most enduringly problematic issues.

The inequalities that faced black and Asian immigrants in the housing sector had been well known for some time; the sociologists John Rex and Robert Moore, in their influential 1967 study of the Sparkbrook district of Birmingham in the south of the city, positioned immigrant communities as a separate underclass worse off than their fellow occupiers of Britain's inner-city slums.[110] Black and Asian communities were often forced to rely disproportionately on the private rental sector, where, as a result of the unscrupulous practices of "shark" landlords, poor conditions continued to belie postwar narratives of increasing affluence.[111] Yet the experiences of organizations operating on the community level suggested that within the immigrant underclass there were significant variations that required particular responses. In 1974, for instance, the black teacher and part-time social sciences student Beresford Ivan Henry completed a dissertation based on field research he had undertaken with Harambee, a Handsworth-based organization that had been established two years earlier to attempt to deal with black homelessness. If groups such as the IWA and ARC found that the familial structures often presumed to be present in Asian households were often irrelevant when it came to the problem of elderly homelessness, Henry suggested that the conservative religiosity of some black parents and the growing disillusionment of black youth in the education and employment sectors had led to young people becoming "alienated from parental or home situations" and in some cases being "rejected from their families" altogether.[112] Some reports suggested that as many as a fifth of local black teenagers could be classified as homeless.[113] Like the ACSHO, Harambee maintained a globalist, Pan-Africanist stance; the group's name was taken from the Swahili word for "all together." But this did not correspond with an interethnic politics based around black as a political color; the commitment to service provision in Handsworth and the particular way in which issues such as housing and homelessness were manifested meant that, like the ACSHO, Harambee focused its priorities elsewhere.

Harambee's organizational emphasis was encapsulated in the fact that it originally called itself Black Social Workers, though many of its members were also trained teachers and lawyers. Maurice Andrews, an immigrant from Jamaica who cofounded the group and was himself a former social worker, cited a "phenomenal tension" within black households, particularly in instances where marriages had broken down and children were living with a stepparent. Andrews recalled that teenagers as young as fourteen were being evicted from their family homes and sleeping in parks or with friends in bed-sits. Harambee's ambition was to develop a "positive initiative in order to begin to retrieve the situation."[114] The group obtained funds to purchase a three-story property on Hall Road, a few hundred yards from the "front line" at the Villa Cross pub. This was turned into a hostel that catered not for visiting sojourners or for elderly Asians, but for local black youths specifically. Addressing this issue had become a central feature of Black Power politics following its emergence in Britain in the late 1960s. One of the first hostels for homeless black youths was the so-called Black House in North London, which opened its doors in 1969 and was run by the controversial Trinidadian activist Michael X's Racial Adjustment Action Society (RAAS).[115] In Handsworth, Harambee's intention was not only to house and feed homeless black youths, but also to make them "feel more aware of themselves, their situation and the role they can play in society," as well as "offer opportunities to black adults to regain the trust of the younger generation." According to the group's 1974 annual report, there were three stages to Harambee's interventions: first, an initial rescue operation took black youths off the streets by providing them with short-term accommodation; second, longer-term homes were allocated, often in partnership with local authorities; and finally, an educational program with the overall aim of making young people "more socially aware and self-reliant" was provided. Within seven days of the hostel's opening all fifteen places in the house had been filled by local homeless young people. By March 1974, seventy young people had stayed at the Harambee hostel, for periods ranging from one night to ten months.[116]

Throughout the long 1980s Harambee expanded its activities in response to what it saw as the needs of the local black community. It purchased other disused properties in Handsworth and turned them into hostels for black youths, setting up its own housing association to provide low-cost housing in the area. Harambee established an advice center that broached the issue of tensions between police and black communities by offering free legal guidance, and ran a black studies course for residents at its hostels; a nursery was opened to cater for the children of black single mothers, and the group also ran a supplementary Saturday school for older children, which in the mid-1970s became the focus of local newspaper attention because of its status as an "'exclusive West Indian organisation.'"[117] These services were named not after South Asian revolutionaries like Udham Singh but African Caribbean figures such as Marcus Garvey and Harriet Tubman. In the 1970s one of its members summarized its ideology as being "'influenced by Pan-Africanism, African socialism, and parts of the black power philosophy,'" with the aim of enabling "'black people . . . [to] carve out for themselves a decent existence in Handsworth.'" As Maurice Andrews saw it, "We had to find our own place in society"; Harambee had emerged out of an insistence that "we had to manage our own affairs. We had our own problems, and it was important *we* solved them."[118]

From the beginning Harambee made a decision that it would seek funding from the state. Unlike the IWA, whose 1978 building of a state-funded welfare center on Soho Road reflected a shift away from the group's Marxist-Leninist roots, for Harambee using state money was a part of its own radical political rationale, which saw the state as negligent in its duty of care toward black communities. As Andrews conceptualized it, "our theory was that we pay taxes, we are a part of this society," and therefore it was the state's responsibility to respond to social problems such as homelessness—if not directly through the provision of adequate services, then indirectly via the funding of locally embedded groups such as Harambee. Although Harambee property was raided by the police three times in the mid-1970s, agencies including the Birmingham Social Services Department, which funded Harambee's main hostel, clearly valued the group's ability to work with a section of the community often treated by authorities as impossible to reach.[119] In 1975 one funder described the Harambee hostel as "one of the best pieces of self-help work" in the area and saw the group as being "ideally placed to work effectively with young West Indians."[120] From the perspective of those who ran Harambee, accepting state funds did not compromise the group's emphasis on "togetherness and self-help."[121] To Andrews, at least, calling for the state to fund a group like Harambee was itself a radical position. This was a politics of "self-help backed up with the demand that the state must pay."[122]

This attitude was a point of cleavage with the ACSHO, which had been established in Handsworth in 1964 almost a decade before Harambee and three years before a Stokely Carmichael visit to London helped stimulate the expansion of the Black Power movement in Britain.[123] The ACSHO became one of the longest-serving black political groups in the country and, like the AYM and the BBS, emphasized the importance of independence from the state. This position was made clear in an article published in the ACSHO's journal, *Jomo*, in response to the announcement by the Birmingham City Council in 1989 of funding cuts. For the ACSHO, the cuts were a signal for groups such as Harambee, who had accepted state money, to "learn the bitter lesson of the enemy's politics." The ACSHO had been "branded extremists for not wanting to collaborate" but argued that the cuts were an example of the state using its "economic strength to divide and rule" and a validation of the group's stress on the importance of self-sufficiency. The cofounder of the ACSHO was the Jamaican Bini Brown. If the lesson drawn by the group in 1989 was "never rely on your enemy for liberation," Brown conceptualized the group's position even more vociferously: "We don't like going with our hand begging, begging, begging. If you have to keep on begging somebody for something, what kind of human being are you? You have no dignity. When you're self-reliant, you do what you do, you're proud of what you are."[124] The group also refused to talk to mainstream journalists and the growing number of white sociologists who, like Rex and Tomlinson, used Handsworth as a case study for their wider explorations of race and immigration.[125] While London-based Black Power groups such as the UCPA and the British Black Panthers were committed to a class-based analysis that left room for alliances with other nonwhite communities, the emphasis within the ACSHO on autonomy stemmed from a version of cultural nationalism that translated into the most ethnically specific politics of any of the organizations discussed in this chapter.[126]

The ACSHO was formed in reaction to the everyday racism that first-generation immigrants experienced in Britain. "People couldn't take the pressure of being called 'wog,' 'nigger,' 'coon,' and so on," Brown recalled. "If you didn't fight back then you'd suffer serious emotional and psychological problems." The ACSHO often framed this fighting back in militaristic terms, in keeping with the idiom of Black Power. Just as in the late 1960s Carmichael envisaged an ensuing transnational "'color clash'" split along binary racial lines, the ACSHO predicted that the collapse of British imperialism and the eventual defeat of apartheid in South Africa would result in the return of "white settlers" to Britain, which would in turn lead to a conflict with an expanded Far Right.[127] Emulating the Black Panthers, in which all new members were given "military training" that included introductions to intelligence work and the use of weaponry, the ACSHO presented itself as a quasi-paramilitary organization in which prominent members were given titles such as Minister for Information and Minister of Defense and new recruits were required to go through a process of "re-education."[128] Concurrent with this vanguardist approach, however, the group also provided a practical program that had the aim of "allowing us to survive in this [the British] environment."[129] In one of the first academic surveys of black Handsworth, the black sociologist Gus John described the ACSHO program as "the most hopeful growing-point for an active and relevant community self-help effort" in the area.[130] Whereas Harambee's core focus was on housing, the ACHSO took the lead in the provision of alternative education for Handsworth's black youth.

The ACSHO supplementary school had been established in 1967 in an atmosphere of growing dissatisfaction among black parents at the way their children were being treated by the educational authorities.[131] Two years later in London, a campaign was fought by the North London West Indian Association against the proposed introduction of a "banding" system in Haringey that was designed to dilute the presence of black pupils in schools across the borough and would thus force many to travel significant distances each day. The campaign eventually forced the Haringey Council to abandon its plans, and the support the campaign gained from other black organizations helped put education at the center of the black political agenda.[132] The focus was often on the disproportionate number of black pupils who were sent to "educationally subnormal" (ESN) schools for children with low ability or learning difficulties. The potential for pathologizing supposed subnormality was obvious, and by 1972 there were five times the number of black pupils in ESN schools than there were in the mainstream system, with the proportion vastly higher in areas of black settlement. Some pupils who had recently arrived from the Caribbean were immediately identified as ESN without ever having attended a mainstream school.[133]

These problems were well known anecdotally among black communities. What demonstrated the true extent of them was the publication of *How the West Indian Child Is Made Educationally Subnormal in the British School System* (1971), a seminal report by Bernard Coard, a Grenadian teacher, postgraduate student, and future key player in Grenada's Marxist revolution. Coard proved the discrimination at the heart of the ESN system and highlighted the effects of an ethnocentric curriculum underpinned by the stereotypes and assumptions of British colonialism. British schooling was shown to have made virtually no accommodation to the growing black presence. Teachers conflated a child's use of the patois dialect with poor ability, and when it came to career planning suppressed aspiration by focusing on manual employment for black school leavers. Where black history was taught it was done so according to a narrative of triumphant colonial expansionism.[134] Coard's research was published by New Beacon Books, the black publisher attached to a radical North London bookshop run by the activist John LaRose, and sold an unprecedented ten thousand copies. At the heart of his recommendations was a call for the black community to set up its own independent or supplementary schools in order to "make up for the inadequacies of British schools" and "teach our children our history and culture." If the ACSHO school in Handsworth was an early forerunner, Coard's work resulted in a mushrooming of black supplementary schools across the country.[135]

It is emblematic of the inadequacies of the state's attitude toward black pupils that it took a report authored by a student and published by a piecemeal publishing house to bring to light the fundamental inequalities in the education system. But it is also demonstrative of the ways in which, in the absence of any serious response from the authorities, black communities developed alternative responses as a result of dialogues taking place across the black globality. Thus, although the growth of supplementary schools occurred as a result of the situation on the ground with respect to ESN schools and black underachievement, the blueprint for how to proceed often came from elsewhere. In Notting Hill in London, for example, the Malcolm X Montessori School was run according to the principles of Hakim Tahar, the director of the Malcolm X Schools Program in the United States, who in 1970 came to London to advise parents on the importance of facilitating creativity and self-discovery.[136] Likewise, it was independent black bookshops like New Beacon and, in Handsworth, the Harriet Tubman Bookshop on Grove Lane that stocked the kind of material mainstream shops refused to sell but that could form the basis of a supplementary curriculum. These bookshops often had links with international sellers such as the Drum and Spear bookshop in Washington, DC, and Liberation Books in Harlem, New York, acting as "transnational magnets" for hard-to-find teaching material on black culture and history, as well as for activists, intellectuals, and educators from across the diaspora who used them as meeting points for discussions and impromptu seminars that played a critical role in shaping the black supplementary school curriculum.[137]

It has been estimated that by the 1980s more than 150 such schools had emerged across the country, in which church groups, parents, and other stakeholders operated alongside organizations such as the ACSHO to offer alternative educational programs on evenings or weekends.[138] The ACSHO's commitment to education was shaped by an ideology rooted in Black Power, Pan-Africanism, and interpretations of Marxism. The chief function of schooling in Britain was held to be to "oppress and brainwash black children into forging the cheap labour force for this capitalist society." In the absence of "a representative number of black teachers" in British schools, the ACSHO advised all black parents to make arrangements so that their children could receive the required supplementary education.[139] By the mid-1970s, many local authorities were actually beginning to move toward a "multiethnic" curriculum that, like the postimperial vision presented by the organizers of the Commonwealth Arts Festival a decade earlier, paid lip service to the importance of diversity and respect for "'different patterns of belief, behaviour and language.'"[140] In contrast, the ACSHO's black educational vision was explicitly separatist in nature. *Black* was a banner restricted to the African diaspora. This meant "those who were called by a variety of names: West Indian, Nigerian, Batian, Trinidadian, Jamaican, Bantu . . . negro . . . black British, etc. etc."[141] It has been shown how black supplementary schools were appreciated by both pupils and parents for their apparent success in facilitating a better level of achievement in math and English.[142] The most overtly political element of the ACSHO's curriculum was the approach to black history. This was a program that presented what was identified as "the true history of our people": African, Caribbean, and African American history. The ultimate aim was to provide students with "a sense of identity which is African"; it was, in Brown's analysis, a program for "re-educating and liberating our people."[143]

In the 1970s the ACSHO Saturday school was attended by an estimated 120 pupils.[144] Although education was the central focus of its activities, the group was behind a range of programs and campaigns aimed specifically at the black community. It demanded "an end to the racist discrimination acts in housing," for example, and "an end to the exploitation of black (African) people by unscrupulous landlords and estate agents." In employment, it called for separate "sections for black people" and declared "that it is very wrong for black people to join the armed forces of this racist capitalist country . . . which are used to repress us and maintain imperialist interest in Africa and the Caribbean."[145] Throughout the 1980s the group was also involved in a campaign against the police in Handsworth. Its journal *Jomo* regularly reported incidents of alleged police brutality and, like Harambee, the ACSHO offered legal assistance to people it believed had been wrongly arrested. Posters were distributed around Handsworth that advised people who had been arrested to use their right to a telephone call to contact the ACSHO, which would provide a "trustworthy and dedicated black lawyer."[146] Utilizing tactics originally adopted by the British Black Panthers—most famously at the 1970 trial of nine black protestors charged with incitement to riot following a demonstration against the police's targeting of the Mangrove restaurant in London—the ACSHO also called for the introduction of all-black juries for black defendants in the British court system. Current black prisoners should be retried with all-black juries or have their sentences overturned. "If these rights are refused," the ACSHO concluded, "then it is apartheid."[147]

The key driver behind the group's operations was an identity-based politics that, shaped by the Black Power of Malcolm X and Carmichael and the Pan-Africanism of Garvey, emphasized the experiences of black people in Handsworth—whether they had been born in the Caribbean or in Britain—as above all part of an African diasporic sensibility. The group summed up its philosophy as being "in the tradition of the honourable Marcus Mosiah Garvey; race first, nationhood and self-reliance together."[148] In 1989 the ACSHO published an article on the legacies of Garveyism that emphasized "all so-called Black people are African and intrinsically and essentially part of the African Nation, irrespective of their geographical location."[149] The long 1980s witnessed a concurrent revival in the cultural politics of Pan-Africanism, stimulated by a growing interest in Rastafarianism. However, as shown in chapter 3, whereas for many Rastafarians an affinity with Africa was largely symbolic, the ACSHO's ultimate aim—following Carmichael—was ostensibly, as Bini Brown explained, to contribute to "re-taking our land and making sure that we actually go back home there. We have the right to the minerals in the ground."[150] This brand of Pan-Africanism at times corresponded with crude, quasi-biological understandings of race that marked it out from the relative importance of class in organizations such as the UCPA. In one leaflet advertising membership in the ACSHO, the group outlined its vision of a world "divided into groups and races," all of which "aspire to be on top." The European was held to compete using a brand of "physical and psychological warfare" called white supremacy, while the Arab competed under "Arab supremacy," a "religious ideology that recognises his race as the 'chosen people.'" "The ACSHO also competes. As Africans, we compete under the banner of Pan-Africanism. A cultural, spiritual and political ideology that is wholly African: An ideology dedicated to the African way of life . . . firmly rooted in our African heritage. How do you compete?," the leaflet concluded by provocatively asking.[151]

This outlook was communicated not only to the participants in the ACSHO's Saturday school or to the readers of its journal. Members were also encouraged to attend the ACSHO's weekly Tuesday seminars, which took place at 104 Heathfield Road surrounded by pictures of Marcus Garvey and Malcolm X and anticolonial posters from Mozambique, Angola, and South Africa.[152] The seminars, according to Bini Brown, were part of the ACSHO's "consciousness-raising programme for the African Race," and each event was advertised as being "strictly an African occasion."[153] The topics discussed ranged from themes such as racism in education, to "the Islamic 'fundamental' threat to Africa," to "Is there a superior race?" Other topics suggest that, like the largely masculine cultures of the IWA and the AYM in Handsworth and sexist attitudes toward women in London-based Black Power groups including the RAAS and the UCPA, the ACSHO was far from comfortable dealing with the subject of women's rights.[154] An introduction to a discussion on abortion, for instance, started with the premise "no one pretends that this is not a gruesome act" and asked whether it was appropriate for women to be condemned by their communities for exercising their right to choose. Another seminar on "Women's Lib" questioned what "a battle . . . between the European sexes [has] to do with African women."[155]

Such positions had consequences beyond the ACSHO discussion groups held at Heathfield Road. For instance, one writer recalled attending a public discussion event in the mid-1980s at which three black women poets were heckled by male ACSHO members and accused of "boot licking" the white establishment, being ignorant of the realities of black inner-city life, and betraying the "revolution."[156] This is not to say women did not participate in ACSHO events. In his 1988 account of his journey through "Afro-Britain," the writer Ferdinand Dennis described encountering a female attendee making her way to an ACSHO seminar on a Tuesday evening in February dressed in "tropical" West African clothing. For Dennis, what was revealing about the encounter was the extent of the attendee's dedication to an "African way of life." When he inquired whether her attire offered adequate protection from the realities of a British winter, she told Dennis in a hybrid Caribbean-Birmingham accent: "'When you know your African identity, the cold can't bother you.'"[157] The ACSHO's Afrocentric agenda seemingly overrode all other considerations. It was presented as a means of "stop[ping] our dependency syndrome." Indeed, whereas other groups in Handsworth struggled to reconcile ideological commitments with their practical programs, the ACHSO's program of consciousness raising complemented the practical work that the group undertook in Handsworth; with respect to the group's educational work, one flowed from the other.[158]

The group's narrow brand of black nationalism had no space for those South Asian organizations who argued for the political benefits of a more inclusive version of black, nor for those immigrants who were in Britain as a consequence of the policies of Africanization implemented in East Africa in the late 1960s and early 1970s. Indeed, in the aftermath of the 1985 rioting, Bini Brown laid the blame for the unrest at the door of this latter community in particular. Speaking to a news crew in the days afterward, Brown declared that "the problem is the striving middle class Asians who were in Africa and were thrown out of Africa. They've come here and they've set up these shops and some of these shops have been collaborating with the police and saying they want to put down the black community."[159] Brown's views were not diluted over time. "The racial group is clear," Brown explained in 2009. "We are one people. We don't need anyone imposing their culture on us."[160] It was an uncompromising commitment to self-help that, in the ACSHO's case, belied the emphasis placed on state multiculturalism as an explanation for the breakup of unified, cross-cultural political alliances. This commitment, manifested in different ways by the ACSHO and Harambee, led to a focus on those issues that were seen to affect the black population in particular. Both groups undoubtedly contributed to meaningful improvements in the lives of residents of black Handsworth, particularly in the areas of housing and education. In one survey, 30 percent of respondents cited Harambee as making the biggest contribution to developments in the area, more than local councilors, churches, and other political groups.[161] With respect to the ACSHO, the Black Power that emanated out of its premises on Heathfield Road was appropriated from America and shaped by a focus on Africa. But this was a vision not extendable to those who were identified as the product of different diasporic formations.

CONCLUSION

What is striking about black politics in the long 1980s is the extent to which it was molded by the kind of transnational dialogues, movements, and exchange of ideas generally associated with an earlier period and the campaigns to bring an end to British colonial rule. While the precise tenor varied from group to group, each organization to some degree adopted an internationalist line of vision that attempted to understand what was happening in Handsworth in relation to the struggles of African Americans in the United States, the campaign against South African apartheid, or contemporaneous anticolonial movements in Africa and elsewhere. The politics of local organizations was shaped by the visits of Malcolm X, Stokely Carmichael, and other African American activists, as well as by representatives from organizations on the front line in the struggle for a postcolonial Africa; by the transatlantic networks that stocked black bookshops and made them a critical facet of the supplementary school movement; and by every donation that was made to help the victims of famine or natural disaster in the developing world. These diverse forms of solidarity imbued the struggles being fought locally against racist violence, the threat of deportation, or educational disadvantage with a potent level of political urgency. Yet inevitably, perhaps, it was also at a local level—in the everyday activities of Handsworth organizations—that contradictions often began to emerge.

Given the separatist nature of the ACSHO's politics, Bini Brown's willingness to accuse sections of the Asian community of causing the 1985 rioting was perhaps unsurprising. Yet the riots also resulted in the ACSHO working alongside other groups in Handsworth, including those South Asian organizations that emphasized the importance of black as a political color. After the first day's rioting, Brown and the ACSHO moved quickly to establish the Handsworth Defence Campaign. Their intention was to ensure that people who had been charged during the unrest received sound legal advice through the provision of sympathetic solicitors. Significantly, the campaign also aimed to "build support in the Handsworth community for the defence of all those who have been charged."[162] Following a meeting attended by both the IWA and the AYM, the campaign released a statement claiming that Handsworth was united both in "condemning the actions of the police" and in the "aim of building up the unity of Asian and African-Caribbeans." A leaflet was circulated that attempted to counteract what was perceived as "the lies and mis-information put out by the police." The leaflet stressed that the riots were "directed against property and the police" and urged the local community to remember that "temples and mosques are side-by-side with Afro-Caribbean social centres and churches."[163] In this particular instance, in spite of Brown's public comments to the contrary and his organization's explicitly narrow racial politics, the ACSHO clearly felt that it was necessary to build alliances with South Asian groups in order to defend the wider community from the actions of the police. It was a version of black as political color that Sivanandan would no doubt have approved of. And it emerged out of a particular practical issue: what were perceived as the divisive actions of the police and the need to support the 380 people who would, in the aftermath of the riots, face police charges.[164]

Each organization discussed in this chapter shared a commitment to responding in practical ways to the needs of the Handsworth community. Events at the local level prompted the turn toward the black globality, as organizations attempted to make sense of, and address, the profound inequalities that were faced by their constituents. Yet the irony of Bini Brown's apparently inclusive Handsworth Defence

Campaign is that for the most part, local issues generally contributed to the weakening of an inclusivist politics of black. Certainly the groups discussed in this chapter were able to make significant advances in countering the effects of the racism that lay at the heart of a host of key British institutions. Certainly too, organizations such as the BBS had some success in their demands for a recognition of the fact that women experienced this discrimination in highly particular ways—even if a regressive attitude toward gender persisted in some organizations. The problem for those adherents to black as a political color was that by the long 1980s inequalities as they were experienced by the residents of areas like Handsworth were increasingly also manifested along ethnic lines: the threat of deportation, the problem of elderly homelessness, the demand for translation services, and the overrepresentation of black pupils in ESN schools. It is indicative of the dedication of local activists that by this time, in their attempts to limit the damage caused by these issues, they had in many ways become social workers as much as campaigners, utilizing their local knowledge to develop responses that could go some way toward filling the gaps left by the state. In the particular conjuncture of the long 1980s, however, the most effective responses were often those that were sensitive to the particular needs of different sections of the local population.

The state's efforts at remedying racial inequality, such as they were, were often restricted to a willingness to provide monetary resources. But the emphasis placed specifically on funding in the breakup of black as a political color has been overplayed. A reliance on state funding evidently made some organizations vulnerable. In 2010, for example, Harambee was forced to close many of its operations following the decision by Birmingham City Council to withdraw financial support.[165] As the examples of the BBS and the AYM show, however, independence from the state was far from a guarantee of longevity. Indeed, Surinder Guru has questioned whether the hard-line stance the BBS took on the issue of funding was the right one. "I've come to the conclusion that state funding can take your independence away," she recalled, "but if your organisation is strong and with a clear purpose, this is not necessarily the case."[166] To the degree that a unitary black politics was ever there in the first place, the picture that has emerged is of a process of fragmentation that was taking place organically in Handsworth—away from, or at least in parallel to, the encroachment of the state.

If it was the white-led AFFOR that was best placed to play the state's monetary game, it was the ACSHO that seemingly combined most effectively a practical politics with its particular ideological reading. Its brand of Black Power combined a focus on Pan-Africanism and the black globality with a program tailored to meet the needs of the local "African" population. The group's politics certainly posited a challenge to the amnesia around Britain's colonial past, symbolized most spectacularly by its decision to stage its inaugural African Liberation Day on the Silver Jubilee weekend. But there were also contradictions. The group's willingness to make alliances with the IWA and AYM in the aftermath of the rioting showed that it was not above the pragmatism of realpolitik. And it was also not consistent when it came to the issue of state funding. In spite of Brown's emphasis on self-reliance and his group's public criticisms of those organizations who chose to accept funding, the ACSHO was in fact also in receipt of public monies. Much of this was small grants for equipment and other items, but in December 1983 the ACSHO was awarded more than £10,000 by the Race Relations Sub-Committee for "various projects to improve community relations." The Handsworth Defence Campaign, and the literature it produced stressing the importance of unity between black and Asian communities, were funded by that committee's newly established Handsworth Disturbance Fund.[167]

This is perhaps an indication that the ACSHO had—in private, at least—moved toward an ideological position closer to that of Harambee, which saw no contradiction in embarking on a program of self-help funded by the state. And as has been argued, it is important not to discount the agency of black activists in using public monies in ways that the funders may not have originally intended.[168] Yet Brown's unwillingness to acknowledge his organization's use of state money was perhaps demonstrative of the discomfort he felt about the issue. What is clear is that it is South Asian activists who have felt the decline of black as a political color most acutely. In the analysis of Ranjit Sondhi, founder of the ARC, while "the Afro-Caribbean community has preserved the political definitions of 'black,'" it is "the Asians [who] have lost it." Among Asian communities, he reflected, there was a desire to "distinguish themselves from the Caribbean community," but "in the process we lost the political power that came with being 'black.'"[169] For some, it is here that the roots of homegrown Islamic fundamentalism can be found, signified by the 1989 spectacle of young British Asians burning copies of Salman Rushdie's *The Satanic Verses* in response to a fatwa issued by an Iranian cleric.[170] In black Handsworth, whatever the contradictions in the ACSHO's eventual decision to accept state funding, the group had, like others, developed a program that undoubtedly resonated in a climate of educational inequality and other structural issues. Yet the politics of Black Power, Pan-Africanism, and diaspora was not restricted to the activities of a relatively small number of committed activists. These themes were part of a much more pervasive structure of feeling manifested culturally, socially, and, as shown in the next chapter, in debates over the politics of representation.

2

Visualizing Handsworth

The Politics of Representation

INTRODUCTION

In January 1987 an argument broke out in the letter pages of the *Guardian* newspaper over the merits of *Handsworth Songs* (1986), a documentary made by a group of young black filmmakers that explored the rioting that had taken place in Handsworth some eighteen months earlier. The argument involved three of the most prominent voices of multicultural Britain: Salman Rushdie, whose Booker award–winning novel *Midnight's Children* (1981) made him a literary heavyweight even before the controversy that would later surround *The Satanic Verses* (1988); Stuart Hall, professor of sociology at the Open University, who by the mid-1980s had been a prominent figure on the British Left for three decades; and Darcus Howe, one of the country's most visible black political activists and a key player in the establishment of a British iteration of Black Power. *Handsworth Songs* eschewed a straightforward narrative of events in Handsworth in favor of a fragmentary method that interspersed scenes from the riots and their aftermath with archival snapshots relating to colonialism and the collapse of the British Empire, the process of immigration, and the experience of diaspora. For Rushdie, however, it was an approach that was unsuccessful. Not only was it couched in what he decried as the "dead language of race industry professionals," but it also failed to offer a view of black Handsworth that was any different to "what we know from TV. Blacks as trouble; blacks as victims."[1] Hall disagreed, arguing that the film represented an attempt precisely to find new ways of narrating black Britain and portraying Rushdie's stance as creating a "false and dangerous dichotomy between 'experience' and 'politics.'"[2] Hall questioned why Rushdie felt that his "songs" were any better than those presented in *Handsworth Songs*—"presumably," he suggested, "because they don't deal with all that dreary stuff about riots and the police etc."[3] Finally, Howe intervened to side with Rushdie. He characterized *Handsworth Songs* as a symptom of an "absence of a critical tradition in the field of black arts" and saw Rushdie's critique as a "timely intervention" that could lay the ground for such a tradition, beyond what he saw as "patronising" tendency to award black artists "ten out of ten for struggling."[4]

As the tone of the debate suggested, this was a critical period for the black arts in Britain and the politics of representation. *Handsworth Songs* was made by the Black Audio Film Collective (BAFC), a London-based group whose work was particularly engaged with a project to address what Stuart Ward has identified as the "potent blend of trauma, nostalgia ... resentment" and "fundamental ambivalence" caused by the legacy of empire in postwar Britain, and what in Sandra Courtman's terms was a "process of constructing a new metropolitan identity and a post-colonial future."[5] In its concerns with empire and the relationship between urban Britain and the black globality, the BAFC in many ways represented an artistic manifestation of the ideologies of the political groups discussed in the previous chapter. Just as the ACSHO had made the decision to stage its inaugural African Liberation Day at the highly symbolic moment of the 1977 Jubilee weekend, for example, so the BAFC sought to emphasize the enduring, if largely unacknowledged, presence of the imperial legacy in postcolonial Britain. Prior to *Handsworth Songs*, the group had made *Expeditions: Signs of Empire* (1983), a slide-tape installation that sought to highlight the links between present-day debates on race relations and the worldview of British colonialists such as the one-time governor of Nigeria, Lord Frederick Lugard. The BAFC was part of a new generation of black British artists that included the photographer David A. Bailey; the multidisciplinary Sonia Boyce; and Sankofa, another film-based collective based in London. For the Nigerian critic and art historian Okwui Enwezor, this was a historical moment of black artistic self-discovery in which there were echoes of the Harlem Renaissance and *negritude* movements in the earlier twentieth century.[6] Whatever the merits of *Handsworth Songs*, the debate among Rushdie, Hall, and Howe undoubtedly helped cement it as a critical intervention into Handsworth's visual cultures. And the film corresponded with a range of primarily photographic work that came from within the area, which had a more specific focus on the peculiarities of the Handsworth locale. What united these art-forms was a desire to undermine the saliency of existing visual representations of black Britain crafted by mainstream media that, as Rushdie recognized, often reduced their subjects to the status of victims or, increasingly, potential aggressors fundamentally at odds with British ways of life.

Such representations had evolved from the postwar period onward. In the 1950s, for example, magazines like the *Picture Post* featured photographs of black immigrants on their arrival in Britain framed by a prominent uniformed police presence, their potential for criminality confirmed by headlines that identified them as "Thirty Thousand Colour Problems."[7] Upon their settlement in areas such as Handsworth, immigrants were pictured in the context of an easily recognizable sign of urban deprivation; black subjects appeared next to crumbling walls, in cramped bedsits, or with litter blowing around their feet. On the one hand, this referenced the long-standing tradition of social reformist photography classically embodied in the work of Jacob Riis and Lewis Hine in turn-of-the-century America, whose subjects were commonly presented as the victims of the acute deprivation that surrounded them.[8] But on the other hand, in postwar Britain the frequency with which black people were photographed in the context of poverty both denied black subjects agency and helped to reinforce stereotypical perceptions of an essential connection among race, dilapidation, and the crumbling slums of postwar Britain.[9]

The moments of Powellism and mugging helped frame the black presence, and black youth in particular, as a potentially violent menace. If in the Powellian imaginary the figure of the lone female pensioner being tormented by "wide-grinning piccaninnies" helped create a framework that cast white society in the position of victimhood, the "mugging panic" of the 1970s emphasized the growing violence of this threat, which had moved on from a focus on elderly women to anyone who happened to be walking the inner-city street.[10] It was the riots that marked the moment that this threat began to be seen in collective rather than individual terms. The 1985 unrest came just months after the conflict between the government and the National Union of Miners, and contributed to Britain's engulfing sense of crisis. Earlier, speaking in July 1984 to the 1922 backbench committee of Conservative MPs, Margaret Thatcher had famously conceptualized Britain as being at being at war with an "enemy within," a "scar across the face of our country" that, like the "enemy without" in the war with Argentina over the Falklands, would have to be defeated.[11] Such discourse helped establish the dominant tone of how black communities like Handsworth had come to be represented. Newspaper reportage emphasized the way in which the notional enemy within had also come to include black, inner-city rioters. News photos lingered on scenes of vandalized and looted shops, indicating that this was not only an attack on the residents of Handsworth but also a wider affront to the values of individual entrepreneurship and private property, which by this time had become widely understood as key motifs in the politics of Thatcherism. Black youths were no longer simply violent; they now represented a "proto-insurrectional" mob propelled, as Paul Gilroy has argued, by what were regarded as "the deviant impulses of their pathological alien culture."[12]

The focus of this chapter is on the wide-ranging attempts at developing alternative visual representations of black Handsworth. The BAFC's innovative approach to form was in part facilitated by the growth of the independent film sector in

Britain following the establishment in 1982 of a fourth television channel. But it was preempted by a photographic movement that had roots in the counterculturalism and alternative arts scenes of the late 1960s. Also drawing inspiration from the work of theorists such as Susan Sontag and John Berger, community photography initiatives emerged across the country, rejecting the traditional documentary practices that have hitherto occupied the primary focus of historians.[13] Although often white themselves, community photographers sought to bypass what they regarded as the fundamentally exploitative power dynamics between usually male, very often middle-class, and nearly always white documentary photographers and their commonly marginalized subjects. The aim was to place photographic skills, techniques, and equipment into the hands of those traditionally rendered the objects of the visiting photographer's gaze, thus opening up the possibility for the creation of images that radically challenged the way these communities were represented. In parallel to this, and sometimes as a direct result of their participation in it, a new generation of black documentary photographers had also emerged from within communities like Handsworth who, rather than venturing into alien landscapes represent the ways of life of the people who lived there, sought to make a photographic record of their own environments and the people that surrounded them. This chapter takes as its starting point two community photography initiatives in Handsworth, before moving on to examine *Handsworth Songs* and the work of Vanley Burke and Pogus Caesar, two prominent Handsworth-based documentary photographers.

No matter the innovative methodology deployed, I argue, the tension alluded to in the discussion among Rushdie, Hall, and Howe—between an abstract search for a visual language with which to tell Handsworth's "songs" and, on a practical level, the reappearance of images that only conformed to existing stereotypes and "what we know from TV"—was one that these artists found virtually impossible to elude. There was a perpetual dialogue between a desire for a more authentic vision of black Handsworth, and the enduring reach of stereotypical images commonly found in the pages of tabloid newspapers. For some community photographers, the only solution to this problem was to remove any visible trace of the Handsworth context, thereby confirming the potency of what Rushdie summarized as the "front page" view. In light of this, the discussion that follows might more properly be understood as providing an insight into the ways in which individual artists used their work to explore their own identities, a process of self-fashioning that examined race and diaspora as part of an increasingly atomized political agenda. Yet while accounts of the self were an important backdrop to this artistic output, this is not to suggest a familiar narrative of 1980s individualism.[14] Rather, no matter how problematic it was, each artist was involved in a collective project that in many ways could be seen as a process of archiving, as much as representation: a shared attempt at establishing an alternative, visual record of postcolonial Britain that could counter dominant stereotypes about Britain's black inner cities.[15] For the BAFC, this meant adopting an experimental approach to form that attempted to make Britain's imperial past a present feature of the metropolitan landscape. For documentary photographers such as Burke, the ambition was to develop a photographic, quasi-anthropological map of what had become Handsworth's extensive black locality.

The following discussion shows that at times, as there had been for Handsworth's political groups, there could be tensions within this body of work between the global and the local, as the ideological emphasis on the black Atlantic rubbed up against the practical politics of the Handsworth locale, and a concurrent desire—particularly among Handsworth's documentary photographers—to faithfully record what was happening in the community. But what Hall identified as Rushdie's "false and dangerous dichotomy between 'experience' and 'politics'" was never an issue for artists attempting to visualize black Handsworth. While this chapter could be seen as a bridge between the previous exploration of political groups in black Handsworth and a subsequent interrogation of its leisure and social lives, it in fact demonstrates the extent to which political questions maintained a pervasive reach. No matter how hard Burke in particular sought to linger on everyday life in black Handsworth—for example, scenes of religious worship, reggae concerts, and individuals pictured on their way to the shops—the politics of urban disorder, poverty, and conflict maintained a continual presence. In the divisive context of Thatcher's Britain, they too were part of what it meant to experience race.

COMMUNITY PHOTOGRAPHY

The ethos of community photography arguably had roots as far back as 1934 when, inspired by a parallel movement taking place in the United States and alongside the Communist Party of Great Britain, the Workers' Film and Photo League was established with the aim of developing film and photographic practices among the working classes. The league partnered with Left Book Clubs across the country and hoped that by giving workers more sophisticated photographic skills they would be able to create images that would act as a propaganda tool in the class struggle.[16] The organization had disbanded by the outbreak of World War II, and although early community photography publications featured essays emphasizing the league's enduring relevance, as a movement community photography was closer to the experimentalism at the heart of the counterculture movement of the late 1960s. Within this latter milieu, initiatives were highly diverse but to some extent united by an ambition to produce alternative perspectives to those seen in the mainstream by giving a greater number of otherwise marginalized voices platforms on which they could be heard. This ranged from the emergence of an alternative poetry scene and radical street theater to an increasingly influential underground press in the form of magazines such as *International Times* (*IT*), *OZ*, and *Time Out*. The physical locus for these activities often came in the shape of "Arts Labs," the first of which was established in London in July 1967 by Jim Haynes, an American ex-serviceman who had earlier played an important role in the development of alternative theater in Edinburgh and in 1966 had cofounded *IT*.[17] Haynes characterized Arts Labs as "an experiment with such intangibles as people, ideas, feelings, and communications," and the activities of the more than seventy Arts Labs that emerged across the country moved fluidly among theater production, dance, experimental art, and cinema.[18] They were nevertheless shaped by an understanding that art should be taken out of the gallery and into the street and a commitment to what would become Arts Labs' guiding principle: "Everybody can do everything."[19]

Although Haynes's Arts Lab had folded by the start of the 1970s, spin-off versions in Birmingham and elsewhere continued throughout that decade and were closely aligned to the birth of community photography. Here the key markers included the 1974 formation of the Photography Workshop in London by the photographers Jo Spence and Terry Dennett, who aimed to provide a darkroom, photography gallery, and other facilities for use by local communities; the 1976 establishment of *Camerawork*, a journal on the ethics and practice of socially committed photography; and the concurrent emergence of small-scale initiatives across the country that were beginning to develop imaginative practices that sought to bypass what was seen as the problematic of "straight" documentary photography. These initiatives included the 1973 Free Photographic Omnibus project, in which the photographer Daniel Meadows converted a double decker bus into a photographic studio and traveled the country offering those he encountered free portraits of themselves, and the 1977 Bootle Art in Action project, which used photographs taken by residents of Bootle, an inner-city area of Liverpool, to campaign against the poor-quality housing stock in the area.[20]

The nature of these initiatives demonstrates how the ethos that characterized late 1960s counterculturalism continued to resonate beyond London well into the 1970s, even after the high-profile obscenity charges that were brought against both *IT* and *OZ* in the early part of that decade.[21] In Birmingham, key players in the developing community photography scene were Brian Homer, an electrical engineer at the Central Electricity Generating Board with an interest in community publishing; the Cambridge graduate and journalist Derek Bishton; and John Reardon, a photography student and aspiring photojournalist. In the first instance they were inspired by what they saw to be the more properly democratic approach of the underground press. In 1971 Homer helped launch *Grapevine*, a magazine envisaged as a less explicitly provocative *Time Out* for Birmingham that would nevertheless provide community-oriented, politically committed news that the mainstream press did not to cover.[22] Its cofounder was Trevor Fisher, a student under E. P. Thompson at Warwick University and then at Birmingham's CCCS. Fisher introduced Homer to Richard Hoggart's *The Uses of Literacy* and the burgeoning History Workshop movement, which, propelled by Raphael Samuel following its establishment in 1966, proposed a radical reorientation of history that was likewise focused on the principles of egalitarianism and, by 1972, was staging events that were attended by more than two thousand people.[23] By the mid-1970s both Bishton and Reardon were contributing to *Grapevine*'s successor publication, *Broadside*, and subsequently left their full-time occupations to set up a dedicated community publishing agency.

Initially this was based at the Birmingham Arts Lab, which was situated next to Aston University, a fifteen-minute drive from the center of Handsworth along the newly opened Aston Expressway. In 1977 the photographers moved into premises at 81 Grove Lane, in between the Harambee hostel for black youth on Hall Road and the IWA's Udham Singh Welfare Centre on Soho Road.[24] Two years later, Bishton, Homer, and Reardon established *Ten.8*, a journal that aimed to develop debates around the community arts but, like *Camerawork* in London, with a specific focus on the photographic medium. The tone of the magazine was initially a humanistic one, and it was always much more earnest in presentation than the deliberately provocative underground magazines of a decade earlier. In spite of this, *Ten.8*'s dedication to the subject of democratization was signaled in its first issue with an essay by Bishton and Homer on the growth of community photography. In it, the authors quoted an earlier article by Jo Spence in which she made clear the wider political objectives of the movement. In Spence's conception, community photography could help people "'look at the world differently'" and, more ambitiously, make their relationship to the media "'less of a one-way concern'" by counteracting the stereotypes they were seen to put forward. If photography was put "'into the hands of a lot of people,'" Spence wrote, "'eventually [they will] be able to dispense with the experts.'"[25] Unsurprisingly, given the increasingly acute issues surrounding the media's representation of race and the inner city—made explicit in Handsworth with the 1978 publication of *Policing the Crisis* (coauthored by a CCCS research group)—it was Spence's aim of demystifying the media to which the editors of *Ten.8* gravitated. Community photography, Bishton and Homer argued, had resulted in a welcome shift away from an emphasis on the quality of a picture and toward "the *act* of pressing the shutter." Concurrently, giving a community like black Handsworth—traditionally the object of the visiting photographer's lens—power over their own representation would, it was hoped, have a much more pervasive impact. It could, Bishton and Homer argued, turn participants into more general "*agitators* for change."[26]

Ten.8 provided an outlet for the community photography being practiced across the country, but in its early issues it often focused on the Birmingham and

Handsworth locales. A long-standing initiative was the Westminster Endeavour for Liaison and Development (WELD), an educational and community arts organization established in 1968 by two teachers at a primary school on Westminster Road, a mile north of the ACSHO premises at 104 Heathfield Road. Alongside dance, arts, woodwork, and other workshops, WELD ran photography classes during school holidays, open to anyone who wished to make use of WELD's darkroom, light box, and six cameras.[27] WELD was also the first initiative in the country to employ a professional community photographer, a post filled in the late 1970s by the photographer Jon Stewart.[28] Homer and the other founders of *Ten.8* concurrently taught photography classes at WELD; for Stewart, the aim was to push participants in the courses away from an understanding of photography that reduced it to something used only "on special occasions or on holiday." Instead, Stewart aimed to encourage people to think about using cameras in order to represent themselves in the context of their own immediate environments, whether they were pictured at ease with that environment or confronting it.[29]

Most of the pictures taken at WELD fitted into the former category. Participants were often lent a camera over extensive periods and were encouraged to document their everyday lives as they walked Handsworth's streets, attended its parties, or spent evenings at friends' houses. One such series of photographs was taken by Hurvin Anderson, whose parents were immigrants from Jamaica and who grew up in Handsworth in the late 1960s and 1970s. Anderson would later go on to become a prominent artist in his own right; in 2017 his oil paintings were nominated for a Turner Prize. Indeed, it is striking that in many of the photographs he took while a participant at WELD—a portrait of a young black woman smoking in a bedroom, for example, behind whom are an ashtray and a half-drunk bottle of beer—the quotidian element that would characterize Anderson's later paintings of black barbershops and domestic interiors was also evident.[30] For all the emphasis Stewart placed on using photography to enable participants to engage with Handsworth's built environment, it was Anderson's ability to document everyday life in the domestic sphere that offered the clearest contrast with the work of established documentary photographers of urban life, for whom the street most commonly functioned as the critical canvas.[31] Elsewhere, another series of pictures taken in 1978 came from a day trip to the countryside organized by WELD. Groups of black teenagers were photographed in the grounds of a church, sitting casually on benches or walls, and eating picnic food. In one image, a group of boys pose for the camera on the steps of a tombstone in the church graveyard; in another, a couple are pictured eating ice cream. In spite of Stewart's insistence on the importance of encouraging participants to move away from an understanding of photography as something that was to be used only on holiday, such scenes can be read precisely as the kind of pictures that are taken on vacation; they are reminiscent of snapshots placed in family photo albums.

Erika Hanna has shown how both amateur snapshots and photo albums can offer meaningful insights into the ways in which historical actors develop modified views of themselves in relation to hegemonic ideas about issues such as gender, sexuality, and nation.[32] It would be tempting to apply Hanna's arguments to the photographs produced at WELD. In lingering on scenes of everyday normality, the participants at WELD were fashioning a version of themselves that contrasted markedly with the increasingly hysterical attitude toward race presented in the mainstream media. Yet unlike genuine amateur photography, in which control rests with the person who both takes the pictures and curates the photo album, in community photography a larger number of people played active roles. Of particular importance was the role of the professional photographer like Stewart, who had a significant influence not only through training participants in basic techniques but also with respect to their choice of subject matter and the eventual dissemination of their images.

Bishton and Homer were evidently aware of this issue. Like many community photographers, they turned to theoretical criticism to make sense of the practical issues they encountered. Following the novelist and art critic John Berger, the photographers introduced a distinction between private and public photographs. Berger had become an influential figure in debates about photography, particularly following his 1972 television series *Ways of Seeing*, which explored the development of the Western aesthetic canon, and his later essay "The Uses of Photography," which was pitched as a response to Susan Sontag and a more nuanced reading than Sontag's overt suspicion of the medium would allow. The categories of private and public were critical in this respect. In his conception of a public photo, Berger echoed Sontag's understanding of photography as a fundamentally exploitative medium. Images used by advertisers or newspaper and magazine editors were, Berger argued, overlaid by ulterior, political motives to sell to or persuade.[33] Berger maintained that private "snaps" of family or friends offered a direct contrast. These images are meant to be seen by a select number of people and are often mediated by someone with a direct connection to the photograph's original context: the person who took the photograph, someone who was in it, or a family member who had some understanding of the people and places it showed. As a result, Berger contended, lived experience is at the heart of a private photograph. For Bishton and Homer, writing in *Ten.8*, these categories offered a way of understanding the liminal position of community photography as amateur snapshots that were nevertheless influenced by professional practitioners.

Bishton and Homer suggested that the WELD series were "both political images and private pictures." When placed in a family photo album, the dominant register of photographs such as these would evidently be that of the family photo. In the pages of *Ten.8*, however, these photographs took on a different meaning. This was influenced not only by the professional community photographer but also by those writing about such images for magazines like *Ten.8*. In Bishton and Homer's analysis, the WELD photographs were unsettling "because they present such a stark contrast between the essentially 'white' associations of the English country church and the unexpected intrusion of 'blacks.'" This was a statement that spoke to the pervasiveness of racialized stereotypes in the long 1980s. But it was also a reflection of the implications of a photograph's passing from the private into the public domain. In newspapers, groups of black youths pictured in the context of the inner city fed into familiar anxieties about the supposed black threat. But when an ostensibly private photograph of black youths in the countryside was placed in the public domain, it too generated significant concern. When an exhibition of WELD photographs went on display at a public gallery, it provoked several complaints from members of the public on the grounds that the photographs were "tasteless."[34]

This was the central contradiction in community photography: on the one hand, practitioners maintained a theoretical commitment to attempting to overcome the power relations seen to be inherent in conventional documentary practice; on the other hand, there was a politicized incentive to create a set of images that would clearly provide an alternative perspective. Stewart, employed professionally as a community photographer, also stressed the importance of generating photographs of Handsworth that countered "the ghetto image of poverty and deprivation."[35] Many of the WELD images indeed do this. Arguably the most powerful photographs were not those taken in the countryside but the brief glimpse of domestic life provided by Hurvin Anderson's image of a woman smoking. The domestic was certainly a sphere that visiting documentary photographers to Britain's inner cities, at least, consistently found themselves unable to access. And it was also a site of a much wider set of shared practices and aesthetics that Anderson himself would later explore in his artwork.

The editors of *Ten.8*, perhaps concerned that the political message of photographs of the domestic would not have the same resonance with their audience, did not include Anderson's work in the magazine. But another photograph, taken on a Handsworth street by Sharon Smith, a local resident and a WELD participant, was featured. Her image makes some of the contradictions of community photography particularly clear. Smith enjoyed photography because she found it otherwise "'hard to express my feelings.'" She recalled encountering a demolition site in Handsworth and stopping to take a photograph with her WELD camera: a black-and-white image of a silhouetted man standing among the rubble of what was once a line of terraced houses. The dust from the demolished bricks is all around the slumped figure, who is dwarfed by the presence of a large digger behind him (see figure 1).[36]

The photograph was originally shown in a small exhibition in Handsworth, where it may have been seen as an example of one of the key aims of community

FIGURE 1. Demolition site in Handsworth, 1979. Photograph by Sharon Smith; reproduced by permission.

photography: to encourage participants to engage with their immediate environments. Yet as Bishton and Homer recognized, when removed from its original context and shown in the pages of *Ten.8*, Smith's picture "could have been taken by any 'concerned' documentary photographer."[37] The focus on urban deprivation and the tone of despondency in the image evoke long-standing documentary tropes in photographs of working-class areas. The emphasis on such an overt sign of poverty is also in keeping with a strong theme within the mainstream media's representation of black Handsworth, particularly in the earlier period of black settlement. For Smith, however, this was not the point. She took the photograph because the scene captured her feelings about living in Handsworth. "'The man hanging his head in despair ... the drooping figure in the photograph,'" she reflected, "'says it all.'"[38] Taking photographs in Handsworth often meant being unable to find images that contrasted with external views of the area. One solution to this problematic was to leave Handsworth altogether for new locations, such the countryside. Another option, deployed by Bishton, Homer, and their collaborator John Reardon in their own photographic practice, was to remain in Handsworth but to remove all visible traces of its physical environment.

Over four weekends in autumn 1979—as the impact of the Conservative Party's landslide election victory that same year was becoming clear—Bishton, Homer, and Reardon constructed a makeshift photography studio outside their premises on Grove Lane, Handsworth. It consisted of a 35 mm camera mounted on a tripod, a plain white backdrop, and a sign in three different languages inviting passersby to come in and take their own photographs. The photographers hoped to generate a set of images that would more accurately capture what they saw as the richness of the area.[39] How and when the photograph was taken was left up to the participants. The camera was attached to a long cable release that each participant would hold; Bishton, Homer, or Reardon would set the camera up, hand participants the cable release, and then stand aside, leaving control over the shutter in the hands of the person whose photograph was being taken. The next weekend, after Bishton, Homer, and Reardon had developed the previous set of images, participants would return to collect copies of their own portraits to keep.

The project arose partly out of the photographers' firsthand awareness that programs like WELD would not, as the photograph taken by Smith made clear, necessarily result in pictures that were "qualitatively different from [those] produced by an outsider."[40] Yet a tension between Berger's notion of the private and public photograph would also characterize the pictures taken by participants in what became known as the Handsworth Self-Portrait Project. In the first instance, what is striking about the pictures is the private intimacy within each frame, the sense of ease upon each participant's face. Participants pulled faces or winked at the camera (see figure 2a), and families and young children featured prominently in a set of images that would ultimately number more than five hundred. What Sontag decried as the "aggression ... implicit in every use of the camera" was seemingly overcome in the Self-Portrait Project by virtue of the fact that the person taking the photograph was also the one being photographed, and because of the familiarity of participants with the local environment.[41] Grove Lane connects Handsworth Park to Soho Road, which was made up of toy shops "crammed with cheap plastic junk," high-street jewelers, and "greengrocers stocking what looked and smelt like every known fruit, vegetable and herb."[42] Opposite the photographers' makeshift studio was a fish and chip shop. As a result, when people took their own portraits, many brought with them into the studio items from their everyday lives outside as they made their way to or from the park or Soho Road shops—bags of shopping, for example, or skateboards (see figures 2b and 2c).

As the trilingual sign the photographers placed outside their studio suggests, the photographers were aiming for—and largely got—a cross-cultural representation of the Handsworth population. Although what funds the photographers had largely came from the Arts Council, the self-portrait project was in many ways an aesthetic in keeping with the moves in local governance toward the multicultural agenda. The majority of participants were black or South Asian, many of whom treated the project as an opportunity for an impromptu family portrait. This was also an echo of the earlier practice of immigrant settlers, who often used commercial photography studios on the high street to create images of themselves and their families that could be sent back to relatives overseas (chapter 4 discusses this phenomenon in more detail). Although not a central part of their rationale for the project, the photographers would also have recognized the potential for their setup to avoid a central critique of community photographers, such as that of Jo Spence, who highlighted the fundamentally constrictive nature of the male documentary gaze. Women featured strongly in the self-portraits, not only as mothers in family shots but also as solo participants, occupying a range of subject positions:

FIGURES 2a–c. Handsworth Self-Portrait Project, 1979. Reproduced by permission of Derek Bishton, Brian Homer, and John Reardon.

from a woman dressed in a full *shalwar kameez*, her one protruding hand operating the camera's cable release, to the young black woman nonchalantly operating the cable release in one hand while holding a smoking cigarette in the other. The photographers owed their inclusivist ethos to the American photographer David Attie, who in 1977 published *Russian Self Portraits*, a collection of images in which a similar technique had been used to attempt to overcome Western stereotypes regarding life in the Soviet Union during the Cold War.[43] Attie's setup appealed to Bishton, Homer, and Reardon because of problems they were encountering in their everyday photographic work in Handsworth. "As young white guys walking around the streets of Handsworth ... trying to engage with young black guys," Bishton recalled, "you were inevitably getting a stereotypical response to your presence. Inevitably, if you've been criminalised in some way, and someone's following you around with a camera, then you're suspicious." The photographers felt that passing control over the camera shutter to the subject of the photographs, as Attie had done in Russia, offered a potential way beyond this issue. The idea, Bishton recalled, was to "allow people to present themselves to the camera" as opposed to the photographer "pre-determining the result."[44]

Yet the politics of the public photograph was also present within these images. Bishton, Homer, and Reardon were from the beginning open about the political nature of the project. The project was undertaken partly in response to Margaret Thatcher's infamous comments about immigration in which, in the run-up to the 1979 general election, she appeared to sympathize with those gravitating toward the NF as a result of concerns about Britain becoming "swamped" by people of a "different culture."[45] Bishton, writing in 1980, regarded Thatcher's comments as "probably ... the most overtly racist comments by any politician in power since Hitler." Building on Jo Spence's ambition for community photography to demystify the media, Bishton, Homer, and Reardon wanted above all to produce images that challenged such portrayals of multicultural Britain. The plain white backdrop removed Handsworth almost completely, in order to avoid "present[ing] people in a context of deprivation and inferiority" and to "confront and challenge racist stereotyping." Instead, the central aim of the project was to communicate what the photographers perceived as being "the unique richness of a community."[46]

Although the Handsworth photographs were technically *self*-portraits, in the sense that it was the participants themselves who controlled the shutter release, ownership of the portraits in terms of copyright belonged to Bishton, Homer, and Reardon. It was they who determined the nature and setup of each portrait, as well as the politicized message of showing black people away from the context of inner-city deprivation. Each participant was required to sign over copyright on the images to the photographers, thereby allowing them to show the images in exhibitions or magazines. The 1979 photographs quickly became increasingly public images; almost immediately, they were published in magazines and newspapers and shown in exhibitions, and they were subsequently donated to the permanent collections of the Birmingham Museum and Art Gallery.

In 2010, as part of a project marking the twenty-fifth anniversary of the Handsworth riots with an exhibition of photography from within the area, the Handsworth Self-Portrait Project was re-created.[47] This time the makeshift studio was constructed on Soho Road itself, in order to attract the largest possible foot traffic. Indeed, the ensuing images captured Handsworth's changing demographics, which by this point, alongside black and South Asian communities, included a significant Eastern European population. But the re-created project also illustrated the way in which, like the WELD project, the influence of the professional photographers over the images being created could be problematic. Most obviously, in their original project it was Bishton, Homer, and Reardon who decided on the setup of the images, the erasing of the Handsworth context, and the subsequent dissemination of the photographs. The 2010 re-creation demonstrated that the professional also retained an influence over the relationship between camera and subject. The ability of subjects to control the shutter via long cable release did not—as Bishton had hoped it would—stop the photographer from attempting to predetermine the result. Those behind the camera often played an active role in directing the subjects in front of them: how they posed, who was standing with whom, and in some instances, when the photograph was taken. The professionals were never entirely able to relinquish their control over the camera's shutter release.

In some ways, this could be seen as a metaphor for the more general problematic of community photography. In WELD, it was the professional who often decided where photographs should be taken and how images should be interpreted for public audiences. The ability of ordinary participants to use photography to fashion private identities for themselves, in relation to the Handsworth locale, was often curtailed by the politics of the professional. This did not mean a complete departure from the countercultural maxim that everybody can do everything. But it did mean that Jo Spence's original hope that community photography would one day lead to experts being dispensed with was always likely to be overly ambitious. Professional photographers retained a commitment to their own expertise and what was undoubtedly a well-meaning faith in the political power of certain types of photographs above others. To the extent that their community photographs constituted an alternative mapping of Handsworth's black locality, these images arguably conceal more than they reveal. The pictures leave behind only small clues about the histories of the people who inhabit each image and how they saw themselves in relation to wider society. For Bishton, Homer, and Reardon, confronting the ethical dilemma of traditional documentary practice meant concealing the street from view. This was in contrast to the BAFC, whose 1986 *Handsworth Songs* announced the group as key players in the politics of visualizing Handsworth. Their attempts at disrupting the documentary eye owed less to the democratized, localized ideal of community photography; instead, the group attempted to develop a cinematic form that could express a globalist, anticolonial agenda that brought to the fore the connections between Britain's imperial past and events in contemporary Handsworth.

HANDSWORTH SONGS

The BAFC was formed in 1982 by seven London-based students enrolled in subjects including fine arts, sociology, and psychology at the polytechnic in Portsmouth, the port city to the southwest of London. The immediate context was significant growth in the independent film sector, prompted by the establishment in the same year of a fourth television channel with a remit to nurture and provide a platform for independent filmmakers. With funding from arts councils and the British Film Institute, Channel 4 backed the formation of new film companies or workshops across the country and offered a guarantee that a selection of the work that was produced would find an outlet on the new channel. In its first year 60 percent of Channel 4's airtime was filled with material from independents. The new channel was an attempt to break up what was seen as the unhealthy monopoly of the established channels' use of in-house production teams by encouraging a broader market and new possibilities for film-based entrepreneurship. Although the proposal for a fourth channel had originally been made in 1977 by the Royal Commission on Broadcasting, it was in these entrepreneurial terms that the first Thatcher government also felt able to justify the idea of a new "publisher" commercial broadcaster. However, as the media scholar Paul Long and others have argued, with the subsequent emphasis on collective ways of working and the provision of platforms and new skills for alternative or previously suppressed voices, it contributed to a milieu in which there were resonances of the late 1960s countercultural scene.[48] The experimental labs that formed the institutional foci of the latter, and which by the 1980s had in fact been in receipt of public monies for some time thanks to an increasingly sympathetic Arts Council, had been joined by government-backed workshops with an explicit remit for film.[49]

John Akomfrah, a founding member of the BAFC who would subsequently go on to direct the film *Handsworth Songs*, conceptualized the members of the group as the "bastard children of '68." There were certainly connections between the group's origins and the community photography moment; one of the BAFC's earliest projects, for example, was a series of screenings that took place at the gallery affiliated to *Camerawork* photography magazine in London.[50] Yet their stated interests in the existentialism of Jean-Paul Sartre and the post-structuralism of Roland Barthes demonstrated the extent to which the BAFC was at the avant-garde end of the post-1968 spectrum—certainly when compared with the humanist agenda of WELD or Bishton, Homer, and Reardon. Moreover, to begin with the group was also detached from the workshop movement ushered in by Channel 4 and did not become a formally accredited and therefore funded workshop until 1986. Race was the main driver behind the group's formation. As the collective explained in its founding artistic statement, its core aims were to develop ways of "extending the boundaries of black film culture," to explore how "racist ideas and images of black people are structured," and to question what black independent filmmaking could mean "when present film culture is a largely white affair."[51]

Prior to the early 1980s, the spaces available for such an exploration were indeed limited in the extreme. On television, it was not until the late 1970s that overtly racist and highly popular programs including *Love Thy Neighbour* and *The Black and White Minstrel Show* were canceled—the latter in 1978, when the BBC finally bowed to growing criticism of the continued use of white performers in blackface.[52] Belatedly, programmers had begun to commission material from black writers that sought to develop a portrayal of ordinary black life in Britain from the point of view of black characters. If a key marker in film was the 1974 release of *Pressure*, a feature about a young black school-leaver that was backed financially by the British Film Institute and directed by the Trinidadian Horace Ové, four years later the English Regions Drama Unit at the BBC's Pebble Mill studio in Birmingham produced for television *Empire Road*, a sitcom penned by the Guyanese writer Michael Abbensetts that was set in Handsworth and focused on the everyday lives and relationships of a well-to-do Caribbean couple at the heart of the community.[53] Although the attempts at crafting alternative depictions of black life in the sitcom were in many ways admirable, and the four episodes that were directed by Ové were particularly adept at dealing with difficult material, the overall tenor of *Empire Road* had a tendency to romanticize its representation of multiculturalism using sanitized and well-worn imagery.[54] Its theme tune, for example, focused on salt fish, roti, chapatti, and other culinary offerings in an attempt to communicate the program's commitment to a comfortable vision of multicultural conviviality. Unsurprisingly, perhaps, the reference to empire barely extended beyond the program's opening credits.

The BAFC was immersed in an altogether different project. Informed by the individual biographies of each member, the group attempted to develop an experimentalist documentary form that could simultaneously articulate the experience of diaspora from the point of view of Britain's black population and the enduring echoes of empire even in a period when explicit references to it could largely be absent from public debate.

These themes were embedded in the collective's earliest interventions. Its first work was a performance that took place at Portsmouth's student union. It featured 35 mm projector-slide images of colonial encounters—*The Scourged Back*, for instance, an 1863 *carte-de-visite* of the extensive scarring of an African American slave's back caused by repeated whippings—which as they progressed were accompanied by members of the BAFC reciting passages from Aimé Césaire's poetic meditation and key negritude text, *Notebook of a Return to My Native Land* (1947).[55] This set out what would become the emblematic BAFC approach: an interest in both the presences and absences of the colonial archive and the extent to which these could be brought to bear in the present, the ambivalent role of memory and its relationship to diasporic identities, and concurrently a postmodern approach to form that rejected linearity of narrative. This approach was developed in the group's subsequent work, *Expeditions: Signs of Empire*, which was made between 1982 and 1983 and formed its name by inverting *Empire of Signs* (1970), Roland Barthes's classic study of Japanese mythology. The collective again adopted an audiovisual approach that meditated on the unacknowledged presence of Britain's colonial past in present-day race relations debates. Fragmented archival images of Queen Victoria, white colonialists surrounded by dead tigers, and mutilated black bodies were accompanied by audio recordings that matched the imperialist bombast of prominent colonial administrator Lord Frederick Lugard with the words of the right-wing Conservative MP and repatriation advocate Sir Ronald Bell, who on the subject of the 1981 outbreak of urban unrest across the country responded to a journalist on the issue of the black presence: "If you look at their faces . . . they don't know who they are or what they are. And really, what you're asking me is how the hell one gives them a sense of belonging."[56]

The 1981 rioting was seen by the BAFC as marking a critical rupture in which the questions of race and national identity had unavoidably taken center stage, even if the group saw the commitment of other socially aware artists to class as an analytical category as blinding them to the growing importance of racial issues. By the time the second and more serious outbreak of unrest emerged across urban Britain in 1985, the BAFC was well-placed to intervene. The funds for the production of what would eventually become *Handsworth Songs* came from monies raised from the exhibiting of *Expeditions* in colleges and universities, as well as from a grant awarded by the Greater London Council, further demonstrating—as Stephen Brooke has shown—the way in which the council operated as a significant facilitator of progressive and often experimental projects in ways that disrupted at a local level the increasing hegemony of Margaret Thatcher's neoliberal project.[57]

The BAFC's interests in archive, memory, and identity were central features of *Handsworth Songs*. Although the funds the collective raised enabled them to shoot a significant amount of their own footage, they eschewed a straightforward narration of the unrest in Handsworth and its possible causes. Instead, contemporary footage of burned-out shops, uniformed police officers, and on-site interviews with black and Asian members of the public are disrupted by archival material of an earlier, ostensibly more innocent period of black settlement. Although the presence of empire is less overt here compared to the group's previous works, it is rendered apparent through the *Pathé* and other news clips of black settlement in the 1940s and 1950s that demonstrate the way in which this generation was composed of colonial citizens who were to varying degrees themselves shaped by empire. Arguably the most poignant moment in the film is the footage of the Trinidadian calypso singer Aldwyn "Lord Kitchener" Roberts, who, having arrived as one of five hundred immigrants aboard the SS *Empire Windrush* in June 1948, was asked to perform for the waiting cameras at Tilbury Docks. Kitchener's stage name was itself a nod to the high point of British colonial expansionism during the imperial century, and his rendition of the opening verses of a song that would eventually be recorded as "London Is the Place for Me" included a line that stressed Kitchener's imperial attachment and "glad[ness] to know my mother country." Although his impromptu recital could be read as part of a familiar narrative of postwar black settlement that emphasizes the unpreparedness of immigrants for British ways of life, weather, and above all racism, in many ways it is, as Kennetta Hammond Perry has argued, more properly an example of the manner in which this the members of this generation asserted not only their attachment to Britain but also their right as imperial citizens to be there. In this sense it was a "moment of claim making with political implications," rendered all the more powerful in *Handsworth Songs* by the juxtaposition with footage of a visibly crumbling 1980s urban landscape and by what had, in the aftermath of the riots, become a near-pathological fixation among politicians and other commentators on the supposed alien-ness of the black inner city.[58]

The film also offers an insight into the production of racialized knowledge in 1980s Britain. The collective's members were there to capture Home Secretary Douglas Hurd's traumatic visit to Lozells Road in the days after the unrest, not far from the headquarters of AFFOR (discussed in the previous chapter), during which he was heckled by angry crowds and pelted with missiles but stuck to the government's line—often repeated in public and elaborated on more colorfully in private—that there could be no structural causes for the unrest, which were instead "senseless" occasions that were "completely without reason."[59] An equally telling moment came when the BAFC was filming at a public meeting about the riots in Handsworth and inadvertently captured the way in which the event was covered by a local news crew, who can be heard discussing what they regarded as a problem: that there were "not too many whites" in the audience.[60]

The film's central message, however, is more abstract. Its deployment of a voice-over disrupts rather than sustains any coherent narrative and instead brings to the fore alternative, poetic "songs" that emphasize both the multitude of stories emanating from contemporary black Britain and also the incomplete and often forcibly erased nature of the colonial archive.[61] The film's refrain that "there are no stories in the riots, only the ghosts of other stories" is emblematic not only of the collective's desire to unpick totalizing narratives but also of their extended meditation on the ambivalent legacy of empire, its absences as well as its presences. In opening the film with archival footage of a black worker tending large-scale industrial machinery, for instance, the BAFC signals a recurring engagement with the relationship among industry, empire, and race, made all the more powerful by the film's geographic location in a region that had once been a driver of Britain's industrial revolution. *Handsworth Songs* was a meditation on what the art critic Kodwo Eshun has described as the "dialectics of belonging" and the "poetics of memory," which—as much as the politics of the ACSHO—sought to disrupt postcolonial amnesia by making present the ghost stories of Britain's colonial past.[62]

It was *Handsworth Songs* that announced the BAFC as a major player in the independent film scene. The film was the recipient of seven major awards, including the Paul Robeson prize for "Best of the Best Diasporic Cinema" at the Pan-African Festival of Cinema and Television of Ouagadougou Film Festival in Burkino Faso.[63] It was a symbolic accolade that drew a connecting line between the BAFC and Robeson's own attempts half a century earlier to use his appearance in *Sanders of the River* (1935), a feature film about colonial relations in Nigeria, to strengthen his own commitment to Pan-African knowledge and the cultivating of cross-diasporic ties.[64] The success of *Handsworth Songs* paved the way for the collective to become a franchised workshop funded by Channel 4. And its subsequent films continued to explore the enduring legacy of empire and what the BAFC saw as its effects on the development of diasporic black identities.

The BAFC's follow-up to *Handsworth Songs*, the 1988 *Testament*, used postcolonial Ghana as a setting to further examine the functioning of memory and identity. It centered on the fictional story of an exiled Ghanaian newscaster who returns to her homeland following the military coup against Ghana's first postcolonial leader, the Pan-Africanist Kwame Nkrumah. The film was also directed by Akomfrah, who envisaged it as a vehicle for him to explore his own family history. His parents had been dedicated anticolonial activists in Ghana and supporters of Nkrumah in the run-up to independence but, following the death of Akomfrah's father and the 1966 military coup against Nkrumah, his mother felt compelled to flee to Britain with her four young children for fear of political reprisals. As the cultural theorist Kobena Mercer has argued, by focusing on the disorientation experienced by an exile returning to a radically altered postcolonial climate, *Testament* demonstrates the "slow time it takes to come to terms with post-colonial trauma."[65] The BAFC's next production, *Who Needs a Heart* (1991), underscored its commitment to avoiding simplistic interpretations of the postcolonial legacy, through a focus on the enigmatic Trinidadian-born activist Michael de Freitas or Michael X, whose mutating career trajectory as a drug dealer, pimp, self-proclaimed British spokesman for Black Power, chaperone to Malcolm X and Stokely Carmichael during their visits to London, founder of a hostel for black youth, and eventually convicted murderer itself defied any straightforward narrative reading.[66]

Although the BAFC has been the recipient of multiple awards and in 2009 was the subject of a retrospective exhibition at the Tate Britain in London, the group's decision to reject documentary realism and embrace the deconstructivist agenda meant that it inevitably also attracted significant criticism, represented most spectacularly by the public argument over the merits of *Handsworth Songs* among Rushdie, Hall, and Howe. Given his status as a high-profile observer of Britain's race relations scene, it is Rushdie's critique that has garnered most attention and prompted Hall's decision to come to the BAFC's defense.[67] As Angela McRobbie has shown, by the mid-1980s Hall had already begun to move on to a phase of his career in which he acted as an important interlocutor for the new generation of black artists that included the BAFC as well as the Sankofa collective, whose 1986 *Passion of Remembrance* adopted a similarly poetic, archive-based approach to the documentary form.[68] For one critic, *Handsworth Songs* in particular should itself properly be regarded as an iteration of Hall's cultural studies project, comparable to key works on race such as the collectively authored *The Empire Strikes Back* (1982) and Paul Gilroy's later *There Ain't No Black in the Union Jack* (1987).[69] If Hall's riposte helped temper Rushdie's critique that the film had failed to find an appropriate language with which to tell Handsworth's songs, given the BAFC's interest in the legacies of Black Power, Howe's comments may well have been more difficult to take. No doubt aware that his career as a political activist and a key player in the establishment of the British Black Panthers marked him out from both Rushdie and Hall, Howe framed his comments by emphasizing his two-decades-long experience in black politics, before going on to agree with Rushdie's objections to the film and to decry what he characterized as a patronizing absence of artistic criticism in the emerging black arts scene.[70]

Rushdie's desire for a more conventional documentary form that could create a better visual archive of black Handsworth was undoubtedly out of kilter with what was in the artistic sphere a rising postmodernist tide. But it was in many ways also a pertinent call to recognize the importance of the political conjuncture, particularly one as fraught as Handsworth in the long 1980s. In this context, urban rioting had cemented mainstream representations of the black inner city in general, and Handsworth in particular, as potentially insurrectionary, as well as fundamentally alien, spaces.[71] In the days after the Handsworth riots, for example, the same photograph of a young black man apparently about to throw a lit petrol bomb appeared on the front page of every national tabloid newspaper (see figure 3). The "black bomber," as the man in the photograph was christened by the press, quickly became emblematic of what was presented as a "war on the streets" against the black perpetrators of an "orgy of fire, looting and murder." In Handsworth, the intersection between Heathfield Road and the Lozells Road, and the forecourt around the nearby Villa Cross pub, were known locally as the black front line. To the media in the aftermath of the rioting, the whole of Handsworth had become

"Front Line Britain."[72] The *Sun* even launched its own campaign to name the black bomber, eventually revealing on its front page that he was "hate-filled" James Hazell, brother of the professional footballer Bob and a father of three, who supposedly held a "massive grudge against the police."[73]

To Rushdie, the BAFC's approach in *Handsworth Songs* had resulted in a perpetuation of such discourse: images of "fire, riots, looted shops, young Rastas and helmeted cops by night. A big story; front page." As a point of comparison, Rushdie advocated the effectiveness of *Home Front* (1984), a collection of documentary photographs that were taken by Derek Bishton and John Reardon in Handsworth alongside their Self-Portrait Project and other community photography activities. In these photographs, Rushdie wrote, "you see Rasta groundations, a mosque, Pentecostal halls, and Hindujain and Buddhist places of worship. Many of Handsworth's songs are hymns of praise. But there's reggae, too, there are Toasters at blue dances, there are Punjabi ghazals and Two Tone bands." It was important, Rushdie concluded, to "tell such stories" in order "to say, this is England."[74] Writing in the introduction to *Home Front*, Rushdie echoed the emphasis the BAFC placed on adopting a postcolonial line of vision by highlighting the myriad ways in which image making had been used to underpin the racist ideology of colonialism. If Handsworth constituted the front line, Rushdie agreed that representations of it were part of a struggle the political implications of which were signified by the title of Bishton and Reardon's photographic collection. The significance of images such as those in *Home Front*, Rushdie argued, was the way in which they represented "new, truer images against the old falsehoods"; they were a means of "chas[ing] out the old."[75]

Rushdie's existing familiarity with Bishton and Reardon's work perhaps meant that he was predisposed toward a negative reaction to *Handsworth Songs*. As Hall was right to point out, he had underestimated the significance of the BAFC's experimentalist approach to form and its ability to speak both to the presences and absences of postcolonial Britain. Even in the context of the radical turn in filmmaking ushered in by the birth of Channel 4, the BAFC's craft was highly innovative, and in its attempts to adopt a perspective that emphasized the enduring relevance of Britain's imperial past, in its own way polemical. Yet for all that some criticisms of *Handsworth Songs* may have been bound up with what Kobena Mercer has suggested were anxieties over the challenge it posed to normative ideas about what constituted black film, Rushdie had also hit on the contradictions—encountered in different ways in the previous chapter—between the invocation of the black globality in theory and the politics of a particular locality in practice.[76] Such was Handsworth's privileged position in the popular imaginary, the saliency of those images commonly found in the pages of tabloid newspapers often retained their currency in *Handsworth Songs*. Just as Bishton, Homer, and Reardon felt obliged in their community photography to remove the visible Handsworth locale from their work in their attempts to undermine external stereotypes, so the BAFC had found itself unable to form an account

FIGURE 3. Tabloid front-page article, "War on the Streets," 1985. Reproduced by permission of Trinity Mirror/Mirrorpix.

of the songs that were taking place in contemporary Handsworth—away from police lines, burned-out cars, and above all, the symbolic image of the black bomber.

The BAFC's members were arguably as much outsiders to Handsworth as the journalists, photographers, and news crews that descended on the area in the aftermath of the unrest. Although engaged in a project to address the incomplete nature of the colonial archive, *Handsworth Songs* should more properly be seen as a semiautobiographical attempt to unpick the experience of postcolonial Britain in the internal as much as the external world. Erased in the Self-Portrait Project, the Handsworth locale was almost incidental to *Handsworth Songs*, a point reaffirmed by the group's use of footage from concurrent unrest in Brixton and Tottenham. In contrast, locally based documentary photographers like Vanley Burke—while also motivated by a process of self-fashioning and a desire to establish a more authentic archive of postcolonial Britain—were, as a result of their embeddedness in the Handsworth locale, better placed to develop a sustained consideration of the specificities of space.

DOCUMENTARY PHOTOGRAPHY

By the time the BAFC arrived in Handsworth, both Vanley Burke and Pogus Caesar were already prolific photographers. Burke in particular has maintained a pervasive connection to the area; he has continued to live and work there for more than five decades. His photographs span that entire period, though he remains best known for the pictures he took in the 1970s and 1980s. Burke was rarely an outsider to the scenes he captured; they were part of a life that he was himself leading.[77] He summarized his aims in straightforward terms: to capture "people in their environment, struggling to establish themselves in that environment."[78] But the insider status that both he and, to a lesser extent, Caesar enjoyed did not mean that they were able to avoid the political considerations that effected each contributor to black Handsworth's visual cultures. In many cases, a near-anthropological ambition to faithfully record life in black Handsworth came up against the familiar desire to present an alternative picture to that which had come to define the area. The work of these photographers allows for an expanded perspective on life in black Handsworth, capturing scenes from inside houses, churches, and pubs. However, decisions about what to photograph were nearly always made in relation to dominant perceptions. As it had been for the BAFC in *Handsworth Songs*, a desire to move beyond the media's external representations did not stop familiar scenes from continuing to appear.

In May 1985, six months before the riots in Handsworth, both Burke and Caesar appeared on *Black on Black*, the newly established arts and current affairs program that was part of Channel 4's remit to cater for ethnic minority communities.[79] "We realised that no one was making a record of the community, past or present," remarked Caesar, who had emigrated to Birmingham from the island of St. Kitts when he was five years old. "So we made it our business to build up a picture of the black community in Handsworth." For Burke, who had followed his parents to Handsworth from Jamaica in 1965 at the age of fourteen, people had "brought with them cultures and traditions" on their arrival in Handsworth, and "a lot of them got changed in the process.... [I]t was just necessary to record them." Caesar explained that "the kids today are trying to find a new identity. For some people this means reaching out to other black communities, some in Britain, some abroad. But both Vanley and I are convinced that the answers about our identity lie here in our local history; that's why we think someone has to collect and record that history before it disappears."[80]

Vanley Burke's focus on the necessity of recording life in Handsworth was counterbalanced by a wider ambition: a desire to foreground a romanticized conception of everyday life in black Handsworth, and a belief that capturing Handsworth's everyday stories was a political act. Thus, Burke talked of the need to show "the architecture, the trees, the park, the parked car ... everything" in his photography. But he also described the recording of Handsworth's stories as a way of bringing about "change in the community, change that is relevant to a specific social and cultural environment." Burke hoped that images of scenes of normalcy in Handsworth might replace the familiar tropes of rioting and conflict. "I made a conscious decision to shy away from the spectacular," Burke remarked. "I wanted to concentrate all my efforts on the ordinary, and hopefully let the ordinary become extra-ordinary."[81]

Burke's photography is powerful, however, precisely because of its ordinariness. Like many of the images produced by participants in community photography projects, his photographs resonate because of their ability to appear as private images. There is a sense of intimacy within each frame. His subjects are not asked to falsely pose for his camera; they instead appear immersed in their own business: a lone figure placing a bet at a bookmakers, a baptism inside a church (see figure 4), a middle-aged couple dancing in front of floral wallpaper. As Stuart Hall reflected in a foreword to Burke's first retrospective catalog, in Burke's photographs people appear "absorbed in *their* lives, *their* activities, *their* troubles, sorrows, joys, celebrations [and] griefs."[82] In one image, a group of friends—known locally, Burke recalled, as "the wild bunch"—sit together on a seesaw in Handsworth Park; in another, a group of older men wearing pork-pie hats play dominoes in a pub.

There is often a generational divide in Burke's photographs of leisure in Handsworth. Older generations are usually pictured in the relatively tranquil environments of the betting shop or pub. Younger people, by contrast, are captured in the context of the liveliness of Handsworth's prominent reggae scene: bands rehearsing in basements (see figure 5), sound systems performing at Handsworth carnival, dances held at local youth clubs. Burke also documents weddings, funerals, and other significant occasions in community and family life.[83] Religious spirituality represents a dominant theme in Burke's photography. Alongside scenes of grief such as a funeral burial, there are moments of elation during worship, a whole congregation singing, and the baptism of a teenage girl.

The romantic, almost poetic element in Burke's photography marks him out from many of his contemporaries. The second issue of *Ten.8* featured a selection of Burke's work alongside a statement from the photographer in which he attempted to encapsulate the nature of the people and places in front of his lens. Burke evoked

Figure 4. Baptism, ca. late 1970s. Photograph by Vanley Burke; reproduced by permission.

FIGURE 5. Band rehearsal, ca. late 1970s. Photograph by Vanley Burke; reproduced by permission.

the "resilience and hope" he saw as "characterising the West Indian," and it is his determination to use his photography to communicate this sensibility that provides a contrast with other photographs of black life in the period. Between 1973 and 1976, for example, Colin Jones, a white photojournalist with the *Observer* and the *Sunday Times*, photographed Michael X's hostel for homeless black youths in north London. The tone of these images is characterized by a sense of realism and harshness, black-and-white photographs that depict graffiti-covered walls, stained mattresses, and boarded-up windows.[84] By contrast, in Burke's first retrospective his photographs are composed of more subtle tones, visually closer to shades of brown than shades of black. It was in many ways a nostalgic aesthetic in keeping with the evident admiration he had for those around him: the "hard working man, who at the end of a hard day," Burke wrote in 1979, "donned his felt hat and with it a spirit of enjoyment"; the "eternal optimist for whom the betting shop is a haven"; the run-down houses that were nevertheless "husks enveloping warmth, vitality and love of life."[85]

In Burke's representations of women in Handsworth, this nostalgia is often manifested as a paternalistic, even patriarchal perspective. Certainly women are not seen as the self-confident urban *flaneuses* they are in, for example, Roger Mayne's mid-century photographs of a working-class district of northwest London or, in a different way, Janet Mendelsohn's images of late 1960s Balsall Heath in Birmingham.[86] Men greatly outnumber women in Burke's black Handsworth, especially in the context of the street. Here, Burke's way of seeing casts men unequivocally as actors and the potential drivers of change. We see men on political marches, for example, in heated discussions with police officers, and in the numerous portraits Burke took of passersby on the street or in the park, confidently returning Burke's gaze. Men are also depicted at work, posing in blue workmen's overalls or operating heavy-duty machinery. In contrast, in spite of the fact that older generations of Caribbean women were as much economic migrants as their male counterparts, women are largely portrayed as the matriarchal symbols of Burke's idealistic vision of black Handsworth's "warmth and vitality." They are generally seen not on the street but in interior settings: in church as brides to be or devout worshippers, or in the home, where Burke's vision of feminine warmth is arguably embodied in his photograph of a middle-aged couple dancing (see figure 6). Here, what Burke captures is almost an embrace rather than a dance. The woman is apparently comforting her partner, whose head comes close to resting on her shoulder. It is undoubtedly a poignant image, but it contrasts markedly with the representation of black femininity presented in the work of other photographers. Maxine Walker, for example, was a contemporary of Burke's in Handsworth, and her 1987 work *Aunty Linda's Front Room* comprises a series of portraits of black women in the home. In this series, discussed in detail in chapter 4, the front room is presented as a feminized domain outside the jurisdiction of men. The assertiveness of "Aunty Linda" is communicated by the formality of her pose and the way in which she is seen to hold the gaze of Walker's camera. Although it is a representation of femininity that again takes place in the domestic sphere, in contrast to Burke's work, it alludes to the power that black women wielded in this space as they constructed often-aspirational versions of black selfhood in opposition to the racialized stereotypes of the 1980s.

In keeping with his gendered perspective, Burke's most famous photograph is "the boy with the flag" (see figure 7). It is the image that is most often reproduced and with which Burke is most closely associated. It is the photograph that has

FIGURE 6. Couple dancing, ca. late 1970s. Photograph by Vanley Burke; reproduced by permission.

arguably come to define his career. Taken in the early 1970s, at a time when the Union Jack had become closely connected with the racist politics of the NF, the political power of such an image is obvious. Indeed, formal political activity also figures prominently in Burke's work, including the events surrounding Handsworth's 1977 African Liberation Day in the run-up to the Queen's Silver Jubilee celebrations (see figures 8a and 8b). The local media all but ignored events in Handsworth, in thrall as they were to what was seen as "a tide of patriotic feeling" that had turned Birmingham "red, white and blue again."[87] In contrast, Burke was there to capture the visual juxtapositions of an alternative story, epitomized in one photograph by the presence of a black marcher whose sign, proclaiming the need to "Bury Imperialism in the Fire of Black Unity," was framed by a hedge-fronted terraced house decked out in Jubilee Union Jack bunting.[88] The political tenor of the Liberation Day event is encapsulated by another photograph in the same series and the slogans on the placards being carried by a larger number of protestors: "Never Again," "Hands off Africa," "Stop the Nazi NF," and "We Are Our Own

FIGURE 7. Boy with a flag, ca. 1970s. Photograph by Vanley Burke; reproduced by permission.

Liberators." A final photograph (figure 8b), taken at the march's culmination in Handsworth Park, gets at a sense of the scale of the Liberation Day event.[89] The artist and critic Eddie Chambers has suggested that in its focus on the multitude in the audience (as opposed to those addressing it) and the predominance of headscarves, dreadlocks, a reggae sound system, and other symbols of the growing centrality of Rastafarianism among a young black generation, no other image better encapsulates the "cultural spaces to which young black Britain was gravitating"; the photograph is, Chambers argued, a "cogent document of a particularly culturally and politically charged moment."[90]

In spite of the political tenor of these photographs, however, and Burke's own unquestionable status as an artist of considerable stature, there remains a sense that Burke would most like his work to be considered photographs that belong in a family album. "Right from the start," he reflected, "it was the private face I wished to capture."[91] In his second retrospective catalog, published in 2012 to coincide with a major public exhibition of his work at the Midlands Arts Centre, Burke

FIGURES 8a–b. African Liberation Day, 1977. Photograph by Vanley Burke; reproduced by permission.

FIGURE 9. "A day trip to Skegness." Photograph by Vanley Burke; reproduced by permission.

captioned each picture with the kind of annotations commonly found in such albums: "Selwyn comforts his sister," "a day trip to Skegness . . . curried goat and cooked rice in the boot" (see figure 9), and "Huw in his Sunday best."[92] Burke emphasized that he wanted people to be able to "reference themselves" in his work.[93] Unlike Bishton, Homer, and Reardon, who in the 1990s each moved away from the area, or the BAFC, whose members visited in the aftermath of the rioting, Burke has remained in Handsworth to document the changing lives of his subjects. And this includes the boy with the flag, Winford Fagan, whom Burke photographed in 2004 at the funeral of his son.[94]

Burke suggested that his work should not be viewed as "some sort of anthropological, sociological manifesto."[95] Yet there is something quasi-anthropological about Burke's desire to capture the defining moments in the lives of subjects such as Fagan, and the ritualistic occasions of baptisms, weddings, and funerals. In the 2000s Burke documented the growing number of funerals of young black men who had died as a result of a violent dispute between rival gangs in the area. And his commitment to recording in an earlier period also meant that both he and Pogus Caesar were often forced to capture scenes that mirrored the view found in the pages of tabloid newspapers, scenes that were not intimate or akin to those found in family albums, but were—in Burke's own term—"spectacular." For Burke, this often meant photographing scenes of violence or deprivation. The police, for example, are a regular presence in Burke's photography. Uniformed police officers are photographed grouped behind riot shields or in verbal altercations with black youths. Similarly, Burke also photographed racist graffiti, burned-out cars, and littered streets. It is in the work of Caesar, however, that this problematic is made particularly apparent.

Like Burke, Caesar has been a longtime chronicler of the changing makeup of both Handsworth and wider Birmingham. He has built up an impressive collection of portraits of prominent reggae musicians and artists, often pictured in the Handsworth locale.[96] Caesar's work depicts the Jamaican reggae band the Mighty Diamonds on a visit to the Soho Road, for instance, or the local reggae group Beshara, or the BAFC's John Akomfrah reading the local newspaper in the days after the rioting, or Vanley Burke sitting on a staircase. The photographs for which Caesar is best known, however, are undoubtedly those that he took during the 1985 Handsworth riots. Caesar's images of burned cars and burning phone booths offer powerful illustrations of the extent of disorder in the area, while his image of Home Secretary Douglas Hurd being jeered on his post-riots visit to Lozells Road symbolizes the extent of the disconnect between the black inner city and the government. When in 2010 the BBC produced a short film exploring the legacy of the riots to mark their twenty-fifth anniversary, it is significant that the decision was made to base it almost entirely around Caesar and his photographs. Caesar was filmed returning to the streets that were most affected by the rioting, explaining to viewers what it had been like to bear witness to a scene that included "bottles flying everywhere . . . stones . . . flames [and] cars being overturned."[97] His commitment to documenting what had happened and his status as a black photographer meant that, even twenty-five years later, Caesar was positioned as the authentic narrator of an event that continued to be understood through the prism of race.

On one level, Caesar's photographs do offer a perspective on the riots that differs from that of the mainstream media. Rather than witnessing the events over the shoulder of uniformed policemen, as in the images of the riots taken by visiting photojournalists, Caesar's photographs present what happened as seen through the eyes of Handsworth residents. These are images from within Handsworth, taken in between local residents. In one image, an elderly resident peers out at events from behind a curtain; in another, a group of people are sprinting away from something. Caesar shows his viewers a street sign that has been snapped in two and a "mug shot" of a man hiding his identity with a balaclava and a pair of sunglasses. When we see the police in these photographs, it is they who are seen as alien and aggressive invaders. Caesar's key image of the riots from within is one taken from over the shoulder of ordinary Handsworth people: an officer jabbing his finger in the face of two black men (see figure 10) or a row of policeman crouching behind their riot shields.

FIGURE 10. Confrontation between the police and two black men, 1985. Photograph by Pogus Caesar. ©Pogus Caesar. All Rights Reserved, DACS, 2018.

Yet on another level, Caesar's photographs are a further reminder of the enduring problem of photographing Handsworth within. For documentary photographers like Caesar and Burke, the desire to create a visual archive of Handsworth's everyday stories also necessitated capturing events that were out of the ordinary, "spectacular," and similar to those found in the pages of tabloid newspapers. Caesar's photographs of the riots may offer a different perspective, but the viewer is nevertheless confronted with Rushdie's front page image of fire, looting, and helmeted cops.[98] Engaging with this issue meant that, perhaps inevitably, photographing Handsworth was as political for Burke and Caesar as was Bishton, Homer, and Reardon's decision to erase it altogether. Burke, in particular, may have been drawn to scenes that encapsulated what he saw as black Handsworth's essential spirit of "resilience and hope," but like Caesar his anthropological desire to record meant that he also captured scenes that potentially incriminated his subjects. Burke was aware that he had amassed a large amount of "sensitive material which, if held in the wrong hands, could be harmful to the people who were photographed."[99] In the days after the riots, Burke attempted to take photographs inside the Acapulco Café. The café was located on Handsworth's front line opposite the Villa Cross pub and, according to reports, was the place outside which a disagreement between a black man and a police officer provided the initial spark that led to the unrest.[100] Burke had gained permission from the owner of the café to take photographs inside but was threatened by a customer, who explained "in no uncertain terms . . . what he would do to me should he see a photograph of himself anywhere."[101] In spite of his insider status, Burke could still be subject to suspicion. During the altercation in the Acapulco, Burke was accused of being responsible for taking the picture of the black bomber, which had become the defining image of Handsworth from without.

Burke clearly felt a great deal of responsibility toward the people whose photographs he took. His politics of being a photographer within the locale was to present a side of Handsworth that those without had not seen before, not one they already had. However, for other photographers operating in Handsworth at this time, these boundaries were not so rigidly maintained. Bishton and Reardon's *Home Front* collection of documentary images was described by Bishton as "our personal testament to what we'd experienced [in Handsworth]."[102] The book's title certainly suggests that even those who operated within the community had to some extent bought into the notion of a "war on the streets" of Handsworth, albeit one that was being fought over the issue of representation. It was this genre of work that Rushdie saw as being able to contribute to a process of "liberation" for the residents of black Handsworth.[103]

If understandable, Rushdie's words were also naïve. Whether attempting to bypass the professional by putting cameras into the hands of ordinary people, experimenting with the cinematic documentary form, or undertaking documentary photography from within the community, there were unavoidable contradictions involved in visualizing Handsworth. The case of John Reardon provides one further example. Reardon was one-third of the group behind the Handsworth Self-Portrait Project, whose aim was explicitly to undermine the front page view of Handsworth. Along with Bishton and Homer, he was a product of the late 1960s countercultural milieu, producing the Handsworth photo journal *Home Front*; tutoring participants at WELD; and contributing to *Ten.8*, a magazine about the ethics and practice of community photography. But Reardon was also a jobbing photographer. During the 1985 riots he was also there to document what happened. But when the opportunity came to sell one of his photographs to the mainstream media, he took it. The image of the black bomber, which made it onto the front page of every national tabloid newspaper and prompted the *Sun*'s front-page campaign to name him, was his. Realizing the moral ambiguity of his decision, perhaps, shortly after the riots Reardon moved away from Birmingham.

CONCLUSION

Rushdie's notion that images made from within Handsworth could eventually "chase out" those that were perpetuated without was always likely to prove overoptimistic.[104]

This chapter has revealed how in practice it was not only the approach of the BAFC that, as Rushdie suggested, strayed close to the perpetuation of existing, stereotypical images. Similar sights were found in almost every example of image making from within Handsworth. This is a reminder that as well as being at the heart of hegemonic stereotypes about black Britain, scenes of conflict, poverty, social disorder, and an invasive police presence were also a significant feature of what it meant to live race during the long 1980s. Photographs like Sharon Smith's image of a demolition site, for instance, taken as part of her participation in the WELD community photography course, was not in keeping with community photography's desire to subvert dominant tropes. But for Smith, its tone of deprivation and despondency encapsulated her own feelings about what life was like in the area. For other, more seasoned photographers, the proximity between within and without often had much more problematic implications. The case of Reardon, who alongside Bishton was the subject of praise from Rushdie for his socially aware photographs of black Handsworth, vividly demonstrates the ethical dilemmas that artists faced when attempting to represent such areas in a period of heightened political tension. That Vanley Burke—with his emotional attachment to black Handsworth and enduring presence in its community—could have been accused of taking the photograph of the black bomber, which for a time came to signify the supposedly subversive, insurrectional nature of the black inner city, was testament to the political intensity around image making and the climate of distrust that this evidently provoked. That it was in fact taken by Reardon, a photographer apparently so embedded in the locale and in debates about the ethics of representation, arguably provides yet another example of the enduringly exploitative potential of the documentary gaze.

However acute, though, the politics and contradictions of visualizing Handsworth should not be seen as rendering this body of work valueless. If nothing else, each approach was part of a shared project to develop an expanded visual archive of postcolonial Britain. For the BAFC, like the political organizations discussed in the previous chapter, critical to this process was the adaptation of a global perspective that disrupted Britain's amnesia about its imperial past. This was seen in what the group recognized as the echoes of imperial discourse in contemporary race relations debates, a narrative that not only evoked concurrent cultural studies work on race but also prefigured subsequent scholarly interventions in what has been called Britain's postcolonial "melancholia."[105] The group's oeuvre was autobiographical, a product of its members' diverse family backgrounds and an attempt by the filmmakers to deal with and articulate the subject of fragmented diasporic memory in light of a sporadic and fundamentally incomplete archival base. It was this that for the BAFC rendered the stories emanating from 1980s Handsworth "ghosts of other stories" and dictated their decentered approach to form.

Other artists adopted approaches that were more closely allied to the Handsworth locale and their perceived status as insiders. In their efforts to contribute to a more accurate visual record of a particular iteration of what had become a patchwork of black localities across the country, Handsworth-based practitioners were also involved in a process of archiving. As Burke and Caesar explained in their 1985 television interview, theirs was a project to "collect and record" the history of black Handsworth as it evolved around them, "before it disappears." Both photographers deployed more conventional methods than either the BAFC or the post-1968 experiments in community photography. In particular, Burke's sense of selfhood was bound up with his desire to be seen as the authentic chronicler of black Handsworth. But it is significant that his boy with the flag photograph was also included in *Handsworth Songs*. And Burke's commitment to a process of recording in fact went beyond the role of the photographer to include that of the quasi-archivist. Alongside his long photographic career, Burke has been a compulsive collector of pamphlets, posters, magazines, and other ephemera from black Handsworth that have rendered his archive one of the most substantive collections relating to race in contemporary Britain. In some ways, it should properly be regarded as the necessary other half of Burke's artistic opus.

In September 2015 Burke's status as a quasi-archivist was recognized when the Ikon Gallery in Birmingham staged an exhibition entitled *At Home with Vanley Burke*. In contrast to Burke's previous exhibitions, the focus of the show was not his photography. Instead, its curators moved the entire contents of Burke's Birmingham flat into the gallery's exhibition space. It was an attempt to communicate the extent to which Burke's commitment to collecting over a period of more than five decades had, in spite of his extensive archival donations to the Library of Birmingham, rendered his living space a museum-like display of archival ephemera. On the walls of the exhibition were the posters and fliers Burke had collected advertising local reggae concerts and political gatherings; in a corner were the suitcases that had accompanied him when he moved to join his mother in Britain in 1965; and on shelves and mantelpieces were records, ornaments, family photographs, and a library of books that included Clive Harris's study of the slave trade, *Three Continents, One History* (2008), Paul Gilroy's *Black Britain: A Photographic History* (2007), and *Policing the Rainbow* (2004), a memoir about his time as a senior police officer in 1980s Handsworth by former chief superintendent David Webb. Such material encapsulated what Stuart Hall understood as a process of "diaspora-ization" among black British artists, a drive to locate their own experiences in urban Britain in the context of family migration and the wider story of the black Atlantic.[106] The exhibition was a complex intervention and, in its willingness to present Burke's bed, kitchen, and other intimate areas of his life, undoubtedly raised pertinent questions about the anthropological gaze of the show's curators. At the same time, however, in visually re-creating the results of his collecting, *At Home with Vanley Buke* was a statement confirming Burke's status as both a photographic chronicler of black Britain and one of its most prolific diasporic archivists.[107]

Inevitably, Burke's perspective was—like that of each of his peers in Handsworth—a partial one. Certainly in his photographic work his male gaze never seriously engaged with the role of women as propellers of change in Handsworth, whether in the domestic sphere, at work, in political movements, or elsewhere. There are also absences in Burke's attempts at representing those political organizations discussed in the previous chapter. His emphasis on the street as the primary backdrop to Handsworth's political life in many ways serves to highlight the extent to which Burke was not able, or willing, to photograph the internal activities of political groups. Burke never took his audience inside the ACSHO headquarters at 104 Heathfield Road, for example, or inside the Harambee hostel for young people half a mile away on Hall Road. And while his archival work should be an essential element in any investigation into the development of Black Power in Britain, the activities of South Asian communities are comparatively absent in both strands of Burke's oeuvre. No photographer cum archivist can be everywhere. But it is striking that this Asian sensibility has a stronger presence in the photographs of Derek Bishton and John Reardon, whose status as white practitioners perhaps meant they had fewer scruples about entering the Sikh *gurdwara* as well as the black Pentecostal church, or about documenting a Punjabi *ghazal* alongside a performance by a local African Caribbean dance troupe. Other practitioners in this milieu were from South Asian backgrounds. In 1969, for example, Maganbhai Patel—an Indian immigrant and former General Electric employee known colloquially as Masterji—opened a studio at his home in nearby Coventry, which for more than four decades was used by its growing Indian community to obtain passport photographs, portraits commemorating weddings and other events, and images that could be sent back to family members in India.[108] But it was arguably not until the first decades of the twenty-first century, in a climate of heightened hostility toward Muslim communities in particular, that a new generation of Birmingham photographers of South Asian descent moved beyond the portrait studio to explore particular Asian formations from the inside.[109]

Bishton, Homer, and Reardon were seemingly attuned to the central importance of a diasporic consciousness around them. In 1986, two years after the publication of *Home Front*, Bishton published *Black Heart Man*, a photojournalistic attempt at a journey into the Rastafarian culture that had, apart from the Black Power embraced by the area's political groups, arguably become the most visible manifestation of the drive to situate the experience of black Handsworth in the historical context of diaspora. This was seen in the photographs Bishton took alongside Reardon of Rastafarian-infused reggae bands and sound systems transporting their equipment around Handsworth, or those Burke captured of the large African Liberation Day crowds made up of young people sporting dreadlocks, hats in the Ethiopian colors of red, gold, and green and other visual signifiers of Rastafarianism. *Blackheart Man* comprised photographs of this Handsworth scene alongside those Bishton took in the Shashamene region of Ethiopia, which the Ethiopian emperor Haile Selassie had set aside in the late 1940s as a place of settlement for those followers of Rastafarianism across the black globality who were committed to the movement's emphasis on repatriation and a "return" to Africa.[110] Notwithstanding John Reardon's highly compromised position, the commitment of Bishton and Homer in particular to a community-oriented form of photography perhaps meant that, in contrast to the hesitancy of an earlier cohort of white leftists, this generation was beginning to grasp the relevance of the imperial context to race relations in Britain.[111] Yet regardless of Bishton's evident admiration for Rastafarianism, he must surely have recognized this was a project that almost by definition required a level of separation from white society. And as the following chapter discusses, its most significant consequences appeared not in the establishment of a five-hundred-acre settler community in Ethiopia, but in the development by a primarily young black generation of a Rastafarian subculture that brought the movement's focus on history, diaspora, and black consciousness to bear on the Handsworth locale.

3

Dread Culture

Africa in Handsworth

INTRODUCTION

In 1978, the Handsworth-based reggae band Steel Pulse released its debut LP, *Handsworth Revolution*, on the Island Records label. Having been established in Jamaica in 1959, Island had by the late 1970s relocated to London and become a key player in the development of a global market for reggae music, thanks to a stable that included artists such as Jimmy Cliff and Bob Marley.[1] Steel Pulse was the product of transnational relationships, which made the band a natural fit at Island. The founding members—lead singer David Hinds, guitarist Basil Gabbidon, and bass player Ronald McQueen—were in their twenties and had either been born in the Caribbean or were the children of Caribbean immigrants. And although each band member had spent his formative years in Handsworth, their influences came from far beyond Birmingham. These inevitably included the rapidly developing sounds of the plethora of Jamaican reggae artists whose music was being imported into Britain by labels such as Island and was stocked in the growing number of specialist record shops that catered for the heightened demand in areas of black settlement up and down the country; in 1975, it was estimated that there were ten such shops in Birmingham alone.[2] But like Marley in particular, Steel Pulse's music was also imbued with the political and spiritual messages of Rastafarianism, a movement that first emerged in 1930s Jamaica and was revived by the reggae artists of the 1970s, who maintained its original stress on the importance of diasporic connections to Africa. On the front cover of *Handsworth Revolution* (see figure 11)—a color drawing depicting a scene from inner-city Britain—there are resonances of these influences. Echoing Rastafarianism's critique of Western modernity and

FIGURE 11. Cover of Steel Pulse's *Handsworth Revolution*, 1978. Reproduced by permission of Island Records.

emphasis on the natural environment, for example, symbols of urbanity such as a car and a concrete tower block are portrayed as decaying and crumbling.[3] The car has been abandoned altogether; buildings are being overrun by green shrubbery and tropical palm trees. In the middle ground a group of black children stand dressed in robes. One of them is beating a drum. In the foreground, an older black youth has turned his back on this urban scene altogether and is pictured moving purposefully toward the greenness beyond.

Steel Pulse is only one of the most prominent examples of what had by the mid-1970s become a thriving black British reggae scene. Although few acts achieved the same success, many shared a commitment to Rastafarianism and a corresponding emphasis on the centrality of Africa and specifically Ethiopia, where the trigger for the emergence of Rastafarianism was the 1930 accession to the Ethiopian throne of the black emperor Haile Selassie (formerly known as Ras Tafari).[4] And reggae bands were only one part of a much wider subculture across black Britain crystallizing around the ideas and symbols of Rastafarianism. In Handsworth, this included theater and dance groups set up by sympathetic community workers and activists who attempted to offer local black youths cultural outlets for their growing interest in Africa. More organically, bands like Steel Pulse were joined by the emergence of a network of "sound systems," a Jamaican concept that centered on playing recorded music publicly at high quality, adapted and refined by black youth in Britain. Here, Rastafarianism had also become transformed into an everyday style, a subcultural uniform designed to express an affinity to Africa by, for example, the wearing of the Ethiopian national colors red, gold, and green, and perhaps most pervasively, by the cultivation of the dreadlock hairstyle. It is the significance of what might be termed Handsworth's "dread culture" to which this chapter now turns.[5]

A critical feature was undoubtedly this culture's transnational, diasporic sensibility. Rastafarianism first emerged in Jamaica, was repopularized as a result of the global success of Jamaican musicians, and advocated a "return" to Africa and specifically Ethiopia. In its transnational nature there are undoubtedly parallels with an earlier black music scene in Britain. In 1930s and 1940s London jazz music had begun to reverberate in the clubs and bars of Soho, prompted by sojourners from across Africa, the United States, and the Caribbean who were drawn to the area because of the unusually large number of establishments owned by black proprietors, who allowed black musicians to play. Musicians would stay in London for short periods before moving on, when their places would commonly be filled by players who had come from elsewhere in the black globality. If, as Lara Putnam has shown, the age of jazz was marked by a transnational politics "embodied in rituals . . . music and moves," half a century later movements across borders were also a feature of Handsworth's dread culture.[6] In 1978, for instance, Steel Pulse performed on a European tour in support of Bob Marley. More prosaically, having appropriated the concept of a sound system from Jamaica, their British operators often cultivated extensive networks of Jamaican contacts to gain access to the rarest of reggae tracks.

However, it was not the physical manifestation of transnationalism that defined dread culture. Although many of its participants had been born in the Caribbean, these people had most often immigrated to Britain as children with their parents. Like those who had been born in Handsworth and places like it, they had gained their formative experiences in Britain and, in contrast to the sojourners of the 1930s and 1940s, were not themselves well versed in cosmopolitan travel. In many ways, rather than any literal manifestation, what defined Handsworth's dread culture was a localized performance of diaspora—one that took place in the youth clubs, bars, and cafés commonly photographed by Vanley Burke. As it did for Handsworth's political activists and visual artists, the black globality functioned as a tool for making sense of events in the locale. Reggae musicians and dancers sketched for their audiences what they understood to be the connections among Handsworth, the Caribbean, Ethiopia, and Africa. And audiences too were able to undertake their own diasporic performances, most pervasively through the cultivation of a hairstyle that had been taken up by the early Jamaican adherents of Rastafarianism, reportedly in homage to widely circulated photographs of East African tribespeople. The contrast that "locks" provided to dominant understandings of black beauty and respectability ensured that the hairstyle provoked anxiety and "dread" in equal measure—not least among an older black generation in Britain, who were often highly suspicious of their children's turn to Rastafarianism because of the movement's historically marginal status in the Caribbean.[7]

As Stuart Hall has argued, Rastafarianism facilitated a reappropriation of blackness through a "rediscovery of Africa."[8] Certainly the presence of dread culture in black Handsworth shows how the Pan-Africanism often advocated by Black Power organizations in this period coincided with a parallel cultural trajectory with a more pervasive reach. Yet in Handsworth in the long 1980s, the Africa that was invoked rarely meant Africa in any literal sense. Often, for example, Ethiopia and Africa were used interchangeably. This could be seen as a further illustration of the enduring reach of Marcus Garvey, who argued that African national boundaries had been entirely imposed by colonial powers and that precolonial "Africa" was simply Ethiopia.[9] But it is also a reminder that the vast majority of this generation had never been to the continent, and that for most people it was a place invoked primarily by album sleeves, dreadlocks, portraits of Haile Selassie, reggae lyrics, and "national" colors, whether those of Ethiopia or the red, green, and black associated with Garvey's black nationalism.

This is not to say that the turn to Africa in Handsworth should be understood as an entirely "invented" tradition. Participants were often fluent in the language of Rastafarianism and its reappropriation of the Bible, which rendered white society Babylon and Africa Zion. But it is to point out that the prospect of a "return" to Africa was something that was commonly referred to in black Handsworth, but rarely enacted. Beginning with a discussion of the Handsworth Community Theatre Project (HCTP) and Kokuma Dance Company—two initiatives that sought to provide creative channels for young people's exploration of African culture—before moving on to examine Handsworth's reggae and sound system scenes, I argue that the physical journey to Africa is not the yardstick by which dread culture should be measured. As Hall recognized, what Eric Hobsbawm understood as the key features of invented traditions—the symbolic invocation of history as a tool for community and the "cement of group cohesion"—also characterized this generation's turn to Africa.[10] The idea of Africa facilitated the development of a black identity that was used as a way of coming to terms with the particular practical situation that, in the context of 1980s Britain, many young black people found themselves to be in. Its cumulative effect was the establishment in Handsworth of Rastafarianism's distinctive reading of the black Atlantic as a central feature of the landscape.[11] This was simultaneously the product of a transnational sensibility and an example of what Benedict Anderson famously understood as an "imagined community," the meaningful effects of which were rooted firmly in the Handsworth locale.[12]

PERFORMING AFRICA

The HCTP was an offshoot of Banner Theatre of Actuality, which had been established in 1973 and was subsequently based on the Lozells Road, also home to the antiracist group AFFOR and, further up the street, the Villa Cross pub and the Acapulco café. Banner's aim was partly to facilitate wider working-class participation in the theater, meaning that there were parallels with the community arts scene that emerged from the late 1960s countercultural moment. The group's primary lineage, however, was the folk revival movement of the 1950s and 1960s. Its founder, Charles Parker, had made his name working as a radio producer for the BBC, where he made programs that explored working-class experience using recordings of interviews he had conducted with miners, fisherman, and workers in other industries.[13] Parker's refusal to add a "standard English" voice-over to these programs contributed to his eventual firing by the BBC, but he retained his commitment to foregrounding the everyday speech of working people with the establishment of Banner. Parker envisaged it as a "'socialist community and cultural group'" that would maintain strong links with working-class communities through the continued use of oral interviews, which Parker referred to as "actuality." The aim was to expand on the approach Parker had developed in radio by exploring the new possibilities facilitated by the use of actuality in live performances.[14]

Despite Banner's being based in Handsworth, however, Parker's background and politics meant that it primarily became a vehicle for communicating his particular reading of and commitment to the concept of class struggle. The group's earliest plays were explorations of trade unionism and the industrial disputes that increasingly dominated the political landscape as the 1970s wore on; one production examined life in the coalfields, for instance, while another was about the Shrewsbury 24, a group of activists who were convicted of public order offenses as a result of their campaign for better working conditions in the building industry. The experiences of black youth in Handsworth, or signs of its nascent dread culture, were absent. There was an awareness within Banner of the problematic nature of this disconnect, particularly when in 1977 the group staged a play that examined the issue of racism in the workplace but encountered strong criticism because of the absence of any black actors in the cast.[15] The HCTP was established in 1979 with the explicit aim of encouraging local black youths to represent their own experiences on stage. It was to be a multiracial documentary theater group which, through the continued use of actuality, would showcase "the richness of [Handsworth's] ethnic cultures."[16] In the early 1980s the project consisted of approximately twenty-five primarily black participants aged between thirteen and twenty, with rehearsals and performances taking place in local schools. For Chris Rogers, the inaugural director of the HCTP, the aim was to develop a celebration of the area's diversity that, mirroring the agenda of Handsworth's community photographers, would challenge the stereotypes that dominated the mainstream media's representation of the area.[17]

But that Banner attempted to deal with the issue of race through the establishment of a new subsidiary organization—rather than incorporating black experiences into the heart of the Banner agenda—suggests that the group struggled to respond to the challenges posed by the rise of identity politics, in ways that mirrored the experiences of other left-wing organizations. This situation came to a head after 1982, when Milton Godfrey, a local musician and playwright, was appointed the first black director of the HCTP. Godfrey immediately found that participants in the project were "fascinated to talk about their own history and culture" and envisaged that the HCTP could fulfill an educational role for black youth similar to the black supplementary school movement discussed in chapter 1. "We'd choose an issue that they thought was relevant," Godfrey recalled, "be it Marcus Garvey, or the police in Handsworth, and discuss it, then try to turn it into art."[18] But discomfort soon emerged in Banner about the direction in which the project was moving. Members were anxious about the prospect of the HCTP breaking away completely from Banner's socialist platform and becoming a separate black project. In 1984 Banner committee members wrote to their "black comrades" in the HCTP in response to a demand that it should be explicitly positioned as a black project with autonomy from the wider Banner agenda, explaining that "the white people in Banner" would feel uneasy about such a development.[19] The relatively conciliatory tone masked the fraught nature of this disagreement. Godfrey recalled being told by members of Banner at a later meeting that he was in need of "resocialization."[20]

To some extent, Banner's position formed part of what Chris Waters has identified as a postwar tendency to emphasize the importance of a specific working-class sensibility, even as racial politics and the growth of feminist and gay liberation movements were making such a position increasingly unsustainable.[21] In this respect it is ironic that Parker chose to base Banner in Handsworth. The group's premises on Lozells Road was in close proximity to the black front line, described by one observer as teeming with "Afro-Caribbean take-away food shops."[22] It would be difficult to imagine an area that more vividly highlighted the way in which Britain's growing racial diversity was challenging homogenized conceptions of class. The relationship between Banner and the HCTP also offers a reminder of the way in which differing strands of identity politics could operate in conflict, rather than in tandem with each other. Parker had died in 1980, and as that decade wore on Banner began to incorporate feminist perspectives into its program. Here, opposition came not just from those who were wedded to its more traditional socialist perspective, but also from Godfrey and his HCTP. Godfrey, for instance, identified as "irrelevant to myself [and] the community" Banner's support for the peace camps that had been set up by feminist groups at Greenham Common in protest against plans for the Berkshire site to be used as a base for ninety-six NATO-backed cruise missiles.[23] To some extent, in his dismissal of one of the largest and longest-running feminist campaigns of the period, Godfrey's stance was as problematic as the way in which Banner had attempted to deal with race. But it also illustrates the way in which the issue of autonomy, which was a central concern for black political organizations in Handsworth, also played a significant role with respect to its cultural groups. Godfrey recalled that many of the participants in the HCTP were increasingly engaged in the question of black identity through the prism of contemporary geopolitics. "If [the] people [who attended the HCTP] were interested in issues like Nelson Mandela," he argued, "I felt the theatre company had to address the issue of Mandela."[24] However, the turn toward Africa—whether its past, present, or its future—was something that could seemingly better be achieved in organizations that had a far greater level of independence.

The Kokuma Dance Company was formed—initially with the name Mystics and Israelites—in 1978 by Bob Ramdhanie, a senior probation officer with responsibility for young black offenders in the Handsworh area. In a PhD thesis he would later complete based on his experiences with the group, Ramdhanie described the founding impetus as being his need to develop "alternative, dynamic and interactive ways of working with black youths." Ramdhanie found that music and movement was a way of communicating more effectively with his clients in Handsworth, and he soon incorporated an African dancing and drumming project in his portfolio.[25] Thus from the start Kokuma was never an entirely autonomous institution. But even before it developed into an independent organization in the early 1980s, the kind of external, explicitly ideological agenda that Godfrey felt was imposed on the HCPT by Banner was never such a problematic issue. Ramdhanie ensured that the drumming and dancing sessions he ran out of his Probation Services office were informal occasions, enabling him to sidestep any concerns raised by his colleagues. Ramdhanie was a Caribbean Asian, which to some extent separated him from many of his white colleagues in the eyes of his clients. The dancers at his workshops were usually young, black women aged between fifteen and eighteen; the drummers were Rastafarian men in their early twenties.[26] No participant had any prior involvement in African dancing. "But all were steeped in reggae music" and self-identified as "Africans in the diaspora"; the "decision to join the African dance classes was the opportunity to express themselves through the language of dance."[27]

The group met once a week and in the early 1980s began rehearsing in the Handsworth Cultural Centre on Hamstead Road, a main thoroughfare connecting Handsworth with the Hockley overpass and a short journey south on the number 74 bus to Birmingham city center. The center had been established by Ramdhanie in 1978 as "an arena or a forum in which [local black youth] can express themselves." As discussed in the introduction to this book, the diasporic nature of its ethos was signaled by the 1981 opening of a mock African village in the center's rear gardens.[28] By this point Ramdahnie was keen to encourage members of the group to take on more responsibility for its general and administrative operation; to mark this transition, the group renamed itself Kokuma, a Nigerian Yoruba word meaning "this one will never die."[29] With an expanding repertoire of stage productions and the introduction of new training programs run by external dance tutors, Kokuma was developing into an increasingly professional outfit. This transition was accelerated by the appointment in 1988 of Jackie Guy, a Jamaican choreographer who had previously worked with the Jamaican National Dance Theatre Company as artistic director. Kokuma incorporated a number of smaller, Handsworth-based dance groups and went from putting on small-scale shows to full-length, theater-style productions. In 1989 Kokuma moved to a new base in the Lozells Methodist Church on Gerrard Street and, with the support of funding from both the Arts Council of England and West Midlands Arts, formally became a professional dance group.

Kokuma articulated a version of black identity that was fundamentally diasporic in nature, as encapsulated in its 1992 production *The History of the Drum* (see figure 12). The central message of the production was explained in the accompanying program notes: the drum was to be seen by audiences as a symbol of "the extended story of the African people"; the aim was to portray it as a tool that "helped people survive ... the painful experiences of slavery" and subsequently became "reshaped, adapted and used in many forms in numerous different societies."[30] In the opening scene of the production, presumably meant to reference precolonial Africa, the drum is represented as a means of communication both spiritually and as a form of language in which a whole community could be seen to participate. This harmony is violently disrupted, however, with the appearance of an intruder on stage. The intruder, whose face is concealed by a mask, confiscates the community's drum and in so doing visibly weakens its spirit. Having taken the drum, the intruder forcibly removes the people from their homes and places them in a new and unfamiliar environment.

FIGURE 12. Kokuma Dance Company performing *The History of the Drum*, 1992. © Dee Conway/Lebrecht Photo Library.

The intruder is victorious and decrees that all drum playing must stop. The following scene is thus in dramatic contrast to the first; whereas in the first, the community was represented as vibrant and joyous, dancing in unison to the drum's beat, in the second the atmosphere is quiet and oppressive. The community is being forced to work, and the slow, laborious dances are suggestive of a people worn out, overridden, and exploited. Yet despite this, the image of the drum eventually reappears. Initially, this is in the form of the rhythms made by the community's tools of work, but soon the drum itself reemerges. The community becomes reenergized, and the drum is presented as a means of resistance to exploitation. The dances now represent a community in harmony again, and this time defiant. The intruder's impositions are rejected; together, marching like an army, the community confronts him. In unison, the people chase after the intruder, their single stride itself forming the beat of the drum, until the intruder is forced to retreat. The intruder is defeated, and the community members dance in celebration.

The rest of the production documents the continuing beat of the drum in different diasporic locations: the audience is transported to twentieth-century America and the emergence of jazz; to the Caribbean, where the drum provides the beat for calypso and ska; and finally, to contemporary Britain. Here the drum emerges in the context of British and imported reggae music in a dance-hall setting. A DJ is playing requests and "toasting" the crowd in front of him. Then the lights in this dance hall dim; the floor is vacated until there is only one man left on stage. He stands and simply beats his drum, slowly and methodically, until three other men, each in African dress, each beating a drum, and each singing in harmony, join him. Finally, as the singing stops, so does the drumming, and the men take their drums and raise them above their heads toward the sky.

The production's ambition was to "assist in the retention of the culture and identity of the Africans."[31] Like the HCTP, an educational remit was a critical feature of Kokuma from the beginning, which only increased once it became a publicly funded body.[32] When Jackie Guy took over as director, however, there was initially a disconnect between his own preconceptions of Britain and the disillusionment felt by participants who had been born and brought up there. It was only later that Guy began to recognize the educational role Kokuma was playing by responding to what he subsequently understood as "a search for cultural identity" among a young, black generation and the sense of rejection this generation felt from mainstream British society. Even before the professionalization signaled by productions such as *The History of the Drum*, a key virtue of Kokuma was that it helped participants gain a more tangible understanding of their diasporic identities. In January 1980, for example, funds were obtained for thirteen of the group's members to travel to Jamaica to take part in dance workshops at the Kingston Cultural Training Centre. Three years later more money was raised, this time for members to visit the University of Ghana Dance Ensemble in Accra, where they were introduced to Ghanaian drumming techniques, dance styles, dress, and food.[33] The trip not only resulted in an improvement in the technique of Kokuma's participants, Ramdhanie argued, but also served as a practical introduction to Africa that "helped them to clarify their own thoughts about the messages of Marcus Garvey and their spiritual connection to the continent."[34] As part of Kokuma's educational remit the group attempted to share these discoveries with wider communities in the Handsworth locale by staging introductory dance workshops. These included sessions on Nigerian, Ghanaian, and Azanian dance forms, "structured to facilitate the process of development, study and general understanding of the history of African and Caribbean people, their culture, religion, languages, dance and music."[35]

For many participants at Kokuma, the exploration of black history was a way of navigating their contemporary lives in Handsworth. One Kokuma dancer, who had joined the group when it was still attached to the Probation Service, commented in 1982 that "through dance, you can get rid of a lot of frustration" that might otherwise have been spent "going around smashing windows."[36] Another participant, Ursella Walker, joined Kokuma as a teenager in 1985 after her uncle, Milton Godfrey—then director of the HCTP—had taken her to one of the group's beginner's workshops. "That was the first time I was exposed to Afro-Caribbean

FIGURE 13. Kokuma Dance Company, 1992. © Dee Conway/Lebrecht Photo Library.

dance," she explained. "I wanted to be a dancer but I didn't have any formal education."[37] Walker reflected on how important it was for her that Kokuma offered a positive definition of black identity through its dancing and performances:

> As I was growing up, there just wasn't anything positive about black people or black culture at all. So I could really identify with what Kokuma were doing. It gave me a sense of pride really.... [T]he black identity thing was really important to me. It gave me a sense of grounding, and something to aspire to as well.[38]

It is significant that from the beginning the vast majority of Kokuma's participants were young women (see figure 13). The growing popularity of Rastafarianism in Britain in some cases coincided with the perpetuation of regressive ideas about gender within elements of the movement.[39] In the view of one sociologist who spent time with a Rastafarian group in Handsworth in the mid-1970s, women were commonly required to dutifully perform the role of "'daughters' and 'queens' which ironically meant the humbling of themselves and the lionisation of their males."[40] Certainly, as shown later in this chapter, the subculture that revolved around reggae bands and sound systems was for the most part dominated by young men. In contrast, Kokuma not only allowed women such as Walker to assert an identity that was simultaneously diasporic and feminine, it also gave them a sense of self-confidence in the context of a wider absence of black women role models in Britain. As Walker put it,

"In my school, there weren't many black teachers, and I suffered from insecurity as a result. Kokuma helped to fill that gap."[41]

Many of these themes were explicitly elaborated by Kokuma in *The Awakening*, a 1994 production written by the Ghanaian playwright Kwesi Owusu and choreographed by Guy. The production represented the contradictions of contemporary urban living and showed how an embrace of history could help to resolve this situation. A young black couple in Britain are represented as being at odds with each other and the world around them. They are shown repeatedly arguing with one another and struggling to negotiate the demands of their everyday lives. The lyrics of the reggae soundtrack reflect the dominant preoccupation: "Everybody's got to work harder." But they are soon visited by a "griot"—an African storyteller or poet—who introduces them to their African roots and culture through dance. The couple are invited to join in and quickly learn to understand the meaning of their heritage. More secure in their cultural identity, by the end of the production the couple appear at ease in themselves, with each other, and with the contemporary lives they both lead.

The program notes to *The Awakening* explained that the production aimed to "reclaim a heritage lost through the passing of time."[42] But the central message of the production reflected the wider Kokuma agenda: reclaiming such a heritage was for use in the Handsworth and the British contexts. Unlike the HCTP, which never reconciled the tension between a desire to work with black communities and Banner's socialist agenda, Kokuma was able to enjoy a significant degree of autonomy. If to begin with this was thanks in large part to the ingenuity of Ramdhanie, by the time Guy arrived in Handsworth Kokuma was established as an organization that—alongside its growing artistic reputation both nationally and internationally—was valued by funders for performing a significant educational function. The black Atlantic was embodied in Kokuma's practices and structures, whether in the backgrounds of the people who ran and participated in it, the visits to Jamaican and Ghanaian cultural centers, or the performances of and workshops in dance forms from across the black diaspora.

This internationalism continued at Kokuma well into the 1990s. In 1995 Guy was replaced as director by Patrick Acogny, a choreographer from a French Senegalese background who brought to the group an expertise in contemporary West African dance. This perspective was appreciated particularly by the female participants at Kokuma, both because it helped them to articulate positive black identities and because of the way it provided a clearer sense of what diaspora could mean in the Handsworth locale. Yet Kokuma did not itself stimulate the turn to Africa in Handsworth. At any one point it never had more than twenty participants, and even accounting for the popularity of its performances and workshops, it was clearly responding to a much more pervasive drive. As Ramdhanie recognized, participants were arriving at Kokuma if not altogether fluent, then undoubtedly extremely well versed, in the language of diaspora and Pan-Africanism. They were "followers of Rastafarianism" and "inspired by reggae music and the philosophies of Marcus Garvey." Black youths were already "looking to Africa for their inspiration and their spiritual guidance"; Kokuma "evolved out of this situation."[43] Kokuma was both an active part and a reflection of Handsworth's dread culture. It was the much more pervasive reggae music and sound system culture, infused with the language and ideas of Rastafarianism, that played the defining role.

RASTAFARIANISM, REGGAE, AND SOUND SYSTEMS

The accession in 1930 of Duke or "Ras" Tafari as Haile Selassie, emperor of Ethiopia, provided the spark for the arrival of Rastafarianism, though Marcus Garvey had long pointed to the significance of Ethiopia as a historically independent African country that had inflicted a famous defeat on the colonial power of Italy in 1896.[44] Some Rastafarians saw the crowning of Selassie as signaling the deliverance of biblical prophecies found in the Book of Revelation regarding the crowning of a black king of Africa and saw Selassie literally as the Living God or "Jah." The power of this belief was such that some subsequently refused to recognize Selassie's death in August 1975.[45] The more significant legacy, however, was the way in which Rastafarianism's use of biblical imagery had initiated what has been described as a psychological revolution in which the core tenets of Christianity were reinterpreted and applied to the experience of the African diaspora.[46] Rastafarians identified the contemporary and historical sufferings of black people as the reincarnation of the plight of the ancient tribes of Israel, whose people had been enslaved by the kingdom of Babylon. The biblical notions of Judgment Day, Zion, and the Promised Land provided for Rastafarians answers to the suffering of black people living in contemporary Babylon. Echoing Garvey's own call for a return to Africa, where he prophesized that all black people would one day live as "'free and dignified human beings,'" Rastafarians emphasized what they saw as an inevitable black repatriation to Africa, which, it was claimed, was also prophesized by the Bible.[47] To the mind of the writer Dilip Hiro, it was this combination of a faith in "African redemption" and "pride in being African" that was to be the most significant legacy when Rastafarianism subsequently arrived in Britain.[48]

For Stuart Hall, Rastafarianism "saved the second generation of young black people in [British] society."[49] Indeed, for the most part Rastafarianism resonated specifically with the black generation who had been born and schooled in Britain, as opposed to their parents, many of whom had encountered the movement at first hand in Jamaica. There, the authorities had been quick to identify Rastafarianism as a criminal cult, its members bordering on the insane and heavily involved in the illegal use of marijuana or "ganja"; in the 1930s Rastafarians could be arrested for selling pictures of Haile Selassie. Three decades later, following a protest about land rights and a crackdown on drugs, the Jamaican authorities decreed that simply being a Rastafarian could constitute an arrestable offence.[50] Stuart Hall recalled that as a child his mother would call him into the house if a Rastafarian was seen begging in their middle-class Kingston neighborhood.[51] Indeed, the movement's emphasis on Africa disturbed a deep ambivalence about African heritage in the Caribbean, something that was bound up with a highly stratified class system based to a large degree on the specificity of skin tone.[52] It is unsurprising, therefore, that these associations established a popular understanding of Rastafarianism that spread across the Caribbean and that many immigrants brought with them on their arrival in Britain. One interviewee, for example, who was born in St. Kitts in 1941 and immigrated to Birmingham in 1959, described Rastafarians as "disgusting" people who "want[ed] their hair washed."[53] In Handsworth, the familial tensions caused by the issue of Rastafarianism were so acute that they were identified as a significant contributing factor to the problem of black homelessness in the area.[54]

In 1930s Jamaica, Rastafarians began growing dreadlocks as a way of emulating the East African Masai tribespeople, photographs of whom were appearing regularly in contemporary magazines such as *National Geographic*.[55] In 1970s and 1980s Handsworth, however, both Rastafarianism's aesthetic and its philosophies were being communicated via reggae albums imported from Jamaica. There, a key marker in the move away from the ska and rocksteady genres and toward Rastafarianism-infused, "roots" reggae was the April 1966 visit of Haile Selassie to the island, which had gained independence less than four years earlier. Selassie was welcomed by tens of thousands of Rastafarians at Kingston Airport and made a public address at a sold-out Kingston National Stadium. In spite of the ongoing hostility toward Rastafarianism and the fact that Selassie publicly renounced the idea that he was the Living God, his visit imbued the movement with a level of respectability that paved the way for reggae to become its key cultural mediator.[56] Within five years one of the earliest Rastafarian reggae tracks was released: "Blood and Fire" by Niney the Observer, which contained the lyrics "Hail Rasta, hail and wail / Hail Rasta don't quit." In 1973 Bob Marley and the Wailers released *Catch a Fire* on Island Records. Not only did songs like "Slave Driver" and "400 Years" contain Rastafarianism's characteristic emphasis on Africa and diaspora consciousness, but the album was arguably the first in which Rastafarianism was utilized overtly as a marketing device.[57] The front cover of the album showed a close-up of Marley—with his trademark dreadlocks in full view—smoking a spliff. "I heard *Catch a Fire* when I was about fourteen," Basil Gabbidon, a founding member of Steel Pulse, remembered. "I just played it to death. I must have gone through about three copies of that album. It was at that point that I decided I had to form my own band."[58]

"Somewhere between Trenchtown and Ladbroke Grove," Dick Hebdige has argued, "the cult of Rastafari had become a 'style.'"[59] For all that imported Jamaican reggae stimulated the emergence of a nationwide network of black British reggae bands, it is unlikely that Rastafarianism could have had the impact it did in Britain without its stylistic packaging. In the context of the affluence of the late 1950s and afterward, youth subcultures had become a progressively more visible presence on Britain's high streets; the Rastafarian imagery found on album sleeves and, increasingly, in the mass media prepared the ground for the arrival of a specifically black subcultural moment.[60] Just as the front cover of Marley's 1976 album *Rastaman Vibration* depicted Marley dressed in khakis and the Ethiopian colors, black youth in Britain began to display the red, gold, and green and to dress in army surplus uniforms. This "sinister guerrilla chic" signified a militancy in which there were echoes of the American Black Panther aesthetic of leather jackets, berets, and sunglasses.[61] It enabled the expression of a commitment to Africa in a much less formal way than with dances, drumming, and stage productions of Kokuma. And in contrast to the "rude boy" style associated with ska music, it was an aesthetic that was difficult for nonblack communities to appropriate. Dreadlocks were critical in this respect. Like the Afro (also known as "the natural"), dreadlocks were understood as constituting a naturally black style in overt contrast to white people, whose hair does not "naturally" grow in such patterns. As the cultural theorist Kobena Mercer has emphasized, both the Afro and dreadlocks in practice require much more careful cultivation than the association with naturalness would imply. With respect to dreadlocks, however, in the context of the wider imagery and ideology of Rastafarianism, the style emphasized both an extenuated version of "blackness" and a "reconstitutive link with Africa."[62] The object was to look "as African and as fearsome" as possible.[63]

This was undoubtedly a male-oriented aesthetic, though by the late 1970s a distinctively feminine Rasta style had also made its way across the Atlantic. In this respect, a critical moment came with the formation of the I-Threes, a trio of women vocalists who in 1975, following the departure of Peter Tosh and Bunny Livingston from the Wailers, became a permanent fixture of Bob Marley's studio and live acts. Marcia Griffiths, Judy Mowatt, and Rita Marley, the Cuban-born Jamaican wife of Bob, not only added a new, more soulful dimension to the music. With their red, gold, and green headscarves and loose-fitting, ankle-length dresses, they helped popularize a powerful image of "dignified Rasta womanhood" that, echoing the feminized African iconography that was evoked by the Kokuma dance routines in Handsworth, centered on the semiotics of the "African queen."[64] This was expanded as the I-Threes developed their solo careers. In 1979, for example, Mowatt released her *Black Woman* album, the sleeve of which featured photographs of her dressed in the feminine Rasta uniform of robes and a headscarf as well as, in a separate image, the more recognizably masculine signifiers of a khaki tunic and dreadlocks—the latter positing an explicit challenge to conservative interpretations of Rastafarian ideology that suggested women should be expected to conceal their hair from public view. Along with her music, which included songs with titles such as "Black Woman" and "Slave Queen," this was, as Gilroy has argued, a "straightforward demand for the validity of 'feminist' Rastafari."[65]

These internal dynamics within dread culture were often masked by the external challenge it was seen to pose to wider society, symbolized most clearly by the reaction to the appearance of dreadlocked Rastafarians in Jamaica, where authorities initially maintained a policy of forcibly shaving people's heads.[66] In Britain, Rastafarian oppositionality was also communicated by the use of Jamaican slang or patois. For Hebdige, patois was a way of mitigating "outside interference" and had echoes of the use of creole languages during slavery.[67] Drawing on his own experiences growing up in an aspirational family in Jamaica, Stuart Hall has recalled how his mother rested her entire understanding of educational value on an assumption about the essential worthlessness of patois.[68] In contrast, for younger generations born in Britain patois could be deployed, in the words of one young woman, "when I'm with white people and I'm talking about them, and I don't want them to know what I'm saying."[69] Within black households, however, the use of patois reveals the complex dynamic between older and younger generations over the issue of Rastafarianism. Patois had become a feature of the Rastafarian subculture, but for young people who had been born in Britain it was something that in the first instance had been learned from their parents, many of whom felt comfortable using it in private if not in public. Brian Bennett, for example, who was born in Birmingham to Jamaican parents, reflected on the significant disorientation he experienced because his parents "talked different" from him.[70] Thus for all that some members of older generations may have been hostile toward Rastafarianism, and in spite of the central position of Africa within Rastafarian ideology, as well as being a symbol of oppositionality the use of patois by younger generations could also be read as a gesture toward their shared Caribbean heritage and the fact that Rastafarianism had been born in the same place as their parents.

What is clear is that a desire for alternative educational forms was an important feature of dread culture. While for the participants of Kokuma this was met through dance forms and drumming techniques, for many others who were more generally active in the Rastafarian subculture reggae music was treated as an educational resource. Bennett saw reggae as a way of overcoming the disorientation he felt at being the British-born child of Jamaican immigrants. He described reggae as "like a knowledge provider for my culture and my history."[71] Reggae certainly provided many with their first point of contact with Pan-African ideas. "I'm not into Marcus Garvey's concepts as much as I'd like to be," one black teenager from Handsworth mused in the 1980s. "But Bob Marley had nice concepts. That's what I'm for . . . his music was an inspiration."[72] By the mid-1970s, just as Bob Marley was urging his listeners to "never forget who you are, and where you stand in the struggle," bands such as Aswad, Matumbi, and Misty in Roots in London, and Beshara, Eclipse, and Steel Pulse in Birmingham were developing their own distinctive reggae sound.[73]

The influence of Rastafarianism on these bands is demonstrated by the titles of their singles: "Jah Bless Africa," "Back to Africa," and "Babylon Makes the Rules."[74] What distinguished their music, however, was their attempts to apply Rastafarian ideas explicitly to the lives and experiences of a generation shaped by their experiences in Britain's black locales.

Steel Pulse was formed in 1975 by Gabbidon and David Hinds, who went to school together at Handsworth Wood Boys School. From the beginning, the band adopted a Rastafarian aesthetic, placing African symbolism at the heart of its performances. Hinds, for example, who was the band's lead singer, wore particularly large dreadlocks that he further exaggerated by tying them up vertically above his head. The band members regularly appeared on stage dressed in uniforms, including the prominent display of the red, gold, and green. The idea, according to Michael Riley, a backing vocalist with the band, was to challenge the expectations of audiences and make a "mockery of the regimentation of this society."[75] Band members also appeared on stage dressed as priests, a powerful emblem of Rastafarianism's reappropriation of mainstream, "white" Christianity.[76]

A critique of present-day conditions was embedded in Rastafarianism. As Horace Campbell, Paul Gilroy, and others have argued, although Rastafarianism focuses on Africa as the true home of all black people, somewhat paradoxically, it is also a movement concerned with the inequalities of the immediate historical moment, "a movement organised around a political and philosophical critique of oppressive social relations."[77] As Basil Gabbidon emphasized, the decision to establish Steel Pulse came largely out of a heightened political engagement: "We thought we had something to say."[78] The band fused an awareness of contemporary events in the black globality with a commentary on the things that its members were experiencing directly in the Handsworth locale. Thus on the one hand, Gabbidon reflected that the growing awareness of the extent of the East African famine in the 1970s "woke us up to a consciousness" that emphasized global unity and the importance of engaging with geopolitical issues. On the other hand, as the title of Steel Pulse's debut album, *Handsworth Revolution*, makes clear, the band members were also concerned with themes in their own lives in Handsworth. As Gabbidon explained, "You get your creativity, your strength, from your environment, and we got ours from Handsworth." In many respects, therefore, *Handsworth Revolution* represented a quasi-sociological commentary from within on the issues that faced black youth in Handsworth at this particular conjuncture.[79]

Handsworth Revolution highlighted themes that could be immediately referenced by black youth in Handsworth and places like it. This included being a victim of racist attacks. "Ku Klux Klan," for example, placed the growth of British neo-Nazism in a transatlantic perspective that capitalized on the notoriety of the American organization but nevertheless, through its first-person perspective, emphasized that what was being referenced was the growth in support for domestic groups such as the NF.[80] The overriding tone of the album, however, is fundamentally not one of victimhood. Lyrics on the album's title track declared that "Babylon is falling" and that "Handsworth shall stand firm, like Jah rock, fighting back":

> We once beggars are now choosers
> No intention to be losers
> Striving forward with ambition . . .
> We rebel in Handsworth revolution . . .[81]

When within three years of the album's release Handsworth erupted into its first major instance of rioting, these lyrics took on an extra level of poignancy. The song cemented the band's reputation for political militancy and in many ways has continued to define its career. For Michael Riley, however, the initial motivation was to "clean the [Handsworth] name up" and provide a source of pride for the local population: "If I wasn't in the band and came from Handsworth, and a group called their album [*Handsworth Revolution*], it would make me feel good."[82] In its formative guise, at least, Steel Pulse shared with Handsworth's documentary photographers and community artists a desire to present an alternative perspective to the hegemonic stereotypes that had come to dominate the representation of Handsworth from without. Its work can also be read as a celebration of the extent to which the turn to a Rastafarian black globality in Handsworth had transformed the district into an assertively black locale. In many ways, this was encapsulated by the oft-repeated line of the *Handsworth Revolution* title track: "Handsworth means us the black people."[83]

Steel Pulse was the most successful of a number of groups who honed their brand of Rastafarian-inspired British reggae in local venues such as the Rialto (renamed the Santa Rosa in the mid-1970s) at 6A Soho Road, a half mile away from the Harambee hostel for young people on Hall Road. This was complemented by the Hummingbird (formerly Top Rank) in Birmingham city center and older, London-based establishments such as the Ram Jam and Colombo's, which also acted as prominent venues in Britain's performative dread culture.[84] Just as Marley had been for Basil Gabbidon, Steel Pulse became an inspiration for other aspiring reggae bands in Birmingham, precisely because of its use of Rastafarianism to narrate what was happening in Handsworth. Amlak Tafari, for example, was born in Handsworth in 1965 and was the founding member of Amlak Band. As Steel Pulse's debut material began to be stocked alongside Jamaican imports at specialist record shops such as Mango Records, based at 104 Grove Lane (a few doors down from the premises owned by the photographers Derek Bishton, Brian Homer, and John Reardon), Tafari—who was a decade younger than the founding members of Steel Pulse—remembered keeping a scrapbook of cuttings relating to the band as it became the subject of increasing media attention. The band's initial success, he argued, came from its ability to speak to "the lives we were leading"; Tafari felt that he himself was "going through exactly the same things they had been through." While this included everyday issues such as racial violence, Tafari suggested that the band's aim to clean up the Handsworth name was also appreciated. Steel Pulse "glorified Handsworth, just as I myself was proud to come from Handsworth," he reflected. "As a young reggae musician, a young Rasta man, a young man from Handsworth, I looked up to them."[85]

Later in his career Tafari's admiration for Steel Pulse would culminate with a formal position as the band's touring bassist. In truth, however, Steel Pulse was always on a different trajectory than most other British reggae acts, particularly following the success of *Handsworth Revolution* and the subsequent tour with Marley. In 1987 the band won a Grammy Award for its sixth studio album, *Babylon the Bandit*, becoming the first non-Jamaican act to win in the Best Reggae Album category. And apart from this enduring success, a shift in the balance of power was in fact already well under way. Marley's death from cancer in 1981 deprived reggae of its undisputed star performer. In truth, however, in both Jamaica and in Britain, the live reggae music scene was already being superseded by one that was based primarily around sound systems.[86]

Rather than writing music or playing instruments, the object in a sound system is to obtain an extensive, exclusive collection of music and to play it with the best possible quality at social events. The concept originally emerged in postwar Jamaica in the context of a shortage of live musicians, many of whom had either emigrated or found employment in the house bands of Jamaica's growing tourist industry. Sound systems were a cheap way of meeting the rising demand to hear first American R & B and then ska and reggae played competently in large dance halls or slum yards.[87] As immigration increased in the 1950s, the sound system emerged in Britain and became a core component of shebeens or "blues dances": organized parties generally held in people's homes, at which an entrance fee would be charged. The concept was reappropriated by a younger generation so that it became a central feature of Handsworth's dread culture.

This generation moved away from the house-party style of their parents and replaced it with a culture of dances held in youth clubs, church halls, garages, and warehouses. Although, like domestic shebeens, such events could be subject to police clampdowns, they were nevertheless significant as relatively autonomous spaces away from mainstream white society.[88] Internally, sound systems constituted a highly competitive world. Systems were maintained by groups who "represented" the particular area they were from; fans from the same area would follow the system wherever it went to play. Sound system events revolved around the concept of a "clash," a ritualized dual that pitted one sound system and its followers against another. In 1980s Birmingham posters advertising such clashes were "plastered over the pillars" of the Hockley overpass connecting Handsworth to the city center.[89] One such flier, dated May 1979, advertised a forthcoming bank holiday clash taking place at a civic hall in central Birmingham:

> This is the Real thing, the Biggest Show [between] Jah Tubby representing London Tape control, Jah Mafia, representing Birmingham [and] Jah Tippertone, a skilful move up to Division 1. Jah Tubby believes no one can play him on music, he says first to go down will be Jah Tippertone ... no bells to save you this time ... Did you hear what happened to the mighty Coxon? So shall it be to you says Jah Mafia.

If the references to skill and "Division 1" are demonstrative of the way in which clashes were couched in the language of sport, the ubiquity of the word *Jah* in the names of the competing systems shows how, like the reggae bands that systems largely played, Rastafarian imagery was a central feature of their acts. The bank holiday clash was, according to the flier, "the show everyone is waiting to see!"[90]

Perhaps stimulated by the publication of *Folk Devils and Moral Panics* (1972), the sociologist Stanley Cohen's highly influential study of the mods and rockers, the 1970s witnessed a rise in both academic and popular interest in the activities of Britain's subcultures. Dick Hebdige's *Subculture: The Meaning of Style* appeared seven years later, the same year as the release of *Quadrophenia*, a film that acquired a cult following as a result of its dramatization of the 1964 conflict between mods and rockers at Brighton beach. In 1980 this was followed by *Babylon*, a feature film by the Italian director Franco Rosso about Ital Lion, a fictional sound system based in Brixton in London. The film was cowritten by Martin Stellman, the writer behind *Quadrophenia*, but its claims to authenticity lay in its input from real-life players in the dread culture the film sought to depict. The star of *Babylon* was Brinsley Forde, a member of the London reggae band Aswad; the film's score was written by Dennis Bovell, founder of Aswad's London rival Matumbi and a prominent sound system called Jah Sufferer.[91] A key driver in the film is the lengths to which members of Ital Lion go to prepare for a clash with a much more well-established system, including stealing a PA system from a school and using a gold pendant as payment for a rare imported reggae track at a local record shop. These actions represented two determinants of a system's chances of success at a clash: the quality and loudness of the music played and the extent to which a system could draw on a selection of hard-to-find, largely unheard records (also known as exclusives or dub plates). A third, critical factor was the performance of a system's DJ or "toaster."

It was the toaster's role to be the public face of the sound and to provide a live element to a system's act. This included taking up the role of master of ceremonies, introducing records, and giving shout-outs to members of the audience.[92] By the 1980s, however, toasters increasingly delivered entire performances of verse or monologues over the top of the music being played. Systems were judged not only on the basis of the breadth, exclusivity, and quality of their music, but also with respect to their toasters' verbal delivery. The toaster had become a distinct role, a precursor to the MC in the later hip-hop and grime scenes and a creolized manifestation of the lyrical battles that had taken place in the calypso genre, which had emerged in Trinidad in the earlier twentieth century. In calypso, performers adopted imperialistic stage names like Lord Protector and Lord Kitchener, and often ridiculed opponents for their poor grasp of standard English.[93] The lyrics of reggae toasters, in contrast, were generally in patois and imbued with Rastafarian ideology; like the lyrics of bands such as Steel Pulse, they often represented a politicized critique of social conditions. *Babylon*, for instance, climaxes with Forde's character, Ital Lion's toaster, arriving at the clash. His performance references his own experiences with racism and police brutality, just as the police are seen attempting to enter the event in order to close it down. The toaster's role was essentially to provide a live experience that gave some impression of spontaneity. Although tape recordings were made of important clashes, few of these have survived, and those that have are generally in poor condition. However, a number of toasters used their experience with sound systems to develop a related art form that placed a greater emphasis on recorded productions and, in some cases, published books. Within what would become known as Britain's dub poetry scene, the most influential player was undoubtedly Linton Kwesi Johnson, who had been born in Jamaica in 1952 and emigrated to Brixton with his parents a decade later.[94] But Handsworth was to produce its own dub poet, one whose status would arguably eventually surpass even that of Johnson.

Benjamin Zephaniah was born in Handsworth in 1958 to Jamaican and Barbadian immigrants and lived in the area until he was in his early twenties. Unlike the work of Johnson, who never identified as a Rastafarian and was instead active in the London-based Black Panthers, Rastafarianism has been a consistent feature of Zephaniah's work since his early performances as a toaster with local sound systems.[95] His dub poetry is indicative of the way in which Rastafarianism prompted, on the one hand, a turn to Africa for an articulation of cultural identity, and on the other hand, a politicized engagement with conditions in the present, as they were manifested locally in everyday life. *The Dread Affair* (1985) is Zephaniah's second collection of poetry, based in large part on his experiences in Handsworth. In their original form, the poems were set to a reggae beat on Zephaniah's debut album, *Rasta*.[96] *The Dread Affair* is dedicated to "all true Rastafarians who seek God and revolution within themselves" and locates Rastafarianism as a movement that gave "understanding unto the children of slaves."[97] Zephaniah's poems conceptualize Africa as a source of inspiration that was required in the context of the dislocation many of his peers felt in Britain. "I was a slave only fit for the grave," Zephaniah wrote in "I Dwell Here." England "did reject me / I must cling to my tree":

> Africa, Africa
> reaching out
> Africa
> very black
> very proud
> shouting loud
> AFRICA.[98]

This was about Zephaniah getting "me back me real true culture," and for him it was "a matter of survival."[99] Zephaniah urged his readers to "listen to the drum" and to "Africa calling . . . African history, African culture / trees known by their fruit / slave ship shackles in our memory / therefore standing firm / flames of victory and liberty / one day we shall earn."[100]

Yet Zephaniah's poems make it clear that for him, an embrace of Africa on its own is not enough; what is also required is an awareness of and engagement with conditions in the present. "One ting I know if you deal with de dead," Zephaniah writes, "den you dead already like I said":

> If you deal with de past said dat nar last
> so don't involve natty dread,
> why deal with dead and deaders
> come reason with living stuff.[101]

The Dread Affair thus also forms a gritty and often satirical engagement with "living stuff": his experiences living as a Rastafarian in Handsworth and later in Brixton, where he moved at the age of twenty-two. His poems speak of the hardships involved for a young black man living in urban Britain, made clear in one of his best-known poems, "Dis Policeman Keeps on Kicking Me to Death":

> Dis policeman keeps on hitting me and pulling out my locks
> he keeps on feeding me unlimited broc-lacs
> dis policeman is a coward he gets me from behind
> he can jail my body but he cannot jail my mind.

At a time when the police's conduct in black communities was the subject of considerable debate, this was the poem that gave Zephaniah his national audience. And it took on even greater personal significance for Zephaniah when in 2003 his cousin, Michael Powell, died from asphyxiation while in police custody in Handsworth. Zephaniah's engagement with contemporary political events echoed a tradition in the art of toasting that went all the way back to its initial emergence in Jamaica.[102] "Dis Policeman" was built on a class-based analysis more associated with Kwesi Johnson's oeuvre. Zephaniah's reference to a "preacher guy" who told "me 'bout some heaven / dat was in the bloody sky" certainly speaks to Rastafarianism's rejection of mainstream Christianity and its simultaneous emphasis on the here and now. "I don't think I'm free," the poem concludes. "If I'm free den why does he / keep fucking kicking me."[103]

Like the trajectory of Steel Pulse, Zephaniah's progression from sound system toaster in Handsworth to a poet of national standing was the exception rather than the norm. More indicative of the experiences of the estimated 112 systems that operated in Birmingham in the 1980s was that of the Jungleman sound, which was founded in Handsworth in 1978.[104] There were other, more established systems in the city, but Jungleman nevertheless quickly cultivated a reputation as one of the most potent performers on the scene. Echoing a commonplace understanding of clashes that portrayed them not only in sporting terms but also as quasi-militaristic events, for Brian Bennett—who at the time ran Rootsman, a rival system—Jungleman's sound was like a "killing machine."[105] Most systems were preoccupied with finding the necessary funds to support themselves, often through gambling or petty crime.[106] Jungleman, by contrast, had been established following a successful application to the Prince's and Cadbury Trusts, the latter of which was playing a particularly active role as a funder of race relations projects. The group maintained this funding stream all the way up until the mid-1980s, which enabled it to invest much more freely in a higher standard of equipment. According to Bennett, this was a "revolutionary" intervention.[107]

Bennett described the experience of attending a Jungleman sound. "All of a sudden, a needle would go on the record," he said, "and a piece of earthquake would hit the room."

> Boom! Even your eyeballs would start to shake with the bass. The whole place would shake. You know when thunder hits? It was like that, if the thunder was right outside your front door. It had a way of speaking to you and saying, "man is nothing." Jungleman were like that.[108]

It was as a result of this impact that at its height in the early 1980s it was claimed Jungleman had a following of thousands in Handsworth.[109] Sound systems were commonly managed by a crew of ten or more people, from the selector and toaster to the engineer and box men, who were responsible for safely transporting the system to each venue.[110] Colin Braham was born in Birmingham in 1961. Having left school at age sixteen and trained to become an engineer, Braham became increasingly influenced by Rastafarianism, changed his name to Ras Tread, and became a founding member of Jungleman. Tread was the system's engineer and photographer throughout its existence. "We were one of the first sounds to have thousands of watts in our amp," Tread claimed. This meant that if a clash was not going well, Jungleman had the ability to "turn up on them"—literally turn the system's volume up so that no matter what the opposing system was playing, it inevitably came across as weak by comparison.[111]

However, Jungleman's popularity was not only the result of the quality of its sound. The group also "had this energy, like an aura," which for Bennett came from the group's overtly Rastafarian emphasis.[112] As it was for Steel Pulse, Rastafarian imagery was a central part of Jungleman's act. Members adopted names such as Pharaoh, Ras, and Boa that referenced Rastafarianism and Africa, and many members also grew thick dreadlocks with the aim of looking as natural as possible. Jungleman members wore uniforms of khaki suits and tunics, and hats specifically designed to incorporate large dreadlocks. It was a style, Tread reflected, that was designed to express an affinity to both Haile Selassie and Garvey and to differentiate themselves from more casual participants in Rastafarianism. "When we saw images of [Selassie and Garvey] looking impeccable in suits, we thought well, why not us? At that time a lot of Rastas looked like real vagabonds, but we thought having smart tunics was important—it was a militant style that showed we were serious about what we were doing." For Tread, the uniforms were an attempt to "say to Handsworth: 'if we can make ourselves better, so can you.'"[113]

For Jungleman's members, Rastafarianism offered a way out of some of the problems in their everyday lives in Handsworth. Tread had found himself unable to secure a job in the engineering industry and recalled that all the members of Jungleman were "what you call disenfranchised youth: we didn't have jobs, weren't qualified . . . we weren't happy with the way we were being treated by the police." Rastafarianism offered a route beyond these issues. The growth in interest in subcultures in the late 1970s coincided, Tread reflected, with "a lot of sociologists [who] came to Handsworth and wanted to know why we were turning to the Rasta 'cult' as they called it." For Tread, its significance was that "it let us take a different road. It was that Rasta ethos of self-help. We wanted to do something good with our lives—self-help, self-reliance."[114] As shown in chapter 1, among political groups in Handsworth who also subscribed to a philosophy of self-help, the issue of public funding proved to be an area of considerable disagreement. Jungleman, in contrast, saw the public money it obtained as a way of expanding its activities beyond the sound system. The members set up their own tailors, who made the uniforms they wore on stage, and a photography venture, which sold photographs of reggae acts performing in Birmingham. The umbrella group for each of these projects was called Exodus, named after the title of the Bob Marley album which, following its release in 1977, had stayed on the British charts for fifty-six consecutive weeks.[115]

Yet Jungleman was different than the other acts that were a feature of Handsworth's dread culture. The band's commitment to Africa went beyond the level of the symbolic and the performative, whether this was expressed through dance, music, speech, or style. The group's uniforms may have helped contribute to Jungleman's aura on a stage in Handsworth, but they were also indicative of a more fundamental commitment to a return to Africa. For Tread, the uniforms were meant to show that Jungleman's members were "righteous soldiers . . . from God." In 1982 the group obtained more funds from the Cadbury Trust, this time to make a trip to Africa. The idea was to emigrate permanently, use their expertise in tailoring to set up a clothing business, and continue with the sound system. Before making the trip, Jungleman sent some of its members, including Tread, to Africa to find out whether permanent emigration would be feasible. Tread and two others made the trip from Handsworth to Ghana, Nigeria, Togo, and the Ivory Coast and, according to Tread, the "feedback was all really positive." Settling on Accra as the location of choice, Tread obtained the required music permit from the Ministry of Culture and had an agreement in principle with the Ghanaian Musicians' Union. He "began to believe that this could actually happen."[116]

However, the planned migration to Ghana ended in failure. While Tread was there, those members of Jungleman who had remained in Handsworth were having second thoughts. Ironically, given the suspicion within Rastafarianism of Western modernity alluded to by the front cover of *Handsworth Revolution*, Tread recalled having "all these stupid arguments about cars.... 'What are we going to do with the cars?'" For Tread, these were the "stupidest excuses I ever heard"; the remaining members of the group simply "didn't have the courage to come." Tread and those members still in Ghana were forced to return to Handsworth, leaving equipment they had purchased there behind. Unlike Benjamin Zephaniah, Steel Pulse, and the participants in Kokuma, Tread clearly understood Rastafarianism's focus on Africa as something more than an imagined community. His commitment to Rastafarianism meant physically making his own exodus to Africa. In the event, upon his return to Handsworth Tread was forced to return the grant Jungleman had received for the African trip. The experience, he reflected, led him to "question my faith in man." For Tread, at least, "the dream had gone out of the window."[117] Within a few years, Jungleman broke up.

CONCLUSION

By the beginning of the 1990s many of the groups discussed in this chapter had disbanded. In 1992 Kokuma moved out of its base in Handsworth to premises in central Birmingham; by the end of the decade, following a series of arguments about the direction of the group, it folded. Other groups changed almost beyond all recognition. Following the release of *Handsworth Revolution* and three less successful follow-up albums, in 1982 Basil Gabbidon left Steel Pulse, the group that he had cofounded. "I couldn't handle it anymore," he remarked. "I was tired and worn out, angry and depressed."[118] The band's core market increasingly became the United States and, following its Grammy win for *Babylon the Bandit*, Steel Pulse performed at President Bill Clinton's 1993 inauguration party. By this time Steel Pulse had already relocated to America and contained only two remaining members of the original Handsworth lineup.

There were other changes taking place within Handsworth's music scene. By the late 1980s, in Handsworth as in other urban areas, parallel developments illustrated the extent to which dread culture was just one prominent element among other, diaspora-oriented musical subcultures. A South Asian scene had emerged with a focus on *bhangra*, a folk music tradition from the Punjab, the large region that runs along the northern border of India and Pakistan. In its British iteration, traditional instruments such as the *dhol* and the *dholki* drums formed the backdrop to songs that evoked an Asian diasporic experience, with the Punjab functioning as the key symbolic homeland. Performed in Punjabi—and often at "daytime disco" events that facilitated the younger generation's critical involvement in the shaping of this scene—songs such as the 1988 "Soho Road *Uteh*" (On the Soho road) by the Birmingham band Apna Sangeet (Our Music) explored the experience of migration through the prism of two lovers attempting to find each other on separate journeys from India to Britain. While undoubtedly less militant than *Handsworth Revolution*, the importance of the reference to Handsworth's Soho Road—which was a pervasive motif in British *bhangra*—was that, like dread culture, this was a diasporic formation that was conceptualized as functioning assertively within the Handsworth and British contexts.[119] In 1990 Steven Kapur, a twenty-three-year-old Handsworth resident of South Asian descent, built on this tradition as he embarked on his own musical career. Under the stage name Apache Indian, and initially sporting dreadlocks similar to those of David Hinds, Benjamin Zephaniah, Ras Tread, and many other figures discussed in this chapter, Kapur released his debut single, "Movie Over India." It single drew on Kapur's two main influences: the British *bhangra* scene, garnered from his upbringing in a Punjabi household, and reggae, an influence from his time spent toasting for various sound systems in Handsworth. In 1992, following in the paths of Bob Marley and Steel Pulse, Kapur signed a deal with Island Records. The following year he released "Boom-shack-a-lak." The single quickly became one of the biggest-selling reggae records in the United Kingdom. With its party-like tone and irreverent lyrics, it has featured on numerous advertisements and film soundtracks around the world. Kapur's story is undoubtedly a testament to the highly innovative, hybrid cultural forms that were emerging from urban Britain as a result of its ongoing multicultural drift.[120] At the same time, however, coupled with the wider growth in influence of African American hip-hop, "Boom-shack-a-lak" was arguably also a symbol that the particular political and cultural sensibilities associated with Handsworth's dread culture were coming to an end.

Of all the acts that have been discussed in this chapter, it is perhaps Steel Pulse and its *Handsworth Revolution* that best encapsulate the way in which, through various forms of performance, Africa provided for a young black generation a source of identity in the particular context of Britain in the long 1980s. As was alluded to in Kokuma's production *The Awakening*, Benjamin Zephaniah's poem "Dis Policeman Keeps on Kicking Me to Death," and *Handsworth Revolution* itself, Africa helped this generation come to terms with a feeling of alienation in their contemporary lives in Handsworth.

"As soon as you leave school," David Hinds reflected in the early 1980s, "you find that all the things you were promised—a job, a future and so on—it's all different. When you realise that, all you've got to turn to is your own culture and yourself. There's nowhere else to look."[121] As reggae fans such as Brian Bennett or Amlak Tafari made clear, Steel Pulse was popular in Handsworth not only because of the quality of its music, but also because, through its focus on Rastafarianism, the band emphasized an African identity that was specifically for use in Handsworth. The same was true of those who participated in Kokuma. African dance had "given me a black identity . . . a sense of grounding," a performer in Kokuma reflected. It "filled the gap."[122]

This was evidently not true of everyone in black Handsworth. The divisions between older and younger generations over Rastafarianism have been widely commented on. Arguably, given that the older generation was responsible for the establishment of Pan-Africanist political organizations in Handsworth and across the country, they have been exaggerated. What has received less attention is the role of gender within Britain's dread culture.[123] While the transnational reggae scene of the 1970s and 1980s did not exhibit the same levels of misogyny as the later dance-hall genre, the world of sound systems and reggae bands was—as the earlier calypso scene in Trinidad had been—undoubtedly a masculine one.[124] In Kokuma, women were the majority of the participants, many of whom found in African dance a blueprint for a vision of black, diasporic femininity. Women also had a greater involvement in Lovers' Rock, a parallel music scene that first emerged in mid-1970s London. Although this also represented a transnational amalgamation of musical forms—particularly Jamaican reggae and the soft soul associated with the Chicago and Philadelphia music scenes—it was one much less influenced by Rastafarian philosophies.[125] Within Rastafarianism, significant strands of the movement were opposed to the sexual objectification of women, and reggae performers such as Judy Mowatt helped stimulate the emergence of a feminine Rastafarian aesthetic. However, as the writer Ferdinand Dennis found when he visited a group of practicing Rastafarians in Handsworth in the late 1980s, there was also evidence of patriarchal attitudes toward sexuality and motherhood.[126] In Jamaica, by the end of the twentieth century an increasing number of women had become high-profile MCs and toasters in their own right. It is indicative of the way in which the black British music scene has been shaped by transnational dialogues that by the turn of the century, and with the emergence of new acts such as the Birmingham-based grime artist Lady Leshurr, Britain finally witnessed the arrival of a cohort of women performers who stamped their own mark on toasting as a musical art form.[127]

Whether it was through dance, reggae, sound systems, or style, what is striking about the dread culture of the 1980s is the extent to which, for those who were able to participate, the concept of Africa created a point of commonality that was at odds with understandings of Thatcher's Britain which emphasize it as a period of rising individualism. This is not to deny the significant tensions within Handsworth's dread culture, including with respect to the frustration figures such as Ras Tread felt at the unwillingness of others to physically embark on a return to Africa. The irony of this position was that in many ways there were echoes of the emphasis placed on repatriation by Enoch Powell and others who were irreconcilably opposed to Britain's racial diversity.[128] However, as Stuart Hall has argued, "the point was not that some people, a few, could only live with themselves and discover their identities by literally going back to Africa." This was not, as it had been in the Soho jazz scene of the 1930s and 1940s, a form of transnationalism embodied by the fluid movement of people. Rather, the importance of Africa in Handsworth was that it allowed people to come to terms with their experiences in the locale and, in so doing, emphasize it as a distinctively black space. To understand Handsworth's dread culture as the construction of an imagined community around the figure of Africa is not to underestimate the critical and entirely real effects this had on the lives of a young black generation. Hall understood this effect as nothing less than a cultural revolution.[129] If that was so, this was a revolution that was—as Steel Pulse recognized—made in Handsworth.

4

Leisure and Sociability

The Black Everyday

INTRODUCTION

C. L. R. James, the Trinidadian Marxist, essayist, and lifelong cricket fan, famously saw cricket in the Caribbean as being inseparable from the question of identity. In his celebrated memoir *Beyond a Boundary* (1963), which focused on the place of the game in his native Trinidad, James contrasted colonial associations between cricket and English "civilization" with the success of black players on the cricket pitch, which, James argued, had contributed to an increasing cultural self-confidence across the Caribbean. If an early marker was the achievements of the Trinidadian all-rounder Learie Constantine during a playing career in England in the late 1920s and 1930s, James would later argue that this blossomed with the distinctive approach of the Guyanese batsman Rohan Kanhai a generation later. Kanhai's batting, James argued, provided a "unique pointer of the West Indian quest for identity, for ways of expressing our potential bursting at every seam." Like the appointment of Frank Worrell as the first black captain of the West Indian cricket team in 1960 and the subsequent rise of Garfield Sobers, another West Indian all-rounder, Kanhai contributed to a "West Indian renaissance." In James's eyes, race was inseparable from the game. For it to have been any other way, he wrote, "we would have had to divest ourselves from our skins."[1]

Having moved to London in the 1930s, James became a key player in making the city an epicenter of radical Pan-Africanist political organization. Later, following a period in the United States that ended in his expulsion in the McCarthyite 1950s, James acted as a sounding board for the development of the British Black Power movement, particularly through his close relationship with his nephew, the journalist and activist Darcus Howe.[2] James's writings were enmeshed with his political commitments. Yet as *Beyond a Boundary* shows, this did not preclude an attempt to take seriously what was happening in the cultural sphere. James's sustained engagement with cricket, in particular, demonstrates the extent to which he embraced an expanded understanding of culture that chimed with the parallel emergence of cultural studies.[3] Alongside his assessment of the style of players like Constantine and Kanhai, James explored the more general practices that accompanied the game: the impromptu "scratch" games of his youth, the rivalries that developed between competing teams, and above all, the importance of cricket's Victorian "puritan" code of conduct. For James, it was not enough to merely be a player on the cricket field. He also attempted to "live the life."[4]

Beginning with the story of a local black cricket club, this chapter examines the practices and sociability that took place in black Handsworth's leisure sites and explores what these say about black identity, community formation, and the experience of race. To some degree, this represents an extension of the previous exploration of dread culture (see chapter 3); it is an excavation of a lived culture that, given the nebulous nature of the subject, necessitates engaging with the work of anthropologists, novelists, and others most attuned to the quotidian elements of everyday life.[5] While the breadth of sociological investigations into Rastafarianism's emergence in Britain in many ways confirmed its significance, this research was part of a subcultural turn in which the allure of the overtly oppositional in everyday life could be underpinned by an implicit dismissal of what, as has been argued, was often presumed to be "an undifferentiated 'normalcy' or 'straightness' among the vast majority."[6] The emphasis here is on unpicking the importance of spaces not ordinarily associated with an idiom of oppositionality, but which were arguably a more pervasive feature of black life, for an older generation in particular, but to varying degrees for their children, too. Following the analysis of a cricket club is an examination of Handsworth's pubs, clubs, and growing number of black churches. Finally, this chapter ends by entering into black domestic life and exploring the significance of the front room space in particular. Moving beyond the domestic front door represents a pivot away from the public sphere and in many ways is a culmination of this book's insistence on the importance of the everyday in the context of race in 1980s Britain.

Experienced in particular ways depending on class, age, and gender, what was manifest in these spaces was a black identity once again shaped by a dialogue with the experience of diaspora. Like the politics of Handsworth's Black Power groups; the artwork produced by its photographers and filmmakers; and the reggae music, dances, and styles that constituted its dread culture, what took place inside the area's cricket clubs, pubs, churches, and front rooms was the product of a "diasporan consciousness." The precise version that developed in these spaces was, however, distinctive in a number of important ways. First, it was not the largely symbolic Africa or Ethiopia that functioned as the critical locus, but the more familiar Caribbean. This indicates the prominent role of older generations in this sociability, people who were often much more ambivalent about the African legacy and who as an immigrant generation could draw on a more concrete set of reference points from memories of ways of life prior to the act of migration. Moreover, this was not a black identity formally communicated by political placards, documentary photographs, or the lyrics of reggae bands. Rather, it was shaped by quotidian practices and shared memories that had the effect of inserting Caribbean cultures and sensibilities into the everyday urban landscape. On the cricket field, for example, it was manifested by playing what was understood to be a distinctively West Indian brand of cricket; in pubs and social clubs, it came across via the emphasis placed on dominoes, a game widely played throughout the Caribbean, which had a number of distinctive features; and in black churches it was there in a style of worship that was seen as a means of evoking emotional connections to what many still considered home, even if the ambition of eventually returning there had in many cases receded.

To some degree, moving toward the black everyday constitutes the examination of an emotional community, defined as a collective with similar interests, values, and goals whose shared emotional registers act as a source of significant cohesion.[7] For example, while the Caribbean that was invoked in Handsworth undoubtedly functioned less mythologically than the figure of Africa, it was nevertheless often filtered through a nostalgic sentimentality many felt for their birthplace, more so as their early lives there began to slip from view. Operating alongside this was commonly an aspirational desire to be seen to be getting on in Britain, in the context of shifting class dynamics and the enduring reach of a colonial legacy that rendered many aspects of Caribbean culture close in proximity to perceptions of "Britishness." As Anne Spry Rush has shown, the Victorian imperial values of domesticity, "Christian morality," and above all respectability had by the early twentieth century become a powerful ideology in the Caribbean, accompanying later immigrants to Britain in ways that have not always been taken seriously.[8] Indeed, it was this legacy that James and a younger generation of West Indian intellectuals in postwar Britain were often seeking to understand. The cricket field notwithstanding, by the 1980s references to the West Indies were increasingly being superseded by "the Caribbean," a label less implicated with the legacies of colonialism. But what this chapter demonstrates is that bound up with the affective sentimentality many had for the Caribbean were elements of a residual "colonial Victorianism" that also operated within the lived cultures of black Handsworth's leisure institutions.[9] In its cricket clubs, for instance, traces remained of the game's Victorian ethical code as described by James; its church congregations emphasized the importance of dressing respectably in one's Sunday best; and, referencing the parlor tradition of the Victorian period, its front rooms were designated spaces reserved for extravagant domestic goods, special occasions, and the reassertion of the class distinctions that many found had been lost in the act of migration.[10]

This was therefore a milieu structured by cultural capital and a class-based politics of aspiration.[11] And black Handsworth's everyday sociability was also gendered. The first half of the chapter interrogates a largely masculine formation, in which a Caribbean street culture centering on bravado and reputation often structured the life that took place inside Handsworth's cricket clubs and pubs. The church and front room were comparatively feminized spaces, but where the question of reputation specifically—manifested in an emphasis on the accrual of spiritual and cultural capital—was also central. Both formations constituted a set of emotional linkages to particular readings of diaspora that contrasted markedly with the racialized, often gendered stereotypes of the 1980s: the pervasive figures of the male mugger or rioter and a portrayal of black women, whose status as economic migrants often denied them maternal, domestic definitions of "respectable" femininity.[12] In this way, though the focus on the everyday in this chapter signals a move away from the spectacularly oppositional in Handsworth, important political currents also flowed through the black everyday. The very existence of black cricket clubs, pubs, and churches was a testament to the pervasiveness of British racism and the long shadow cast by the color bar. In the context of the 1980s, the political battles that needed to be waged were no less acute. But tracing the development of Britain's nascent 1950s "black locality" into the later twentieth century allows for an expanded line of vision in which the presence of these leisure institutions can be read as the products of a black community that not only rejected dominant stereotypes, but also had established itself in the topographical landscape of postcolonial Britain. Although less immediately visible in the historical archive and lacking the overt political agenda of Handsworth's Black Power groups, artists, or Rastafarians, this was nevertheless a sociability that also represented a highly significant, diasporic reordering of Handsworth. As James himself suggested in the early 1980s, what that sociability arguably underscores is the arrival in Britain of a black British sensibility.[13]

CRICKET

Throughout the 1960s and 1970s, James Brown, a Jamaican migrant who had moved to Britain in the late 1950s, was a member of the Handsworth Continental Cricket Club. The club had been founded in the south of the city in April 1960, then moved to Handsworth Park in the mid-1970s to be closer to a greater number of black players. Having retired from playing in the early 1980s, Brown approached a community arts center with the idea of writing his memoirs. Initially these were handwritten by Brown on the back of leaflets advertising sound system clashes and other events. The memoirs were never published, but the draft suggests that what concerned Brown was not his early life in the Caribbean, the process of immigration, or his attempts to establish himself in a hostile British society. Brown was no C. L. R. James, though the two did share a passion for cricket, which Brown evidently envisaged as forming the sole focus of his writing. This was to be less the story of Brown's life and more an account of Handsworth Continental itself, told using Brown's apparently encyclopedic knowledge of every shot, catch, and wicket ever taken during his association with the club. "I have watched the Continental cricketers demolish and drive many teams out of the park," Brown wrote, recalling how one particular game "started off with glorious shots and boundaries" from the opposing team, but this "soon came to a stop. Campbell took a glorious catch to dismiss Erick the flashy captain. They did not stand a chance. We won the game by 71 runs."[14]

In Brown's relative silence on race there are to some extent parallels with the work of white, working-class amateur memoirists, who often passed over class as a concept in favor of what was seen as the more neutral concept of the "ordinary."[15] To all but the keenest of cricket fans, Brown's evocations of countless amateur matches, shots, and catches could certainly appear banal. Yet if nothing else, they demonstrate the absolute centrality of cricket to Brown's life. Matches are described in minute detail, decisions about which team to field are agonized over, and the merits of a particular player's stroke-play are dissected. For Learie Constantine, writing at the end of his own playing career in England, it was dedication to cricket that above all defined the Caribbean spirit of the game, which "makes us, with our small islands, our lack of unity [and] our few proper pitches . . . able to produce a team that can challenge England."[16] Although others involved in Continental were not moved to write about it, many shared Brown's commitment to cricket and, like Constantine, conceptualized this as part of their own Caribbean formation. Francis Nation was born in Manchester, Jamaica, migrated to Britain in 1960 at age seventeen, and also became a key player in the establishment of Continental. "A young man in Jamaica wanted to be a professional cricketer," he recalled. "If you can't be a professional cricketer, you become a professional supporter. All my life I've loved cricket, and when I came to Birmingham I thought it was a fantastic opportunity to start my own club."[17] It was the cricket itself that emphasized the blackness of Continental. Its members played in what was understood as a distinctively Caribbean style: an attacking, playful, sometimes aggressive approach. Yet this was never completely at the expense of what James understood to be cricket's traditional code of conduct. There remained room for a simultaneous emphasis on the puritanical spirit of cricket, which had its roots in the game's expansion in England during the Victorian period.

In this context, a convoluted system for ensuring class privilege prevailed. The game was structured around the distinction between amateurs and professionals. The latter were working-class players who played for money, the former "gentlemen" of a supposedly higher stock who ostensibly did not require payment but in practice obtained covert sponsorship and expenses deals that dwarfed professional payments. Indeed, it was the gentlemen who administered the game, captained the teams, and most often took what was seen as the more skilled role of batsman (in opposition to the role of bowler, which involved a greater degree of physicality, for which working-class players were presumed to be better suited). Such a system symbolized the more general values of morality and fair play that were seen to set cricket apart from other sports. This was embodied by the gentlemanly amateur, who was both disciplined and principled, openly admitted if he was out whether or not this had been seen by the umpire, and treated both victory and defeat with an equal measure of reserve.[18] In the late nineteenth century this worldview was transposed to the colonies along with the game, with Protestant missionaries envisaging that cricket could function as a means of "civilizing" the black population. Inevitably, therefore, the game was infused with the racialized hierarchies of empire. In the Caribbean, cricket and its associated values became a feature of the private schools that had been set up to cater for the white elite and the light-skinned middle classes. Teams were established along the lines of skin color; the darker the skin of a team's players, the closer they were seen to be to the masses. Following the West Indian cricket team's establishment as a Test team in 1928, black players of any skin tone were barred from captaining it. In spite of this, the game's Victorian moral code was widely reproduced and often internalized, particularly by those such as James who had received an exclusive Caribbean schooling.[19]

Cricket's class and racial distinctions proved to be durable; neither the categories of the professional and amateur nor the ban on black players captaining the West Indies was abolished until the early 1960s.[20] But the game's popularity across the Caribbean combined with the anticolonial movement, with matches between the West Indies and England taking on particular significance. The West Indies beat England for the first time in 1930. However, of greater symbolic importance was the 1950 series between the two teams in England, which resulted in the West Indies' first overseas series victory over the colonial power.[21] The result was celebrated across the Caribbean and was also important to the early black émigrés in Britain. Although there were only a few dozen black spectators present at each match, the audibility of the West Indian support was widely commented upon. The *Times*' cricket correspondent, for example, criticized the "unpleasant" booing that came in response to a decision from the umpire in the final test.[22] Lord Kitchener, the Trinidadian calypso singer who was asked to perform for the news crews upon his arrival in Britain aboard the *Empire Windrush*, remembered leading a celebratory congregation from the final match into central London; his fellow musician, Lord Beginner, who had also been aboard the *Windrush*, wrote "Victory Test Match" as an ode to the win. For others, meanwhile, the success helped inspire the establishment of localized West Indian cricket clubs in areas of black settlement across the country.[23]

FIGURE 14. Francis Nation (r.), Handsworth Continental Cricket Club, ca. early 1980s. Reproduced by permission of Francis Nation.

In the Caribbean, given that cricket facilities were commonly attached to private schools, involvement in a cricket club was seen as a means of maintaining status distinctions; cricket clubs were spaces in which an individual could "mingle with advantageous acquaintances and extend his range of connections."[24] Stuart Hall recalled refusing to join his father's club because he reacted against the airs and graces of the other members.[25] The establishment of black cricket clubs in Britain worked in a different way. In the first instance, they were often valued as alternative spaces away from the racism to which black players were commonly subject in their everyday lives. For example, Francis Nation (see figure 14) recalled dressing "smart in ties and go[ing] to clubs" only to be told "'we don't have blacks in here'"; cricket provided what Nation saw as an essential alternative form of weekend entertainment.[26] Subsequently, however, clubs arguably functioned less as a line of defense against the racism of white society and more as a space for the articulation of black identities. Most obviously, this was manifested by playing what was regarded as a distinctively West Indian style of cricket. The formation of the West Indian cricket side provided an early and unexpectedly durable identity that was to a large degree able to transcend interisland rivalries. It far outlasted the West Indian Federation, the political alliance established in 1958 that was ostensibly based on a mutual sense of West Indianness across the British Caribbean but was dissolved in 1962 in the context of a gathering momentum behind a nationalistic vision of postcolonial independence.[27] For James, it was the batting of Rohan Kanhai—who played for the West Indies for almost two decades and in 1973 became the team's captain—that, with his "cat and mouse" approach and distinctive hook shot, best embodied the West Indian style.[28] At the opposite end of the cricketing spectrum, for the players of Continental Caribbean cricket seemingly meant one thing above all else: an emphasis on attacking play.

To some extent, this mode of play was influenced by the "street cricket" that had begun to emerge in parallel to the elite form of the game in the Caribbean; the former often reappropriated the general tenor and style of the latter, so that skills such as speed and aggression in the bowling and fast-scoring and bravura in the batting were emphasized.[29] At Continental, the club's literature repeatedly dwelt on an individual player's attacking prowess: a "specialist slip fielder" who was "not afraid to hit the new ball for six"; a "utility player" who was also "a potential match winner"; a lower order batsman who could nevertheless "give the ball a good thump."[30] This is not to say that players at Continental had internalized what had become the well-worn stereotypes about West Indian cricket. If calypso artists often used their art form to memorialize the achievements of West Indian cricketers, in the 1950s and 1960s English commentators often used the phrase "calypso cricket" as shorthand for a portrayal of Caribbean cricketers as talented but volatile, "'jolly Caribbean beans'" who provided an entertaining aside to the "real cricket" played by England or Australia. This narrative undoubtedly owed much to the stereotypes presented in the 1920s by writers such as Neville Cardus, the *Manchester Guardian*'s cricket correspondent, who saw West Indian cricketers as impulsive and childlike, their skills hindered by a supposed inability to understand the game on an intellectual plane.[31] Rather, the emphasis on cricketing expansiveness at Continental was part of a wider street culture particularly prominent in Jamaica, in which play and bravado occupy central positions, something often depicted in the fiction of Caribbean writers such as Errol John and V. S. Naipaul.[32] In Handsworth, according to Brown, this translated to instances in which one Continental batsman "upset the bowlers by turning the back of his bat, pretending he was not ready," before "jumping down the wicket [and] driving Robinson for two beautiful fours right over his head." On another occasion, Brown wrote, Continental's batsmen hit "at least ten sixes and were amused at the way many shots had to be retrieved from the river adjoining the . . . ground." Continental summarized the team's style as "built around a pattern of natural ability, attack and defence only as a last resort"; attempting to "hit the ball at every opportunity" was, it was emphasized, "typical West Indian cricket."[33]

The 1980s witnessed a developing professionalism at the club, in part as a result of the growing sponsorship Continental was able to attract. This included Handsworth-based businesses such as Hope's "wholesale distributors of American & Continental Cosmetics," and Caribbean Bakery Ltd. (both based at the foot of Soho Road); Gees Salon, specialists in Afro hair styles (based around the corner on Grove Lane, en route to Handsworth Park); and West Indian Fig Tree Ltd. (based on Lozells Road), demonstrating how, by the 1980s, a concentrated black commercial topography in Handsworth had seemingly recognized the importance of supporting a corresponding leisure sector. Echoing the advertising found in an earlier period of black settlement in magazines such as *The West Indian Gazette*, Continental also enjoyed the support of Caribbean-based corporations, including Red Stripe Lager. If in the early 1960s Red Stripe was actually only available to purchase in Jamaica, by the mid-1980s it was marketing itself to black Handsworth as "the true taste of the Caribbean."[34]

In 1983, having hitherto played without changing rooms, the club constructed a pavilion and clubhouse and joined the Birmingham Parks League. Continental also used its sponsorship to put on end-of-season tours. Initially these took place in the rural village settings that had long been romanticized as providing the backdrop to the purest form of English cricket.[35] But they also began to include tours of the Caribbean. The tours served as a way of physically enacting the transnational connections Continental's players saw their style of cricket as embodying. That tour parties often numbered more than forty and included players' families was a testament to the difficulty many people otherwise had in raising funds for such trips. The tours certainly acted as a means of reinforcing the Caribbean identities of Continental's players. In 1986, for example, Continental embarked on a series of matches against the National Police Cricketers of Trinidad, birthplace of both C. L. R. James and Learie Constantine. The tour's brochure attempted to explain to its readers what could be expected. The "typical Trinidadian batsman," it opined, was "fully aware that the easy paced wickets are a bowler's purgatory." Alongside this was a more general introduction to the island, its climate, its history, and rum punch, which, it was advised, needed to be "treated with the fullest respect."[36]

Unlike the growing numbers of South Asian cricket clubs in Britain, which were often made up of players from specific regions and religious backgrounds, Continental players came from a variety of Caribbean islands, though Jamaican players undoubtedly represented the majority.[37] As has been suggested, immigrants from the Caribbean were often the most enthusiastic proponents of the development of an inclusive West Indian identity, in part because of the widespread ignorance about the region's national specificities that they encountered once in Britain.[38] Yet the introduction to Trinidadian cricketing culture the Continental tour brochure provided may well have been for the benefit of Jamaican players like Brown and Nation, and a recognition of the way in which forms of "island chauvinism" could potentially reemerge when the Caribbean went from being a place nostalgically evoked in Handsworth to one that was physically visited.[39] The author of the foreword to the Trinidad brochure was Viv Richards, the Antiguan-born batsman who moved to Somerset as a professional in 1974 and, by

FIGURE 15. Handsworth Continental Cricket Club, ca. early 1980s. Reproduced by permission of Francis Nation.

the mid-1980s, had become captain of the West Indies and one of the sport's undisputed global stars. That Richards, or someone acting on his behalf, had agreed to write a few platitudes for Continental was undoubtedly a coup in itself. And Richards ended his short foreword by paying the club what must have been received as the ultimate accolade: "The lads even play cricket like they do back home."[40] For Nation, who was part of the touring party by this point in his capacity as club secretary, the result of the matches played in Trinidad was beside the point. In the end, Continental played six games and lost them all. But it didn't matter, Nation concluded. Continental had, as Richards suggested, already demonstrated its Caribbean credentials.[41]

For the sociologist Ben Carrington, the cultivation of a Caribbean style of cricket by black players in Britain was a form of resistance to the racism of white teams and the colonial legacies symbolized by English cricket more generally.[42] Nation recalled that in the club's early days, in particular, Continental experienced considerable racism during games; when the players (see figure 15) had a match against "a pure white team," for example, and were "very vocal and shouted, 'how is that, umpire?', the umpire would take offence to it."[43] Like the language used to advertise sound system clashes, fliers for which Brown had used as paper for the first draft of his memoirs, Brown often couched his subject in quasi-militaristic terms. Derek Bell, a former captain, was described as "a moody black, friendly only if you came to his terms," and Getting, another ex-captain, was likened to Napoleon: visiting teams "dreaded Continental under [his] command" because nothing "could stop him marching on."[44]

This discourse was influenced by the cricketing conjuncture in which Brown was writing. From the mid-1970s onward the West Indies enjoyed an unprecedented period of success, based to a large degree on a fast-paced bowling attack that was widely criticized by English commentators in particular for overstepping the ethical spirit of the game. During the 1984 test match between the West Indies and England at the Oval in London, for example, which confirmed a record 5–0 series win for the tourists that was celebrated as a "blackwash" by West Indian fans, one correspondent decried what he saw as a nasty performance of "bowling brutality."[45] Such depictions were undoubtedly underpinned by deep-rooted racial stereotypes regarding black physicality and aggression. For all the historic connections between cricket and calypso, the players themselves increasingly adopted political positions that evoked the anticolonial race consciousness of Rastafarianism discussed in chapter 3. Viv Richards often took the field sporting a wristband in the Ethiopian red, gold, and green, for example, and in 1983 famously refused a "blank check" offer to break an international boycott of matches against a whites only South African cricket team. Richards—echoing depictions of cricket in Caribbean literature in which the bat is commonly portrayed as a hypermasculine "phallic weapon"—saw himself as having "carried my bat for the liberation of African and other oppressed people everywhere"; his success on the cricket field was in his view "a step beyond sport," where "a whole lot of things needed defending rather than the cricket ball itself."[46] In this context, for Michael Holding, the most prominent of the West Indies' fast bowlers, matches against England were a means of "showing the Englishmen, 'you brought the game to us, and now we are better than you.'"[47]

To understand the sociability at Continental solely in these terms, however, is to miss a central ambivalence within the Caribbean inheritance. While the rapidly growing number of victories by the West Indies over England were important sources of pride across the Caribbean diaspora, some have argued that the fact these took place on the cricket pitch was a confirmation of the ongoing grip of the colonial legacy.[48] Certainly James was unequivocal in his understanding of cricket as being inseparable from a particular English frame of reference learned from his own elite schooling: P. G. Wodehouse, *The Boys Own Paper*, the English public schools Eton and Harrow, and an emphasis on a stiff upper lip.[49] The parallel, street form of the game had certainly watered down such associations. Yet traces were left behind and arguably retained a presence in Handsworth, alongside the bravado and attacking shots on which Continental's players prided themselves. In Nation's recollection, for example, Continental simply accepted racism during games "because we were like professionals."[50] On one level, this illustrates the commitment that individuals like Nation and Brown had to the development of the club. But it also shows how, knowingly or not, the historic divisions between the gentlemanly amateur and hard-working professional—who in the Victorian period would also be responsible for the upkeep of the cricket ground—remained an implicit presence in the discourse around Handsworth Continental. Similarly,

Brown wrote of his admiration for another former Continental batsman, Edwards, a "very good fielder and a very stylish batsman" who was above all a "gentleman" who had "the game at heart."[51] These examples are not quite in keeping with James's own perception of himself as a young cricketer of a Puritan discipline, one who "never cheated . . . never appealed for a decision unless I thought the batsman was out" and "never jeered a defeated opponent."[52] But they do suggest that among the swashbuckling stroke-play and heroic captains idealized by Brown, at least some element of the Victorian sensibility lived on.

The erection of the clubhouse in 1983 enabled Continental to fulfill a more varied role in the Handsworth locale. In particular, it allowed the club to become an active site of sociability during the long cricketing off-season in the autumn and winter months. In part, this provided another symbolic connection to the Caribbean. There, Nation recalled, "the social scene was part of cricket"; the establishment of the clubhouse was for Nation a means of "bringing [that scene] here with us." To some extent, the clubhouse became a social space for younger people and players' families. Nation remembered that his children would regularly come to watch him play for Continental, helping to keep score, shouting words of encouragement from the boundary and "lambasting" opponents. Another important element was dominoes, a game that enjoyed a close connection with cricket in the Caribbean. In Jamaica, one player explained, "when the cricket is on, you have a good game of dominoes—when there's a wicket, you stop." Dominoes quickly became a feature of the Continental clubhouse. The game has a long history in Britain, though what was played at Continental was a distinctively Caribbean iteration. In Caribbean dominoes, for example, winning hands are slammed onto the table in order to rile and jeer at opponents. "Coding" is also a central feature, a way of covertly communicating to teammates critical information about an opponents' hand using signals designed to be hidden from view. During the close season dominoes became the primary game played at the Continental clubhouse. "You used to come down the club in winter and there would be five tables with dominoes on," one player recalled. "It was competitive, people played as if they were playing in a tournament. Everyone would have a partner who they would play with."[53]

In light of the popularity of the game, in the late 1980s some members of the club attempted to establish an official dominoes team that could represent Continental during the off-season. The idea was that the team would join one of the nascent black dominoes leagues in Britain and thus give the club an alternative sporting identity. Dominoes offered Continental's members another potential means of communicating their Caribbean identities in Handsworth. The game's performative dimensions, particularly the focus on slamming down a winning domino in celebration, seemingly chimed with the focus that was placed on an attacking, West Indian style of cricket. This was undoubtedly just one element in a long-standing, multifaceted process of unsettling and recasting the British influence in the Caribbean.[54] And in the context of the racial hostilities of postwar Britain, its political implications were evidently significant. For all that James Brown maintained a tight focus on the shots, catches, and wickets he witnessed in Handsworth Park, his willingness to reach for militaristic analogies when describing matches between black and white teams perhaps indicates that he too recognized the wider importance of this cricketing sociability with respect to the articulation and assertion of black identities in Britain.

Yet as has been suggested, this sociability never entirely superseded the ambivalent influence of a historic affinity to a particular version of Britishness. This is further evidenced by the example of dominoes. In spite of the game's apparent synchronicity with West Indian cricket, the attempts at establishing a formal Continental dominoes team ended in failure. Members of the club's managing board, including Nation, were reluctant to become officially associated with anything other than cricket. Moreover, the central components of dominoes—slamming a winning domino to rile opponents, as well as the use of covert codes to gain an advantage—were in fact seen to be at odds with cricket's core ethos of respectability. The potential of dominoes to provide another means of symbolizing this generation's diasporic identity and affinity with the Caribbean could not outweigh Continental's more conservative commitment to a sense of "fair play." Just as English moral guardians of the game a generation earlier had emphasized that "'taking a mean advantage of another'" was anathema to cricket's core values, the management at Continental decided that dominoes was "just not cricket."[55] It was necessary to find a less well-regulated space in which dominoes could function more freely. In the Caribbean itself, this included "barbershops, rum shops, betting shops, or street corners"; in Handsworth, as will be discussed in the next section, that space became the pub and the social club.[56]

PUBS AND SOCIAL CLUBS

In *The Pub and the People* (1943), the classic exploration by Mass Observation of the role of the pub in prewar Bolton or "Worktown" and the forensic observations of the sociability taking place inside pubs—the practice of round-buying, for example, what and how much was being drunk, and the behavior of the bar staff—the authors included a section on the presence of pub games. Although betting and other pastimes were generally banned, various games were permitted, including dominoes, which, it was observed, was played in an estimated two-thirds of local pubs and therefore represented the town's most popular pub game. The dominoes themselves were described by Mass Observers as comprising "oblong bone, wooden, or composition pieces, about half an inch across and two inches long," the faces of which were split in two with a different number of dots on each side, usually ranging from one to six. Players received nine dominoes each, with the aim being to "construct a chain by matching a number on the free end of the chain ... until no one is able to match the numbers." When this point was reached, players added up the numbers of the dominoes left in their hands; the winner was the player with the lowest number.[57]

Dominoes is believed to have originated in China and been introduced to Jamaica by the Spanish in the sixteenth and seventeenth centuries. For the anthropologist Diane Austin, drawing on the field research she conducted in the Selton Town and Vermount districts of Jamaica in the early 1980s, dominoes was the most popular game played in Jamaican bars.[58] To Bert Williams, a Jamaican immigrant to Birmingham and founder of his own dominoes team in Aston, an area adjacent to Handsworth, dominoes was like a national sport in Jamaica. Williams framed his understanding of the importance of the game to his generation in terms of his own trajectory as an immigrant. Like the role of cricket in Francis Nation's early life in Birmingham, Williams saw dominoes as having "helped us settle in the UK" and enabled him to "meet other people from the same background." Others understood dominoes as having functioned as a form of ritual in the absence of more established community events. "When the Caribbean people came to this country," explained Anita Witter, who was of Jamaican heritage, had begun playing dominoes in the 1980s and would subsequently become chairperson of the Anglo-Caribbean Dominoes League (ACDL), "all they had was christenings, weddings and dominoes."[59] Though undoubtedly hyperbolic, Witter's remarks also demonstrate the way in which dominoes was perceived in both practical and symbolic terms: as a way of meeting people and establishing a sense of community among the nascent black population and, like religious ceremonies, as a ritualized signifier of community itself.

If dominoes functioned as a means of community formation, it could only do so because the game that was played was recognized as a specifically Caribbean iteration. This was manifest in various ways. Unlike in the pubs of prewar Bolton, for example, where Mass Observers noted that dominoes players aimed to construct a chain using multiples of fives and threes, Caribbean players commonly worked to multiples of seven.[60] The centrality of coding was also critical. In competitive games consisting of two teams of pairs playing around a table, players attempted to gain an advantage over their opponents by communicating information about the dominoes in play through covert signals such as a tap of the wrist, scratch of the nose, or "kiss of the teeth."[61] More than these technical differences, however, what was arguably the clearest signifier of the game's distinctiveness was the style in which it was played. In Jamaica, Austin observed how a winning hand was commonly marked by a player who would "slam his dominoes down on the table, cry out, and tease the opposing pair to illustrate that he is, after all, the master." To another observer, Caribbean dominoes players appeared to "spend as much effort on joking and riling their opponents as they do on the inherent mental gymnastics of the battle."[62] The tactical awareness required to code could render the presence of bravado and one-upmanship all the more effective. For many players, slamming down a winning domino epitomized the Caribbean nature of the game. "We always slam the domino down," one player remarked. "It's to make it exciting, it's a craze. You say, 'take that.'" The game is "all about the banter," another player suggested. "If I know you haven't got any threes, I bang my threes down on the table." Amongst "the West Indians," another player concluded, slamming was "part and parcel of the game."[63]

These practices provided a means for members of an immigrant generation to assert their Caribbean formations within the confines of the British inner city. Dominoes players were at pains to emphasize the Caribbean nature of the game they played. Players understood it as "an Afro-Caribbean sport" played in a "Caribbean style"; for Johnson Gowane, captain of the Bromfield Stallions dominoes team in Birmingham and a "new arrival" in Britain, having migrated to Birmingham from Jamaica in the 1990s, "no one plays [dominoes] like we play it. It's unique to us—the Chinese wouldn't understand how we play."[64] To some extent, echoing the example of cricket, the distinctiveness of Caribbean dominoes was defined in opposition to the style adopted by the English. Players observed that "English people ... just put [the domino] down" and often misinterpreted slamming as "something aggressive." Conversely, Gowane argued that slamming was less an act of aggression than a way of "demonstrating our control" and signifying that "you are masterful."[65] If other players admitted that the humiliation of opponents was the ultimate objective of slamming, there was an insistence that the aim was to do so "in the nicest possible way."[66] It spite of the emphasis placed by players on the distinctive nature of Caribbean dominoes, then, slamming arguably represented a form of jocularity that was in many ways consistent with the masculinity of the English working-class pub.[67]

Among those who shared the experience of immigration, dominoes was bound up with a nostalgia many felt for their childhoods in the Caribbean. This was illustrated in a 2014 BBC radio documentary on the Caribbean domino club presented by Benjamin Zephaniah, the poet and one-time Handsworth sound-system toaster. Zephaniah began by referencing his own memories of being taught dominoes by his Barbadian father in Handsworth, then encouraged other players to talk about their personal attachment to the game. One player from Guyana recalled being nine years old, "sitting under the mango tree" and playing dominoes until the early hours of the morning; another who began playing at an even earlier age remembered his father admonishing him for the mistakes he made during a game. "Sometimes," he reflected, "I wish he was still alive and could come and see me play.... [H]e'd be proud." While on one level such testimony is both nostalgic and highly personalized, it is also suggestive of the important role that shared emotions play in community formation. Dominoes functioned as a conduit for a set of feelings the unifying undertone of which was often the experience of migration. Discourse around the game was intertwined with memories of the Caribbean and the sense of disorientation that came with leaving it behind. In the Caribbean, one player remembered, "anywhere cricket was there was a few tables around playing dominoes"; there, another player reflected, dominoes was a game that "went well with the barbeque" but was played in "bars, shops, houses . . . everywhere"; in Britain, by contrast, dominoes was understood as being about "bringing the communities together" in an often-hostile environment.[68]

In Britain, the topography of black dominoes playing was inevitably restricted, particularly in the early period of immigration. "When we first came here," Don Williams explained, "you couldn't go into a white pub and play dominoes. People wouldn't play a game with you."[69] Later, while a number of pubs were recognized as being predominantly black spaces, these could often be the primary terrain of younger generations, for whom dominoes did not necessarily have the same appeal. Handsworth's most prominent black pub in the 1980s was arguably the Villa Cross, on the front line at the junction of Lozells Road and Heathfield Road and in "undisputed Rasta territory." It was the subject of numerous police raids as a result of allegations that it was a site of drug dealing and prostitution.[70] Dominoes was the product of a different formation. In the 1950s and 1960s the game was sustained by a nebulous network of venues that often centered on the home, particularly when these were opened up on the occasion of a blues dance or used as the premises for new businesses such as barbershops. By the 1980s, establishments such as the Villa Cross coexisted alongside other black pubs that were more attuned to the requirements of serious dominoes players. This included the Frightened Horse on the corner of Soho Road and Stafford Street and, a short walk from the Villa Cross and less than a mile from the Continental Cricket Club in Handsworth Park, the Bull's Head.[71] A photograph taken inside the latter by Vanley Burke in the 1980s provides an insight into the distinctive sociability that was at play (see figure 16). A group of middle-aged black men are pictured congregating around the dominoes table, dressed in pork-pie hats and blazers. In the corner of the photograph, a white barmaid is seen serving the players a tray of drinks. It was a scene replicated at other black pubs frequented by older generations, such as the Brighton and the Coach and Horses, a bus ride into town and then two miles south to the Balsall Heath district of the city. In the Villa Cross, the tables were reportedly knife scarred as a result of the "cutting of countless bars of cannabis resin." Pubs such as the Bull's Head, in contrast, would commonly feature specialist tables for games of dominoes.[72]

These pubs existed alongside private members' clubs, set up by immigrants in the context of the reluctance of existing clubs and community centers to cater for the black community. The most prominent of such venues in Handsworth, the Faith and Confidence Finance (FCF) club, opened its doors in 1971 at 178 Soho Hill, a short walk south of the premises of Caribbean Bakery Ltd., the sponsor of the

FIGURE 16. Men playing dominoes in the Bull's Head pub, ca. early 1980s. Photograph by Vanley Burke; reproduced by permission.

Continental Cricket Club. The role of the FCF was multifaceted. In the first instance, it was established to bypass any need to rely on the goodwill of white venues when it came to putting on community events. For Roy Richards, whose father coestablished the FCF and who took over the management of the club in the early 2000s, members of the black community felt it necessary to have their own place. If "anyone wants to have a birthday party, or a funeral," Richards continued, "we are there for that." Clubs like the FCF also became sites of other forms of sociability. The FCF was a venue for wedding receptions and weekend dances, for example; it was home to an annual Jamaican independence day celebration; and it also sponsored Continental. Inevitably, dominoes also occupied a central position. Althea Crawford, a player on the BCA Slammers dominoes team in Birmingham, suggested that the importance of clubs like the FCF was that they offered freer spaces where the facets of Caribbean dominoes could be enjoyed without inhibition, if necessary "late into the night or early morning." Games of dominoes were a core part of Richards's memories of his childhood spent around the club. He remembered being continually drawn to the coded form of the game because of the wide variety of symbols that were in play. "I used to look through the window," Richards recalled, "see these signs and think to myself, 'what's going on here?'"[73]

It is in some ways unsurprising that dominoes players gravitated toward these independent, comparatively private spaces where the more idiosyncratic elements of the game could be embraced. According to one player, "if you're lucky" a domino slammed particularly hard could break the table in two.[74] Yet the game's undoubted machismo did not define the wider sociability that took place at the FCF. In spite of the perception by the management of the Continental Cricket Club that dominoes was anathema to the gentlemanly spirit of cricket, in the notion of humiliating one's opponent "in the nicest possible way" there were echoes of the Victorian emphasis on fair play. Moreover, in order to be used as venues for weddings, funerals, and other formal occasions, clubs like the FCF needed to be seen as respectable establishments. At the FCF, this was epitomized by its strict admissions policy, barring entry to those who were deemed "unfit" or "likely to cause trouble." In an ironic twist on the discriminatory practices that had blighted the activities of black immigrants in the 1950s and 1960s and that made autonomous black clubs necessary in the first place, it was a policy that reportedly meant that Rastafarian youths were repeatedly refused entry.[75]

This stance was perhaps justified by the club's owners in light of the other strand of the FCF's business: the provision of credit and financial services to its members. The "finance" in the club's name originated from an investment scheme that the group set up, a variation of the "pardner" system used in the Caribbean in which, in small groups usually consisting of between five and twenty members, each person makes a weekly contribution of a fixed sum of money. This would be kept by a designated banker, who organized a system of withdrawals in which every member would eventually be entitled to a "hand." In a pardner consisting of six people, each contributing £5 per week, for example, the weekly hand would be £30.[76] The funds to purchase the FCF premises on Soho Hill were initially raised through such a scheme, and the club subsequently operated as a source of credit for those members looking for a means of financing holidays, deposits for mortgages, and other large outlays. Given that the pardner was itself a Caribbean tradition in some respects, like dominoes, its very existence was a way for its members to re-create more familiar systems of sociability. A desire for respectability also imbued such systems in their institutionalized form at clubs such as the FCF. On the one hand, the FCF needed to maintain an ethos of reliability in order to maintain the trust and custom of its members. On the other hand, the participants who used such schemes to raise funds for new cars, radios, and other consumer items were often motivated by the politics of conspicuous consumption, and the pardner system was particularly valued by those who viewed themselves as being on the cusp of a middle-class lifestyle.[77] This is not to suggest that every dominoes player was also involved in a pardner. But the close proximity of these two apparently contrasting forms of sociability within the FCF shows how dominoes was part of a world in which nostalgia for the Caribbean evoked by the game's distinctive practices coexisted alongside an aspirational drive for a greater degree of social status in Britain.

In 1989, following various abortive attempts in the 1970s and 1980s, the components of dominoes were formalized with the establishment of the ACDL.[78] Birmingham-based teams such as the Bromfield Stallions, BCA Slammers, and Hampton Hawks competed against other clubs from across the country in matches that took place annually between April and October, culminating in a grand final that determined final league position. What ensured that the ACDL succeeded where previous attempts had failed was the league's success in attracting sponsorship from major Caribbean companies (such as Grace Foods), or those for whom the Caribbean represented an important market (including Guinness beer and the American money transfer company Western Union). The organizers instilled a level of professionalism within the league. New rules were introduced, including the wearing of team uniforms and fines for wearing the wrong colors, swearing, and the use of mobile phones.[79] If this signaled a radical departure from the roots of a game originally played at the pub, it was also a nod to the importance of respectability that—though not as fetishized as in the game of cricket, and often masked by the slam of a winning hand—had always been a component of Caribbean dominoes. As one female competitor in the ACDL remarked, "You've got to have rules. . . . Swearing? No, no, no, no. Talking rough to people, haven't got no manners, trying to fight people? No, no, no, no. We don't want that. Domino is a decent game, and therefore we should keep it decent."[80] Encouraged by its increasing professionalization, by the end of the twentieth century the ACDL began to attract new participants, including younger women, who regarded the game as an important part of their cultural inheritance. For Bert Williams's daughter Andrea, who was born in Birmingham, "dominoes is a heritage thing. I always remember my dad had a table in the house and the hustle and bustle of it. I wanted to learn about it, and I want my son to learn about it." By the early 2000s the ACDL could boast as many as three thousand registered members, including a growing number of women players.[81]

The expansion of the ACDL was in some ways a measurement of the way in which such institutions had by the later twentieth century become as much about community sustenance as formation. They continued to offer the residents of black Handsworth spaces where what were understood to be distinctively Caribbean forms of sociability could be freely practiced. The importance that was attached to such spaces was undoubtedly emphasized by the evident insecurity of others around them. For example, unsurprisingly, given the Villa Cross's associations with various forms of criminality, in the aftermath of the 1985 riots the city council moved to revoke its license, and the pub has for more than three decades been unoccupied. For other public houses, demographic shifts and a diminishing local population that drank alcohol meant that they ceased to be going concerns. By the end of the first decade of the twenty-first century the Clifton, in the Balsall Heath district of the city, had become a fast-food joint; in 2012, planning permission was granted to turn the Bull's Head pub, photographed by Vanley Burke in the 1980s, into a mosque.[82]

The decision of the ACDL to specialize and implement a nationwide structure that was not tied to any one venue meant that it was less likely to meet the same fate. And its professionalization was undoubtedly a factor in its ability to attract new players who might not have been instinctively at home in the less-regimented environment of the pub. Yet this did not result in the eradication of what were understood to be the key components of Caribbean dominoes. Coding remained legal and, for all the emphasis that some placed on the game's decency, bravado and braggadocio were actively encouraged. Caribbean dominoes, an ACDL promotional leaflet explained, comes down to an "understanding of the power of words and sounds." Players employ sound "to intimidate opponents"; the "bang of a table is often used to humiliate a defeated player. Incessant conversation, jokes, red herrings and wordplay are used to antagonise opponents into submission."[83] These practices were themselves symbols of a connection to the Caribbean, whether this meant romanticized memories of childhoods or—as they were for Andrea Williams—more distant diasporic connections through family ties. The ACDL's name encapsulated the transnational nature of the game. Shaped in the Caribbean, dominoes had become a significant site of sociability in urban Britain. If in an earlier period dominoes was an important means of community formation in the context of the color bar, in the late 1980s even the increasingly professional ACDL had seemingly recognized that dominoes functioned above all as a form of leisure. In the ACDL, matches started at four in the afternoon and stopped at seven for food, and after the game was over, "people go on to enjoy themselves by having a recreational dance." It was the responsibility of the home team to provide the postgame entertainment. "We put on food like rice and peas, and play music until three or four in the morning," one player remarked. "Win or lose, after the game it's fun; you keep on playing dominoes until the music stops."[84]

THE CHURCH

The initial absence of pubs and social clubs that were willing to cater to the growing black presence in Britain meant it was the church that was commonly identified by newly arrived immigrants as the most likely place where social networks could be established. In the 1980s churches continued to perform a central role, as the Irish travel writer Dervla Murphy found during a sojourn in Handsworth that was part of her wider project to explore the sights and sociability of multicultural Britain. Writing in 1987, Murphy evoked the religiosity of the growing number of black Pentecostal churches in Handsworth, which she described as being made up mostly of elderly black men and women who "stood and sang and clapped and swayed," pausing occasionally to "weep on the shoulder of a Brother- or Sister-in-Jesus." There was, she recognized, an unmistakable authenticity to the religious fervor around her; in place of set liturgies there were creative, unpredictable services and "rousing musical content." At many of the services she attended in Handsworth, Murphy "didn't notice the time passing." She observed there to be a powerful sense of community among such congregations. In spite of her own ability to penetrate this world, in the context of Handsworth on a day-to-day basis Murphy perceived these to be highly autonomous spaces, "organised by Blacks for Blacks and on which Whites rarely impinge."[85]

In the Caribbean during the 1950s, it was estimated that more than 60 percent of the population was either members of or regular attendees at church.[86] The majority were members of the Methodist or Baptist denominations, which had maintained a strong presence in the English-speaking Caribbean as a result of the work of nineteenth-century missionaries, or the Anglican tradition, which was the home denomination of the original British planters.[87] In 1980s Britain, however, while overall church membership had dropped significantly among the Caribbean community, the proportion of worshippers affiliated with Pentecostal denominations had risen to two-thirds.[88] To some extent this was part of the wider story of Pentecostalism's rapid global expansion from its initial emergence in turn-of-the century California to, by the late twentieth century, its significant presence across the United States, the Caribbean, Latin America, and beyond. In the Caribbean as elsewhere, members of Pentecostal churches largely came from working-class backgrounds.[89] In Britain, however, this became less pronounced as black-led Pentecostal denominations began to attract relatively middle-class worshippers, who had upon their arrival in Britain experienced significant levels of discrimination at their more established "home" churches. While this is further evidence of the pervasive nature of the color bar in the postwar period, according to one report commissioned by the Church of England, the hostility of some congregations toward black worshippers persisted well into the 1980s.[90]

For Pastor Gerald Edmund, who helped establish the Bethel United Church of Jesus Christ in 1950s Handsworth, the climate of racism exacerbated people's need to congregate together. In the case of Bethel, this initially occurred in a worshipper's home, in keeping with the trajectory of other black churches and the later establishment of South Asian mosques and temples, a development that often provoked concern among local authorities because of the supposed potential for the stirring up of intercommunity tensions.[91] In summer 1955 the Bethel church moved to a permanent residence at Gibson Road, a short walk from the Continental Cricket Club house in Handsworth Park and a mile away from Arden Road, where one of Handsworth's first mosques was established in a private residence.[92] From a negligible presence in prewar Britain, then, by the mid-1980s Pentecostalism had grown to some twenty-five hundred congregations made up of approximately 100,000 members.[93]

Although there were a number of Pentecostal churches in Handsworth, according to John Rex and Sally Tomlinson's 1979 sociology of the area, these accounted for 17 percent of the local black churchgoing population, still far in excess of the small number of local white British Pentecostals, but lower than the 22 percent of the local black community affiliated with the Church of England and the 37 percent affiliated with Methodist or Baptist traditions.[94] These differentiations may be explained by the sociologists' use of a sample-based approach less attuned to a period marked by considerable fluidity in black churchgoing. Moreover, it was arguably also a reflection of the fact that demographic shifts in inner-city areas had meant that those who maintained loyalty to an established denomination were likely to have witnessed a process of white flight, whereby inner-city Methodist or Baptist churches had themselves become largely black spaces.[95] By this period, therefore, both established churches and newly formed Pentecostal denominations had become significant sites of black sociability in which black identities were articulated through what was understood to be a distinctively Caribbean style of worship, often in opposition to that which black worshippers had initially encountered in white congregations.

For those who had arrived in Britain as Pentecostals, this style of worship stemmed from the distinctive nature of their religious beliefs. Pentecostals emphasize a fundamentalist belief system and the role of the Holy Spirit in religious life. At the center of the Pentecostal doctrine is the biblical notion of the Day of the Pentecost, on which Christ was held to have empowered his disciples with the gifts of healing and prophecy. Pentecostals seek to re-create the deep spirituality symbolized by the original Pentecost, which is seen to have been diluted in other forms of worship. Thus at Pentecostal churches in Handsworth, such as Bethel in Gibson Road, the First United Church of Jesus Christ in nearby Beaudesert Road, and the New Testament Church of God, which occupied a building on the corner of Lozells Road and George Street, members would commonly be referred to as "saints." Services were understood to be led by the spirit rather than the pastor, and there was a concurrent emphasis on prophecy, healing, and glossolalia or speaking in 'tongues', an often unintelligible verbalization that indicates a member of the congregation is experiencing an intense spiritual revival.[96] According to Rex and Tomlinson, the congregation at Beaudesert Road would "dress up in their best clothes and take part in an enthusiastic, spontaneous service, playing tambourines, and testifying or preaching if the spirit moves them."[97] This was a style of worship that was participatory, ritualized, and, as has been argued, in spite of its American origins and global development, understood by black Pentecostals in Britain as being rooted in the specific iterations that began to thrive particularly in Jamaica from the 1940s onward. As one member of the New Testament Church of God put it in the early 1990s, the church was "'a part of culture kept from Jamaica [and] brought with you.'"[98]

Although they were less pronounced, black congregations in established churches also emphasized the importance of practices that evoked previous experiences in the Caribbean. For instance, in an anthropological investigation conducted in the early 2000s at the Villa Road Methodist Church, a church close to the Villa Road pub and which by the 1980s had a significant black congregation, it was noted that worshippers maintained an affinity with the "blunt" services and strong oratory that they had been used to in the Caribbean; there was a demand for services that were "worth getting dressed up for," were delivered with added "salt and pepper," and contrasted markedly with what was seen as the cold, understated approach taken in majority-white churches. Quotidian practices were found to evoke memories of childhood experiences in the Caribbean. One woman, for instance, explained how she placed fresh flowers on the altar each Sunday because this reminded her of "flowers blowing through open windows when she was a girl in Jamaica."[99] Like the symbolism that accompanied hitting the cricket ball for six or the slam of a winning domino, such memories were undoubtedly nostalgic. Yet they also demonstrate the way in which affective registers such as homesickness, displacement, or even nostalgia itself are often embodied through everyday practice. And in the established churches in Handsworth these practices took place alongside activities that were explicitly aimed at community formation and sustainment. In the mid-1980s, for example, Cannon Street Memorial Baptist Church—where the congregation was approximately one-third black and two-thirds white, and which was based on the Soho Road, next door to the IWA's Udham Singh welfare center—ran the Olive Branch Community Centre, which provided a free daily luncheon, advice meetings, and, indicating the shift that had taken place in the makeup of the church's congregation, an annual Caribbean night.[100]

Throughout the 1980s, black churches had joined local political organizations in providing services that catered to the needs of black communities in particular, often in partnership with local authorities. And it was at Pentecostal churches that fellowship activity was most valued. The New Testament Church of God is one of the oldest black Pentecostal denominations in Britain, having been established in 1953 at a YMCA hall in Wolverhampton. It too ran an annual Caribbean night, during which oxtail stew, Escovitch fish, and other Caribbean dishes were served, and passages from tourist brochures detailing the history and culture of particular Caribbean islands were read out.[101] In the Handsworth branch one of the most active members was Esme Lancaster, who had been born in Jamaica in 1918 and migrated to Birmingham in 1950. Lancaster moved to the New Testament Church from her original Anglican denomination, where upon her arrival in Britain she had encountered a significant degree of hostility. It has been estimated that as many as 50 percent of worshippers at black British Pentecostal churches had similar trajectories, which is all the more surprising given that in the Caribbean, affiliation with a church was itself an important signifier of status. The Anglican Church in particular was invested with a privileged level of respectability given its association with the British monarchy. Newer Pentecostal denominations, in contrast, were commonly dismissed as "'clap-clap'" churches.[102] For Lancaster, her embrace of the pastoral and community dimensions of Pentecostal religious life enabled her to overcome the depression she endured following her rejection by the Anglican

Church. In *My Journeys Through Life* (2006), Lancaster's autobiography and account of her spiritual development, she detailed her key role in the establishment of a senior citizens club at the New Testament Church, as well as a day-care center for local children. For Lancaster, who also volunteered at the Harambee hostel for young people in Handsworth (discussed in chapter 1) and fostered more than forty children, such community work was a critical part of her religious commitment. "God is counting on me," she reflected; "when I pledge, I must pay."[103]

Lancaster's valuing of Pentecostal fellowship was echoed by other worshippers. In one sociological survey conducted in Handsworth in the late 1970s, 54 percent of a sample of black churchgoers commended their Pentecostal church for making people feel at home and helping their members.[104] But Lancaster's experiences are also suggestive of a problematic within Pentecostal churches, in particular, in which the division between the management of the church and the implementation of its wider activities was often highly gendered. In 1990 it was estimated that women made up 65 percent of Pentecostal congregations. In keeping with what Claire Langhamer has shown was the gendered division of organizational labor in other leisure areas in this period, it was women who, like Lancaster, most often took responsibility for running related church activities such as Sunday schools or choirs, as well as organizing the catering for church activities.[105] Yet only 39 percent of black churches were led by women, repeating a pattern in the Caribbean in which female evangelists often played a critical role in the spread of Pentecostalism but were overlooked when it came to positions of leadership.[106] Moreover, the physical presence of women inside churches was also tightly regimented. At the New Testament Church of God there was a much more pervasive dress code for women than for men, with sleeveless dresses, low necklines, and trousers forbidden. Women were also not allowed to sit next to a man to whom they were not related. This was in no small part due to the church's fundamentalist reading of the Bible; the continued emphasis on passages such as I Corinthians 14:34, in which women are prohibited from speaking in church; and the more general circulation of highly regressive representations of women either as potentially susceptible to temptation or as idealized mother figures whose proper role was as the domestic guardian of the family.[107]

The implementation of these structures was conceptualized as part of a quid pro quo that facilitated women being seen to lose control of themselves in church when they felt they were being led by the Holy Spirit.[108] And Pentecostal churches were similarly regimented when it came to age divisions, with the majority of the leadership of black churches being of an older generation.[109] Young people did, however, feature in the life of the church more generally, particularly as the role of the church shifted from helping to establish a sense of community among newly arrived immigrants to performing a wider role in everyday family life. Although some young people joined the church later in life, for most the point of entry was childhood attendance at Sunday school and the other activities that were put on by the congregations of their parents. An oral history project conducted with the Cannon Street Baptist Church, for instance, revealed that young people oscillated between valuing the church as a site where pool, table tennis, and other leisure activities could be played at its weekly youth club, to enjoying more formal religious activity such as communion marches down the Soho Road.[110] Young people who joined the church relatively late in their lives expressed a particular dedication that echoed the attitude of older worshippers such as Lancaster. Deleyen Smith, for instance, was born in Handsworth in 1962 to Caribbean parents but was not baptized until he was seventeen. In the 1980s his commitment to the church was such that he had begun to play guitar for the church band, organize outreach events, and evangelize in the wider community.[111]

It was perhaps inevitable that others would have a much looser connection to the church, especially given the antiworldliness that was at the heart of Pentecostalism and included an emphasis on an abstinence from alcohol, drugs, swearing, and sex before marriage, as well as other "inappropriate" activities such as attending the cinema or going to a pub.[112] That this milieu existed in such close proximity to dread culture in Handsworth meant that it was unsurprising that black households could be sites of significant tensions. In *Tales from Two Cities*, one of Murphy's informants explains how young people had been driven to the fringes in Handsworth because of the "authoritarian" hyper-religiosity of Pentecostal families, with eighteen-year-old men reportedly "getting thrashed by their fathers" for coming home at eleven rather than ten at night.[113] Yet there was at least some degree of fluidity between the church and other sites of leisure; younger generations were able to move between the apparently contradictory worlds of church and sound system. In a short story written by the black writer Beverly Wood, whose fiction is based on her own experiences growing up in 1980s Birmingham, two young women are depicted visiting a Sunday service at a church in Handsworth, having attended a sound system event the previous night. The women join in the gospel choruses "pepped up to dancehall standards" and eventually become "lost in the rhythm," just as they had been the night before while "dancing slowly" with "the best looking men at the party."[114] In the conception of some, attendance at church was compulsory. For Jacko Rankin, who grew up in a district adjacent to Handsworth with Caribbean parents, "unless you were sick and dying in your bed . . . you had to go to church. Sunday school, Sunday best, all of it, you had to go." It was in church that Rankin "found out that I had a voice." While Deleyen Smith restricted his playing to the Cannon Street church band, moving the church "in a *Top of the Pops* direction," Rankin and others began toasting in sound systems and singing in reggae bands in their leisure time. Rankin became the lead singer in Eclipse, one of the city's most prominent reggae outfits.[115]

As has been recognized by Callum Brown, the growth of Pentecostal churches and the endurance of older denominations in areas like Handsworth complicate narratives about the decline of Christian Britain.[116] If the establishment of Pentecostal churches initially performed an important practical function in the context of the failure of established denominations to cater to black communities, and for individuals like Esme Lancaster the church became an enduringly pervasive feature of everyday community life, by the 1980s local black churches of whichever denomination were places where black identities were articulated through what was understood as a distinctively Caribbean style of worship. Undoubtedly this was seen most clearly in the Pentecostal emphasis on evangelism, the spirit, and healing, but as black worshippers began to form the majority in the established churches, they too emphasized the importance of "blunt" sermons, for example, and services that were "worth getting dressed up for." This latter theme was often particularly important to women churchgoers. For Esmee Mignott, who had immigrated to Birmingham from Jamaica in 1954 and joined Cannon Street Baptist Church in 1969, "dressing up is important to me because whatever you have, God has given it to you." In the Caribbean, dressing up was a means of visually communicating the respectability that was seen to come with regular attendance at church, which often also maintained a close connection to the elite schools. "I like to dress up," Mignott remarked. "The men as well, they are properly dressed in their suits. You always put your Sunday best on. We are worshipping God . . . give him the best."[117]

This idea resonated more widely with those who shared with Mignott the collective experience of migration. Press photographs of Caribbean immigrants from the 1950s showed how they journeyed to Britain dressed in their Sunday best: the "best thing that you had in your wardrobe," which would otherwise have been reserved for church. As Stuart Hall has argued, embedded within these images was the performance of a class-based aspiration in many ways inherent to the act of migration; these were the clothes of people who aimed to "make their mark" and "make a favorable impression."[118] If in the pages of newspapers and magazines these images were overdetermined by narratives stressing the problems that black immigrants would inevitably pose for British society, settlement in places like Handsworth gave immigrants the ability to craft their own visual representations. Establishments such as the Earnest Dyche Studio on the Moseley Road in Balsall Heath, Maganbhai Patel's premises in Coventry, and Harry Jacob's studio in Brixton in London responded to the demand from immigrant communities for high-quality images that could be sent back to families and friends overseas. Central to this was a potent desire to construct new identities in and of the metropole, whatever the reality of the subjects' everyday lives beyond the studio walls. The dominant message of the ensuing portraits was one of advanced status, emphasized by a range of visual strategies, from subjects posing at desks or while talking on fake telephones, to the ostensibly subtle yet unmistakable displays of expensive-looking watches and fountain pens. It was the formality of the sitters'

FIGURE 17. Photograph taken at Earnest Dyche Portraiture Studio, ca. early 1960s. Reproduced by permission of Library of Birmingham.

attire that in most cases united them. In the Caribbean, the semiotic resonance of three-piece suits, bow-ties, ankle-length dresses, and pocket handkerchiefs would have been obvious; these were people who were dressed as if they were attending church (see figure 17).[119]

Like a game of dominoes, therefore, religion functioned in close proximity to aspiration in black Handsworth and the desire to be seen to be "getting on." Inside Handsworth's churches, those who maintained their affiliations with Anglican or Baptist denominations in Britain could continue to enjoy the status that was associated with attending an established congregation in the Caribbean. In the newer, more conservative denominations, the notion that material items could be used as a means of communicating one's cultural capital would undoubtedly have been frowned upon. But the pervasiveness of the Sunday best in these churches offers a reminder that, as Tina Campt has argued, for this generation spirituality operated alongside class in the projection of respectability.[120] For one sociologist writing with respect to the early growth of black Pentecostal churches in Britain, black worshippers saw participation in the church as a way of obtaining the status denied to them by mainstream society.[121] In the high-street photography studios, the cost of using the studio and often the outfits worn by sitters would commonly be paid for using credit. By the end of the 1980s there were other forms of conspicuous consumption on offer, particularly as home ownership among the black community began to rise. As one woman user of high-street photographic studios reflected of her own experiences after arriving in Birmingham from Jamaica in the 1950s, "when we took the photos in the studios we didn't have our front rooms. Once we started to get them, that's where we would take the photographs—we wanted to show them off."[122] This chapter ends by moving from the church into the home and, within that sphere, lingers on the cultural significance of the black front room.

THE FRONT ROOM

The concept of the front room as a space kept apart from the rest of the house and reserved for particular occasions has its roots in a Victorian tradition in which the consumption of luxury domestic items was used by the well-to-do to communicate their social status. Among the aspirational middle classes, having a best room was seen as a way of emulating the tasteful arrangements of Victorian upper-class country houses; working-class households, meanwhile, took inspiration from the drawing rooms often found in the houses of the wealthy middle classes.[123] In 1980s Handsworth, however, black immigrants perceived the front room—like an attacking brand of cricket, the slam of a domino, and church services that were delivered with added 'salt and pepper"—as a discernibly Caribbean practice. As Esme Mignott reflected, the front room was "a tradition people brought from home [in the Caribbean]. You have your settees, and you may have a little cabinet where you put your special cups and saucers that only your special guests use. We are like that—we like to keep one place clean."[124]

The widespread discrimination experienced by immigrants in the housing sector has become a central motif in narratives of black Britain, with the signs barring black people from entry to potential lodgings often used as a shorthand to signify the pervasiveness of the British color bar. However, by the time Margaret Thatcher had outlined her vision of a "property-owning democracy" at her first Conservative Party conference as leader in 1975, a significant proportion of Britain's black population had already become property owners. In the late-1970s more than half of Handsworth's black residents were owner-occupiers and by some measures enjoyed a better overall standard of housing than the local white community.[125] In this context, the concept of a front room was a means of extending the cultural capital that came with owning one's own home. Fictional accounts of this process suggest how, like the photographs taken in high-street studios in an earlier period, it was at least in part a performance of status designed for a Caribbean audience, in which a key signifier of middle-class respectability was the ability to lead a privatized domestic life, in contrast to working-class areas, which often consisted of shared amenities in communal "yards."[126] In "Letters A Yard," for example, a semiautobiographical short story by the Birmingham-based novelist Maeve Clarke, the attempts by immigrant couple Munchie and Nico to buy a house are juxtaposed against what Munchie relays in letters home to her mother in Jamaica. The difficulty that Nico has persuading white homeowners to sell to a black couple do not feature in the letters. Rather, Munchie tells her mother that, having raised funds through a pardner scheme, the couple have bought a house in an affluent district of the city. In contrast to her mother's living conditions—implied in the story's title by the reference to "yard"— Munchie explains that their new home has three bedrooms, "two rooms downstairs," and a garden. To mark the birth of their second child, Munchie writes, her husband has bought her "a wooden cabinet as a present. It so pretty, Mamma, I can't wait till I have some nice plates and glasses to put in there."[127]

This was a fictional representation of the letters home often accompanied by photographs taken in high-street studios. By the 1980s, however, rising home ownership and the increasing affordability of cameras meant that the use of high-street studios had declined.[128] For many, as a backdrop for photographs that could be sent to relatives, overseas portrait studios had been replaced by the front room; the jewelry, watches, and other items used to signify status in studio portraits had by the 1980s been replaced by display cabinets, televisions, and other consumer items that had become staples of the front room space. Handsworth-based photographers referenced this growing strand of domestic photography in their own professional image making, exploring what was often the central position of women within the front room space. Vanley Burke, for instance, photographed his mother in her front room, framed by the ornaments, display plates, and pictures that dominated her mantelpiece. In another photograph taken inside a Handsworth front room in the mid-1980s as part of the photographers Bishton and Reardon's Handsworth photo essay, two women pose for the camera on a leather armchair in front of a floral-wallpapered wall on which a framed painting of Jesus has been hung next to a wooden ornament featuring gold figurines; atop the adjacent bookshelf there is a vase of flowers next to a painting of the Virgin Mary.

Material items coexisted alongside a strong religious dynamic in the black front room. This was a more general feature of the growth in home ownership in postwar Britain, where being able to own a home was commonly conceptualized by first-time buyers in religious terms, for example as being like moving "'from purgatory to heaven.'"[129] Religion had a particularly strong presence in the domestic arrangements of South Asian families; Hindu households, for example, often maintained a *mandir* or temple that functioned as the locus for *aarti*, a particular type of daily prayer.[130] The religiosity of the black front room specifically was indicated by the way families commonly dressed up in their Sunday best for the photographs they took there, thus signaling the links between the studio photographs of an earlier period and the physical act of migration, as well as the respectability that was seen to come with regular church visits. There were also often prominent displays of items of religious faith that, while much less formal than the domestic *mandir*, nevertheless acted as signifiers of a family's religious commitment. In the mid-1980s Dervla Murphy described the home of Theodore and Evelyn Graham, a middle-aged Caribbean couple who lived in "a quiet, tidy, tree-lined road of semi-detached stucco houses with rose-filled gardens" near Handsworth Park. Inside, Murphy observed, invitations to "Pentecostal jamborees" were displayed on the mantelpiece; on the pink-wallpapered walls "photographs of Caribbean beauty spots" hung next to "elaborately embroidered religious texts."[131] The sacred nature of the black front room was emphasized by the manner in which it was used. It could be used for prayer meetings, for example, thus mirroring the way black churches often initially emerged in the much more limited domestic spaces available to recently arrived immigrants. For Esme Mignott, it was important to "secure" a room; "when you have visitors, you put them in there. The minister might come and visit you. You can sit in there in comfort and you are not disturbed by anybody."[132] Securing the front room commonly meant keeping it under lock and key. This practice emphasized the front room as a space that needed to be demarcated from everyday domestic life, simultaneously because of the prominence of valuable consumer items, its association with religious spirituality, and the need for a private, comfortable space in case the minister came calling.

Status functioned in complex ways in the black front room. One interviewee described it as akin to a showroom, where consumer items were put on display alongside the trophies and educational certificates that had been obtained by the household's children and the cutlery and other items that had been given to parents as wedding presents.[133] Yet as the practice of locking the front room made clear, this was not a show that was meant for all audiences. Elaborate net curtains were commonly hung over the windows to ensure that the privacy of the meetings taking place inside could not easily be breached. In some ways, delineating the front room both spatially and visually gave the things inside a greater degree of status than if they had been on display in a more public domestic "gallery" such as the hallway.[134] The front room contained messages restricted to particular types of visitors: church members, travel writers, or friends from the right social backgrounds. For instance, James Pogson, who was born in Birmingham in 1969 to Caribbean parents, remembered his mother staging Tupperware parties in the front room. This was a marketing technique developed by the plastics company that explicitly targeted what were seen as status-conscious women consumers. At the parties, put on at the home of a designated host, friends and neighbors would be able to sample Tupperware containers and other items before subsequently being given the opportunity to purchase them. The Tupperware company understood that guests would be more likely to purchase items from someone they knew and deemed respectable, while hosts would value the opportunity to project an image of exclusivity and sophistication.[135] The front room, with its carefully crafted messages of status and respectability, was the ideal venue for such parties. "Me and my brothers would be in the living room, all the women would be in the front room," Pogson recalled. "We would try and go in there to get a glimpse—we were like, 'wow, people are actually sitting down.'"[136]

This exclusivity exemplifies the differences between the black front room and the domestic arrangements of working-class communities in an earlier period, such as the Hunslet memorialized by Richard Hoggart in *The Uses of Literacy* (1957), in which the primacy of the home as a familial space meant that those outside the immediate family unit were rarely invited to enter it.[137] The black front room, in contrast, was in many ways primarily structured along the lines of the middle-class notion of entertaining. The sociability that took place inside was correspondingly regimented, particularly from the perspective of a household's children. On occasion specific tasks may have been assigned to children, but these were always under close parental supervision. Jacko Rankin remembered that his father would occasionally "tell me to go in there and play some records on the radiogram," a stand-alone piece of furniture that included a built-in record player and radio and was often one of the few elements of the front room controlled by men.[138] But the playlist was generally restricted to parental musical tastes, which were largely calypso, ska, or the country and western music of the American crooner Jim Reeves.[139] If calypso and ska were the musical forms that dominated the listening habits of older generations in the pre-reggae Caribbean, the idiosyncratic popularity of Reeves was a product of the religious imagery that was at the heart of much of his music, his reputation for clean living, and the way in which these themes chimed with the front room's core themes of spirituality and respectability.[140]

Pogson characterized the front room as primarily a "generational thing" that his parents had "brought over from the Caribbean."[141] If age was an important factor, it was gender that was the most influential dynamic. As Stuart Hall has argued, although men and children could occupy the front room, it was women who owned it.[142] The gendered dynamics of black households in this period were distinctive in light of black women's status as economic migrants and active members of the paid workforce. This did not mean that domestic labor was necessarily more equitably divided between men and women in black homes than in white, and black women's status as wage earners also carried a level of cultural stigma in the context of what was, certainly in the earlier period of black settlement, the centrality of an idealized image of the domestic mother. Black mothers thus not only encountered at first hand the racism of the British workplace. Their status as economic laborers often meant that they were denied the "mother mandate" and were consequently commonly portrayed as inadequate guardians of the family.[143] That the front room was often used as a leisure space for women in particular—as the example of the Tupperware party suggests—undoubtedly did run counter to well-established divisions of domestic labor, in which it was considered the mother's responsibility to facilitate leisure activities for other members of the family.[144] But more than this, homemaking also acted as a means of black women undermining long-standing British stereotypes, which not only pathologized the supposed inadequacies of black mothers but also portrayed them as overly fecund and therefore an increasing burden on the welfare state. In this context, for black women the front room represented a significant avenue of autonomous cultural expression that enabled them to undermine the salience of such narratives. In so doing, as Kennetta Hammond Perry has suggested, women "paralleled and appropriated" dominant understandings of gendered British citizenship.[145]

These themes were elaborated on by Maxine Walker, a Handsworth-based photographer born in 1962 to Jamaican immigrants, whose 1987 project *Auntie Linda's Front Room* comprised a series of photographs taken inside local front rooms. Like her contemporary, the London-based artist Sonia Boyce, Walker's work is a meditation on the importance of the domestic space in general and the front room in particular.[146] The material trappings of the black front room are obvious in her photographs: wall ornaments, wooden cabinets, patterned wallpaper, and pictures of Jesus. What is critical, however, is the physical presence of "Auntie Linda," a position taken on by a number of middle-aged black women posing for Walker's camera in the front room space. In some respects, the photographs represent a play on the amateur family photographs taken in the front room and sent to relatives overseas. However, what is most striking is the assertive way in which the character of "Auntie Linda" returns the gaze of Walker's lens, projecting an image of authority both with respect to the way in which the photograph is shot and the material items that surround her. As has been argued, black women often used their status as wage earners for the attainment of domestic goals, "reversing the way in which their construction as workers denied them a domestic or familial identity" and using their financial independence from men to signal their aspirational mobility.[147] This is particularly suggestive in one of Walker's photographs in which "Auntie Linda" is pictured on her settee next to a cabinet full of ornaments (see figure 18). Her gaze is fixed resolutely on Walker's lens, and her hands are resting in her lap; her nails are painted in the same shade of red as her lipstick. It is a confident projection of femininity, respectability, and domestic authority that undermines not only popular discourses around black women but also the dominant racialized anxieties of the 1980s, which centered on the supposed violence of young black men in the context of the inner-city street.[148]

The way in which class operated in the front room was bound up both with what some experienced as a downward class shift as they moved from lower-middle-class

FIGURE 18. Photo from *Auntie Linda's Front Room* series, 1987. Photograph by Maxine Walker; reproduced by permission.

professions in the Caribbean into working-class occupations in Britain, and with the effective dissolution of the Caribbean "pigmentocracy" once immigrants arrived in Britain and found that they were perceived as uniformly black regardless of their particular skin color. In this context, the front room provided a potential means of reasserting class distinctions among black communities, which were represented in the television dramas that had by the late 1970s begun to be made from the perspective of black characters as a counterpoint to the perpetuation of crude racial stereotypes found in highly popular programs such as *Love Thy Neighbour* and *The Black and White Minstrel Show*. While they could at times be in danger of repeating the stereotypes they sought to move beyond, soaps like the BBC's *Empire Road*—which was written by the Guyanese Michael Abbensetts, set in Handsworth, and pitched as a black *Coronation Street* when it first aired in 1978—also often displayed a sensitivity to the realities of everyday black lives in Britain, including black domestic life.[149]

The central characters in *Empire Road* are Everton and Hortense Bennett, an aspirational couple who own numerous properties in the area, and Miss May, a single mother who runs the local fish and chip shop. In the book that accompanies the first series, which was also written by Abbensetts, Hortense is shocked to find out that her brother has started a relationship with Miss May, whose job Hortense regards as a sign of "common[ness]." The status anxieties of the well-to-do Hortense were often played out in the domestic sphere. In the book, one scene is pitched around Hortense's supposed displeasure at the prospect of May paying her a visit. Hortense "looked around her living-room. She had chosen all the furniture in this room. The thought of someone like May . . . *dirtying* her chairs made her shudder. . . . 'I'd have to cover our nice, nice chairs wit' newspaper.'" But it subsequently becomes clear that both Hortense and her husband are in fact relishing the chance to show off their home. As Everton shows May into the house, he catches her stealing "a glance at the Bennett's expensive stereo, the drinks cabinet and the colour television set." With particular relish, Hortense asks her guest if she will have something from the drink cart. "A little sherry . . . some white wine? *Chilled* white wine? Some rum, brandy, you like brandy, or dere's gin, vodka, Martini, Rosso. Take your pick."[150] The provision of drinks that were popular in the Caribbean—including cocktails such as Guinness punch and Irish stout—was one of a number of symbolic associations with the Caribbean in the front room. And for Caribbean women, the consumption of alcohol could also be bound up with the question of respectability, because a women who drank alcohol except on special occasions were commonly perceived as "flighty."[151] Thus in *Empire Road*, immediately after Hortense offers Miss May a beverage from the drink cart, she makes it clear that she herself does not drink alcohol. Abstinence offers Hortense another means of demonstrating her superior cultural capital. Having offered May her choice of refreshment, Hortense "threw in the clincher. 'Of course, *I* don't drink.'"[152]

In 2005 the black front room was re-created as part of *The West Indian Front Room*, an exhibition at London's Geffrye Museum of the Home. It was curated by the playwright Michael McMillan, who was born in the nearby market town of High Wycombe to parents from Saint Vincent and the Grenadines. The centerpiece installation (see figure 19) was made up of the front room's defining features: religious iconography, floral wallpaper that "sort of but never perfectly" matched the patterned carpet, china displayed in glass cabinets, plastic protective coverings on settees and antimacassars over the chairs, elaborate ornaments, and the ubiquitous radiogram.[153] By physically re-creating the front room space using items borrowed from friends and family, McMillan hoped to provoke "flashbacks, memories, and anecdotes" of the everyday "events, conversations, customs, rituals, encounters, colours, smells and images" that took place there.[154] If, as has been shown, the front room was primarily the realm of women in the context of shifting class and status identities, the reaction to McMillan's exhibition suggested that this was nevertheless

FIGURE 19. *The West Indian Front Room*, Geffrye Museum of the Home, 2005. Photograph by John Nelligan; reproduced by permission of Michael McMillan.

an experience that was widely shared among black communities. In the comments books that the museum kept open for the duration of the exhibition, younger generations remarked that the exhibition brought back memories of their own childhoods. Visitors wrote that the exhibition "brought a shiver to my spine and a tear to my eye." One wondered why "people's front rooms are the same, no matter which West Indian island they come from." Another commented that "if my aunty was here she would say, 'have you been to my house while I was out and taken all my furniture?'" There were similar themes in a discussion of the exhibition on Blacknet, an African Caribbean social networking website. Users reminisced nostalgically about "those small whiskey glasses neatly stored in the posh black cabinet in the posh front room" and "the plastic floor covering which was obligatory." One user commented that these were items that "all black folks had back in the day," while a visitor to the exhibition wrote that that walking around it was "like going to my Aunt's, cousin's or any other West Indian house in the 1980s."[155]

Like the sociability that took place inside Handsworth's cricket clubs, pubs, and churches, the practices inside the front room were often a way of evoking previous lives in the Caribbean. For those who had enjoyed a more middle-class, privatized way of living prior to migration, the idea of a room apart from the rest of the house was a tradition that they themselves had brought with them to Britain. The Caribbean was also evoked by the photographs of island beauty spots that hung alongside embroidered religious texts and ornaments, the presence of calypso and ska music, and a drink cart that allowed hosts the opportunity to offer their guests a wide variety of Caribbean cocktails. That the front room was the product of a diasporic sensibility is illustrated most clearly by the way in which it quickly replaced the high-street studio as the backdrop for the visual performance of status for those family members who remained in the Caribbean. Such images were in many ways part of the currency of diaspora. But what is arguably demonstrated most of all by the front room is the strength of this community's aspirations in Britain. While by no means economically viable, or desired, in every black household, the front room was for many an expression of a black identity in which the themes of respectability, status, and being seen to be getting on were all encompassing. This might be regarded as a continuum of one of the original drivers behind the act of migration. As one interviewee remarked, the front room was the place "where you show off the things that you've gathered around you since you've arrived."[156] At the most basic level, however, the purchasing and careful maintenance of a house are also signifiers of a shift from the temporary to a greater degree of permanence. The product of "transnational identities of citizenship and belonging," status anxieties, gendered identities, and the politics of respectability, the 1980s front room was also a symbol of the growing rootedness of black Britain.[157]

CONCLUSION

At the beginning of the 1980s C. L. R. James gave a series of lectures in London, at the invitation of *Race Today* magazine, on the occasion of his eightieth birthday. The series culminated with James turning to the status and future prospects of Britain's black population. Looking out onto the 1980s from the vantage point of Margaret Thatcher's first election victory and a tense atmosphere in areas of black settlement that within months would lead to the decade's first outbreak of major rioting, James emphasized the necessity of black immigrants and their children recognizing that their lives and experiences were part of a discernibly British trajectory. If the emphasis he placed on black participation within the labor movement was couched in terms of James's characteristic political militancy, the general tenor of his remarks made it clear that for him this was also a question of identity. Typically, almost two decades after the publication of *Beyond a Boundary*, James reached for an example from cricket by way of illustration. He pointed to what he saw as the significance of the decision by the Barbadian batsman Roland Butcher in August 1980 to accept a call-up to play for England, thus becoming the first black player to represent the English national side. Although Butcher was concerned about the reaction his decision might provoke in the Caribbean, his conclusion, he explained to the press, was that "I've been [in England] for almost half my life, settled here with my family and play my cricket here.... [M]y home is

England."[158] James had the feeling that Caribbean audiences would be sympathetic. His own transatlantic trajectory and oscillation among the Caribbean, Britain, and the United States meant that he was in many ways the embodiment of a twentieth-century diasporic life. This bestowed a further poignancy on what was arguably the most powerful line of James's lecture, delivered to his predominantly black audience toward the beginning of his address: "You belong here."[159]

The sociability taking place during the 1980s inside black Handsworth's cricket clubs, pubs, churches, and front rooms suggests that this may have been a sentiment that was already being felt organically within this "emotional community." While considering the black everyday has shown how transatlantic dialogues and diasporic perspectives were a central feature of this milieu—for example, the emotional connections to the Caribbean that were evoked by hitting a new ball for six, a game of dominoes, or the act of placing fresh flowers on the altar each Sunday—their key significance is surely the transformative effect they were having domestically on the British metropole. Too often dismissed as a naïve attachment to the mother country, the traces of Victorianism on black Handsworth's cricket pitches or inside its front rooms illustrate the enduring reach of the colonial legacy and of perceptions of Britishness. What was signaled as black communities built their cricketing clubhouses, developed their churches, and carefully furnished their front rooms was that they had moved toward a level of permanence in Britain. Building on the initial claims to British and imperial citizenship that underpinned postwar immigration from the Caribbean, by the 1980s the presence of these spaces, and the sociability taking place inside them, speaks to a community with an understanding of its own belonging, navigating the social anxieties and aspirations of everyday life.[160] As James implied with regard to Butcher's decision to accept the call-up from England, the cricket clubs, pubs, churches, front rooms, and other sites that constituted Britain's everyday black topography were arguably the physical manifestations of what was becoming a black British sensibility.

This is not to downplay the importance of parallel South Asian formations, in which places of worship, cricket, and other social spaces were structured by a comparable, if highly particular, set of circumstances. Nor is it to suggest that this was part of any "irresistible" rise of black Britain.[161] To the extent that it was irresistible, this could only have been as a result of the myriad, long-standing political battles that were fought by black communities, many of which have animated the pages of this book. These included struggles over the need for suitable housing and for better forms of education; the necessity in the arena of representation of undermining highly damaging depictions of the black presence; and the emergence of other sensibilities such as a reggae scene that was able to narrate the experience of a young black generation in an explicitly Pan-Africanist register. And although less obviously oppositional, there were also significant political currents running through the black everyday itself. If the presence of the leisure institutions described in this chapter could by the 1980s be read as examples of the growing rootedness of black Britain, in many cases their initial formation in an earlier period came as a necessarily defensive reaction against British racism and the pervasiveness of the color bar.

Alongside this, the pivot toward the Caribbean that to a greater or lesser degree was evoked by practices such as the slam of a domino, cricket played in a "typically West Indian" style, or the careful furnishing of the front room had important resonances for white British society. Certainly the sociability taking place within these sites challenged contemporary stereotypes about blackness that centered on images of male violence and disorder and perceptions of black women that denied them the "mother mandate." In their place was posited the muscular yet ordered masculinity found in the cricket club and pub, and the assertive, status-oriented version of femininity that took place in the church and, in particular, the front room. Moreover, as much as the African imaginary central to Handsworth's dread culture, these practices were also helping to render Britain's colonial past present. As James suggested in his eightieth-birthday lectures, and as has been elaborated by others elsewhere, this was an ongoing encounter that demonstrated the extent to which the history of empire and decolonization is "still of our time." Having lived through decolonization in the Caribbean and often situated their subsequent struggles in relation to anticolonial movements elsewhere, those who established a black locality structured by assertive readings of diaspora and the black globality posed a challenge to the widespread amnesia in Britain over its imperial past. In this sense, the presence of institutions like the Continental Cricket Club in Handsworth had implications that were in their own way as political as the inaugural African Liberation Day march on that Jubilee weekend of 1977, which culminated in Handsworth Park just a few meters away from where Continental played its home matches. As Bill Schwarz has reflected, this might be regarded as part of an ongoing process of "decolonizing metropolitan Britain itself."[162]

It may seem paradoxical to draw attention to the black everyday in the context of a period that has come to be defined by its racial tensions, and above all by the violence that was played out on the streets of Brixton, Moss Side, Handsworth, and elsewhere at various points in the 1980s. The aim here is certainly not to underplay the extent to which black communities felt under siege in this period, or the pressing nature of the political campaigns that continued to be fought. But it is to point toward the presence of a concurrent milieu, less immediately visible in the historical archive but no less important for that. Informed by the legacies of colonialism and a particular reading of diaspora, a black everyday had emerged as an assertive presence in the landscape of the British metropole. Undoubtedly itself a diverse entity, and viewed from different vantage points depending on issues such as class, age, and gender, this was a structure of feeling that nevertheless spoke to a collective sense of black British belonging.

Epilogue

At the start of the 1980s, when the Trinidadian probation worker Bob Ramdhanie opened his African village on Hamstead Road—where this book began—the black globality had already become a significant feature of the surrounding landscape. A half mile east from Hamstead Road, for instance, at 104 Heathfield Road, the ACSHO refined its Pan-Africanist ideologies at the discussion seminars it held every Tuesday evening, and on Saturday mornings at the supplementary school it ran for local black youth. A short walk from there, toward the outer limits of Handsworth along Soho Hill, a different, more quotidian version of the black globality could be found at the FCF club, embodied by the Caribbean dominoes games that took place there. Heading back north along Soho Road, running adjacent to the New Testament Church of God (the largest Pentecostal church in the area), before turning off onto Grove Lane, and past Mango Records (stocker of imported Jamaican reggae) and Gees Salon (specialists in Afro hair styles), was Handsworth Park, where the Continental Cricket Club played its home matches in the distinctively West Indian style on which its members prided themselves. Finally, circling back onto Soho Road, the sounds of the black globality could be heard on an almost nightly basis at the Santa Rosa, the club where Steel Pulse played its earliest gigs before the 1978 release of its debut album, *Handsworth Revolution*.

In many respects, with its front cover depicting a scene from urban Britain interspersed with African imagery, the album carried the same message as Ramdhanie's Hamstead Road village: black globality was something that was for use in the Handsworth locale; it was here that its most significant effects were to be found. In reaching out across the black Atlantic, the residents of Handsworth developed reappropriated versions of "blackness" manifested in the lyrics of the sound system toasters; in the styles of the Rastafarians; and in every front room that was carefully maintained with drink carts, display cabinets, and patterned wallpaper. These were crucial resources for navigating the many inequalities of the "long" 1980s. And paradoxically, embracing the diverse elements of the diasporan consciousness enabled a black community to arrive at a growing sense of rootedness in Britain. This was a structure of feeling experienced in different ways: as ideology, art, leisure, and everyday practice; through affective communities, "invented" traditions, and the politics of aspiration; and with respect to the determinants of class, age, and gender. But as C. L. R. James suggested in the final stage of his own oscillation among the Caribbean, the United States, and Britain, what this signaled cumulatively was the flowering of a nascent sense of black Britishness.[1]

This was an immensely significant moment, and it also had important consequences for British society. The diasporic reordering of places like Handsworth, undertaken by formerly colonial peoples and their children, disrupted the widespread popular and political amnesia around empire in Britain and the concurrent inability to recognize postwar immigration not as an external encroachment but as a historical process that was itself a central element of the national story. In Handsworth, this sometimes took the form of explicitly political interventions. When those local residents took to the streets for Handsworth's inaugural African Liberation Day in summer 1977—carrying placards with slogans such as "Bury Imperialism" and "Hands off Africa"—they provided uncomfortable reminders about Britain's history of colonial expansionism and what had become its greatly diminished global standing. Similar interventions were made by Handsworth's Rastafarianism-inspired musicians and sound systems and in the film art of the BAFC, which in the context of the inner-city rioting of 1985 emphasized the links between the contemporary politics of race and the historic racial hierarchies of colonialism. More often, though, this was an organic process. In asserting resolutely diasporic versions of blackness through everyday practices and patterns of sociability—through forms of religious worship, the domestic aesthetics of the black front room, the cultivation of a dreadlock hairstyle, and every ball that was given "a good thump" by Continental cricketers—the residents of black Handsworth were problematizing the narrow, ethnocentric versions of Britishness that found their political voice most spectacularly with the interventions of Enoch Powell, and on which the politics of Thatcherism subsequently capitalized. This undoubtedly helps to explain the intensity of popular anxieties over the black inner city which, in the 1980s, was seen as a front line in a wider conflict against an enemy within. The long-term implications of this encounter, however, are complex. In many ways, they have yet to reach their conclusion.

The opening decades of the twenty-first century have been marked by periodic spikes in support for various strands of nationalism, both in Britain and across

Europe. The electoral breakthroughs made by the neo-Nazi British National Party (BNP) between 2005 and 2009, for example, coincided with the rising influence on the Continent of figures such as the Dutch politician Geert Wilders, who established his anti-immigration Party for Freedom in 2006 and quickly made substantial electoral gains. In Britain, while the BNP imploded after 2010, there was a marked growth in support for the UK Independence Party (UKIP), whose campaign for Britain to withdraw from the European Union (EU) was enmeshed with anti-immigration rhetoric that often recalled the interventions made almost fifty years earlier by Powell.[2] If such sentiments chimed with parallel political movements in the Netherlands, France, and elsewhere, they were undoubtedly crystallized by Britain's June 2016 referendum on its future membership in the EU.

Although the political establishment backed a vote to remain in the EU, the nationalistic campaign of UKIP and its leader, Nigel Farage, often set the tone and played a critical role in the eventual outcome of a 4 percent majority vote to leave. With the often-repeated mantra that Britain should "take back control," especially of its borders and ability to restrict immigration, this discourse had tapped into sentiments that were apparently widely felt. This was in many ways a fundamentally defensive, inward-looking imaginary that spoke to an enduringly acute disorientation over the legacies of empire, understood by Paul Gilroy as a form of postcolonial "melancholia."[3] And it was one that mainstream politicians were increasingly willing to articulate. When David Cameron resigned as British prime minister immediately after the EU referendum, for instance, his successor, Theresa May, moved quickly to echo a feeling that had, in different ways, been marshalled by Powell, Thatcher, and others before her. In a speech in central Birmingham, a bus ride from Handsworth, and a short walk from the hotel inside which Powell had delivered his "rivers of blood" speech, May encapsulated what seemed to have become the ethos of the time, in Europe and, with the election of Donald Trump as president in November 2016, in the United States as well. "When you are a citizen of the world," May told her Birmingham audience, "you are a citizen of nowhere." As the process of Britain's departure from the EU was set in motion, one commentator argued that it not only heralded the leaving of an institution, but also the abandonment of a particular "idea of Britain."[4]

What this book has attempted to provide is a reminder of the importance of adopting a line of vision that moves beyond the arena of formal politics. Focusing on those ordinary practitioners shaping events at the level of the locale allows radically different social formations to be brought to the fore. The black structure of feeling I have sought to reconstruct from 1980s Handsworth represents just one chapter in a much wider story, one that reaches back to include the intellectuals and activists who made interwar London a locus of the black Atlantic, comprises the parallel rise of South Asian and other diasporic sensibilities, and takes in major cities across postcolonial Europe. The subsequent history of the dramatic expansion of multicultural Britain at the end of the twentieth century has not yet been written. But by the 2000s and 2010s, to traverse the inner areas of Britain's major cities was to be left in little doubt about the presence of diasporic routes and global perspectives that—apart from the political ascent of ever-more-restrictive ideas of Britishness—continued to reach across oceans and national boundaries. At the most basic level, this is evident in the way in which *halal* butchers, African Caribbean beauty shops, Turkish barbers, and other businesses catering for people from across the globe have arguably become the dominant features of inner-city geographies and physical emblems of new processes of "diaspora-ization." The movement between the local and the global is also demonstrated by, for example, the campaigns that have at different points been developed in solidarity with Palestine; by the take-up of the Black Lives Matter movement in Britain following its initial emergence in the United States in 2013; and by the inner city's innumerable languages, religious networks, and cultural practices that are played out in different ways in the domain of everyday lived experience: in the school playground, on public transport, and on the high street.[5] To spend any length of time in these spaces requires at least some familiarity, or what sociologists have underscored as a form of competency, with what has become their fundamentally global dimensions.[6] As Stuart Hall reflected of Britain at the turn of the millennium, "When I ask somebody where they're from, I expect nowadays to be told an extremely long story." This was a reference to a milieu quite different from that which Hall and his generation of Caribbean immigrants had originally encountered on their arrival in Britain in the 1950s and 1960s, or that invoked by Theresa May in the aftermath of the 2016 referendum: one much less frequently articulated in political discourse, but no less significant.[7]

By the early part of the twenty-first century, the inner city had become the backdrop to an expanded range of racialized folk devils, with the figure of the perennially violent black youth (now primarily conceptualized as a gun-toting gangster) having been joined by the asylum seeker, "benefits tourist," and—most acutely, following a series of attacks in London, Paris, and elsewhere—the "home-grown" Islamic terrorist.[8] In this context, many of the inequalities faced by black communities in 1980s Britain continued to be stubbornly entrenched. In 1999, for example, the official inquiry into the metropolitan police's handling of the racist murder of the black teenager Stephen Lawrence in London marked a belated recognition of the endemic nature of civil society's problem with racism. Six years later, when rioting once again erupted on the streets of Handsworth, the issue of a lack of suitable housing—which the Harambee group had earlier sought to remedy with the establishment of its hostel for black youth on Hall Road—remained severe. Negotiating these issues could be a fraught process, and a plethora of political battles needed to be waged, with a continuing sense of urgency.[9] At the same time, the wider historical implications of what has been described in this book should not be overlooked. As the residents of black Handsworth reached out across the black globality, they were part of a wider process of establishing, in myriad forms, the diasporan consciousness as an irrefutable domestic presence. As was communicated by the African village on Hamstead Road, by the African Liberation Day march that culminated in Handsworth Park, and by every slam of a winning domino at the FCF social club on Soho Hill, Handsworth and similar inner-city locales acted as the primary crucibles for this process of postcolonial reordering. But with ethnic diversity expanding in Britain and becoming an everyday feature of new, often suburban geographies, as well as further indications in the realm of popular culture of Britain's continuing multicultural drift, by the new millennium this was no longer a story that could be contained by the inner city. In spite of the periodic rise of political nationalisms, fueled by the enduring anxieties of the postimperial moment, this sensibility had become an irreversible feature of the fabric of modern Britain.[10]

NOTES

INTRODUCTION

1. Edwards, *The Practice of Diaspora*.
2. Travis, "Rates Grant for Rain Dance Lessons in Ghana," 10. See also Handsworth Cultural Centre, *Handsworth to Jamaica*, 1980 (MS 2478/B/6/20, Derek Bishton archive, hereafter DBA); Walia, *African Oasis*.
3. By the mid-1950s, a quarter of the work undertaken in foundries in the Midlands was car related. See Wills, *Lovers and Strangers*, 195.
4. James, "Immigrants to Britain," 15–16.
5. Nigel Lawson, quoted in Smith, *New Right Discourse on Race and Sexuality*, 11.
6. Patterson and Kelley, "Unfinished Migrations," 14–15.
7. Perry, *London Is the Place for Me*, 48–63. See also Hansen, "The Politics of Citizenship in 1940s Britain," 67–95. On the citizenship claims made by black communities in interwar Britain, see Matera, *Black London*.
8. Rex and Tomlinson, *Colonial Immigrants in a British City*, 74–75. In 1961, 2,307 of these people had been born in the Caribbean; a decade later that figure had reached 3,291.
9. Birmingham City Council, *Handsworth/Soho/Lozells*, 11; Bhavnani et al., *A Different Reality*, 22. These statistics vary depending on where the Handsworth boundary is drawn. The area often known colloquially as Handsworth actually includes parts of the city technically in neighboring electoral wards such as Lozells and Soho. Following Rex and Tomlinson, *Colonial Immigrants in a British City*, this study adopts the looser definition of Handsworth as it was understood in local, popular discourse.
10. Rex and Tomlinson, *Colonial Immigrants in a British City*, 70.
11. Schwarz, *Memories of Empire*, Vol. 1, 4–6. On the ways in which empire resonated domestically during the period of high empire, see Catherine Hall's pathbreaking work; for example, Hall and Rose, eds., *At Home with Empire*.

12. For a sociological report on the black presence in St. Ann's and Nottingham more generally, see Lawrence, *Black Migrants, White Natives*.

13. Solomos, *Race and Racism in Contemporary Britain*, 56–58.

14. Whipple, "Revisiting the 'Rivers of Blood' Controversy," 717–735; Schwarz, *Memories of Empire*, Vol. 1, 4–6; Schofield, *Enoch Powell and the Making of Post-Colonial Britain*; and Corthorn, *Enoch Powell*.

15. For a history of the Centre for Contemporary Cultural Studies (hereafter CCCS) in its first fifteen years, see Connell and Hilton, "The Working Practices of Birmingham's Centre for Contemporary Cultural Studies," 287–311. For the context of CCCS involvement in Handsworth, see Critcher, "Action Not Words," in Connell and Hilton, eds., *Cultural Studies 50 Years On*, 247–256.

16. On the gendered nature of postwar racialized anxieties, see Collins, "Pride and Prejudice," 391–418.

17. Hall et al., *Policing the Crisis*. See also Eley, "The Trouble with 'Race,'" in Chin et al., eds., *After the Nazi Racial State*, 165–166; and Connell, "Review Essay: *Policing the Crisis* 35 Years On," 273–283.

18. Hall, "The Great Moving Right Show," 19.

19. On the British Nationality Act of 1981, see Dixon, "Thatcher's People," 161–80.

20. Lord Scarman, *The Scarman Report*. For an assessment of the role of public inquiries in this period, see Peplow, "'A Tactical Manoeuvre to Apply Pressure,'" 129–155.

21. Thatcher, speech to Conservative Party conference, Blackpool, 11 October 1985, Margaret Thatcher Foundation archive (hereafter cited as MTF), www.margaretthatcher.org/document/106145 (accessed 12 June 2017); Dear, *Handsworth/Lozells September 1985*, 48–49.

22. Geoffrey Dear, quoted in Rees, "Handsworth Ablaze Again after Night of Horror," 1; Nicholas Fairbairn MP, quoted in Bhavnani et al., *A Different Reality*, 13.

23. Wilkinson, "The Tinderbox Towns about to Erupt," 6. For a study of the concept of "white flight" in its original US context, see Kruse, *White Flight*. Thanks to Laurence Connell for bringing this to my attention. See also Hulme, *After the Shock City*.

24. Brown and Deakin, "The Bleeding Heart of England," 15; Gysin, "War on the Streets," 1; and Sir Kenneth Newman, quoted in Sivanandan, "UK Commentary—Britain's Gulags," 81.

25. See Hilton, Moores, and Sutcliffe-Braithwaite, "New Times Revisited," 145–165; and Brooke, "Living in 'New Times,'" 20–32.

26. De Certeau, *The Practice of Everyday Life*, 93.

27. Williams, *Politics and Letters*, 159.

28. Hall with Schwarz, *Familiar Stranger*, 198–199. On Thatcher's marshaling of Powellian nationalism, see Smith, *New Right Discourse on Race and Sexuality*, 9.

29. Eley, "The Trouble with 'Race,'" 167, 176.

30. In terms of school-leavers, the key turning point was arguably the introduction of the 1962 Commonwealth Immigrants Act, which persuaded many parents to send for their overseas dependents and bring them to Britain. In Birmingham, two years after the passing of the act it was reported that in at least ten primary schools in Birmingham one in three pupils was black. This cohort would have reached school-leaving age by the mid-1970s. See Rex and Tomlinson, *Colonial Immigrants in a British City*, 145–147, 176–178.

31. 1976 Race Relations White Paper, quoted in Bourne, "The Life and Times of Institutional Racism," 10.

32. Hall, "From Scarman to Stephen Lawrence," 188.

33. Gilroy, *After Empire?*, 139.

34. See Matera, *Black London*; James, *George Padmore and Decolonization from Below*; Adi, *Pan-Africanism and Communism*; Whitall, "Creolising London"; and Geiss, *The Pan-African Movement*.

35. On the Victorian practice of colonial exhibitions, see Mathur, "Living Ethnological Exhibits," 492–524; and Qureshi, *Peoples on Parade*. For a European perspective, see Ames, *Carl Hagenbeck's Empire of Entertainments*.

36. Quoted in Walia, *African Oasis*.

37. On Malcolm X's visit to Birmingham, see Street, "Malcolm X, Smethwick, and the Influence of the African American Freedom Struggle," 932–950. On the Rastafarian semiotics of *Catch a Fire*, see Hebdige, *Cut 'n' Mix*, 79.

38. Dennis, *Behind the Frontlines*, 99.

39. James, "Migration, Racism and Identity Formation," in James and Harris, eds., *Inside Babylon*, 239.

40. Stuart Hall, quoted in Grossberg, "On Postmodernism and Articulation," in Morley and Chen, eds., *Stuart Hall*, 141.

41. For an overview of the difficulties in the use of *black* with respect to African-Caribbean and South Asian experiences in Britain, see, for example, Brar, "Difference, Diversity and Differentiation," in Donald and Rattansi, eds., *Race, Culture and Difference*, 127; and Webster, *Imagining Home*, xvii.

42. Williams, *Culture and Society*, 18; and Williams, *Politics and Letters*, 159.

43. Williams, *Politics and Letters*, 159.

44. Stuart Hall, quoted in Schwarz, "Claudia Jones and the *West Indian Gazette*," 282. On Hall's reflections on 1960s Birmingham, see Stuart Hall, quoted in Connell and Hilton, eds., *Cultural Studies 50 Years On*, 289; and Phillips and Phillips, *Windrush*, 197–198. Fanon's seminal text on this subject is *Black Skins, White Masks*.

45. Lawrence, "'In the Abundance of Water the Fool Is Thirsty,'" in CCCS, ed., *The Empire Strikes Back*, 116; and Webster, *Imagining Home*, 48, 123.

46. See Carby, "White Women Listen!," in CCCS, ed., *The Empire Strikes Back*, 181–210.

47. Gilroy, *The Black Atlantic*. The phrase was initially elaborated by Robert Farris Thompson in *Flash of the Spirit*.

48. On the individualism of the long 1980s, see, for example, Lent, *British Social Movements Since 1945*; Lawrence, "Class, 'Affluence' and the Study of Everyday Life in Britain," 273–299; Wetherell, 'Painting the Crisis," 235–249; and Robinson et al., "Telling Stories about Post-War Britain," 268–304.

49. Gilroy, *After Empire?*, 2.

50. Ross, *Fast Cars, Clean Bodies*; and Schwarz, *Memories of Empire*, Vol. 1, 5.

51. It has been suggested that by 1966 as much as 60 percent of the Caribbean population in Britain had come from Jamaica. See James, "Migration, Racism and Identity Formation," 257.

52. The scope of this literature is far too large for a single note. In relation to twentieth-century Britain see, as an indicative example from the last fifteen years, Houlbrook, *Queer*

London; Mort, *Capital Affairs*; Laite, *Common Prostitutes and Ordinary Citizens*; Bell, *Murder Capital*; Matera, *Black London*; and Perry, *London Is the Place for Me*.

53. Houlbrook, *Queer London*, 9. See also Neale, "Research in Urban History," 570. On the enduring importance of regionalism in late-twentieth-century Britain, see Smith, "Working-Class Ideas and Experiences of Sexuality in Twentieth-Century Britain," 58–78.

54. Walkowitz, *City of Dreadful Delight*, 15.

55. See Tabili, *Global Migrants, Local Culture*; Tabili, "The Construction of Racial Difference in Twentieth-Century Britain," 54–98; Paul, *Whitewashing Britain*, 114; Hall, "Rethinking Imperial Histories," 5. For studies of Toxteth and St. Paul's, see Brown, *Dropping Anchor, Setting Sail*; and Ken Pryce's classic *Endless Pressure*. Birmingham was home to a small prewar black population, but this was not on the same scale as in port cities such as Cardiff. On the prewar black presence in Birmingham, see Dick, "Locality and Diversity," in Dyer et al., eds., *New Directions in Local History Since Hoskins*, 86.

56. On the earlier sociologies of race relations, see Waters, "'Dark Strangers' in Our Midst," 207–238. See also the opening chapter of Bailkin, *The Afterlife of Empire*, for a further discussion of the emergence of a social science of "race relations."

57. Quoted in Bishton and Reardon, *Home Front*, 101.

58. The limitations of oral history in particular have been well documented. For an overview see, for example, Tonkin, *Narrating Our Pasts*; and Perks and Thompson, eds., *The Oral History Reader*.

59. Eley, "The Trouble with 'Race,'" 164.

60. Burton, *After the Imperial Turn?*; Schwarz, *Memories of Empire*; Bailkin, *The Afterlife of Empire*; Schofield, *Enoch Powell and the Making of Postcolonial Britain*; Burkett, *Constructing Post-Imperial Britain*; Perry, *London Is the Place for Me*; and Bocking-Welch, *British Civic Society at the End of Empire*. For an overview of these historiographical shifts and their wider implications, see Vernon, "The History of Britain Is Dead," 19–34; and Buettner, *Europe after Empire*, 7–18.

61. As has been pointed out, a significant number of postwar immigrants from the Caribbean came from middle-class backgrounds. Rush, *Bonds of Empire*, 12.

62. Hall with Schwarz, *Familiar Stranger*, 14–16. On the Caribbean's pigmentocracy, see Lewis, "Race Relations in Britain," 78–80; James, "Migration, Racism and Identity Formation,", 234; and Perry, *London Is the Place for Me*, 81.

63. On Hall's role in the black arts scene, see McRobbie, "Stuart Hall," 665–683. For the independent "review panel" that investigated the causes of the 1985 riots, see Bhavnani, et al., *A Different Reality*. For Hall's reflections on the legacies of the "*Windrush* generation," see Hall with Schwarz, *Familiar Stranger*, 173–200.

64. Ginzburg, "Microhistory," 11.

65. Putnam, "To Study the Fragments/Whole," 618.

66. Gilroy, *After Empire?*, 3–5; Pomeranz, "Histories for a Less National Age," 1–22; and Vernon, "The History of Britain Is Dead," 24.

67. Gilroy, *The Black Atlantic*, 6.

68. On the black locality in 1950s London, see Schwarz, "Black Metropolis, White England," in Nava and O'Shea, eds., *Modern Times*, 194; and Schwarz, "Claudia Jones and the *West Indian Gazette*," 272.

69. For an overview of the key policy reforms in this area, see Grosvenor, *Assimilating Identities*.

70. For an overview of this new, largely socialist history, see Dworkin, *Cultural Marxism in Postwar Britain*, 182–218.

71. For example, Roberts, *The Classic Slum*; Yeo, "A New Life," 5–56; and White, *Rothschild Buildings*.

72. Hoggart, *The Uses of Literacy*.

73. hooks, *Killing Rage*.

74. Williams, "Culture Is Ordinary," in Mackenzie, ed., *Conviction*, 74. See also Hilton, "Politics Is Ordinary," 230–268.

75. James, "Immigrants to Britain," 15–-16; Schwarz, introduction to Schwarz, ed., *West Indian Intellectuals in Britain*, 2; and Schwarz, "Black Metropolis, White England," 194.

76. Hall, "New Ethnicities," in Morley and Chen, eds., *Stuart Hall*, 448.

CHAPTER 1. SHADES OF BLACK

1. Williams, *The Politics of Race in Britain and South Africa*, 195.

2. Johnson, "From Popular Anti-imperialism to Sectarianism," 485–487.

3. Henry, "The Growth of Corporate Black Identity Among Afro-Caribbean People in Birmingham, England," 473–475; "Independence Day Festival," *Birmingham Evening Mail*, 6 June 1977, 4. For more on the role of jubilees in the imperial Caribbean, see Rush, *Bonds of Empire*, 51.

4. Williams, *The Politics of Race in Britain and South Africa*, 197.

5. Matera, *Black London*, 49, 62–63.

6. Quoted in Perry, *London Is the Place for Me*, 182.

7. Quoted in Abernethy, "'Not Just an American Problem,'" 295; and Street, "Malcolm X, Smethwick, and the Influence of the African American Freedom Struggle," 939.

8. Perry, *London Is the Place for Me*, 17.

9. These groups included the Afro-Asian Caribbean organisations and the Campaign Against Racial Discrimination. See Perry, *London Is the Place for Me*, 178. By 1960 the *Gazette* was selling fifteen thousand copies. See also Ramdin, *The Making of the Black Working Class in Britain*, 225.

10. Angelo, "The Black Panthers in London, 1967–1972," 17–35. See also Bunce and Field, "Obi B. Egbuna, CLR James and the Birth of Black Power in Britain," 391–414.

11. Kenan Malik, *From Fatwa to Jihad*, 51; Sivanandan, "Challenging Racism," in Sivanandan, *Communities of Resistance*, 66. On Carmichael and Third World ties, see James, "Black Power," 362–374.

12. Malik, *From Fatwa to Jihad*, 68.

13. The term *multiculturalism* first emerged in the United States in the middle of the twentieth century and had become increasingly prominent in Britain by the later 1970s. For a good overview of this history, see Chin, *The Crisis of Multiculturalism in Europe*, 8–18.

14. There is a wealth of literature that adopts variations of this analytical stance. See, for example, Kundnani, *The End of Tolerance*, 44; Bryan, Dadzie, and Scafe, *The Heart of the Race*, 179; Troyna and Williams, *Racism, Education, and the State*, 24; Sivanandan, "Challenging Racism," 66; and Ramamurthy, *Black Star*, 69.

15. Solomos and Back, *Race, Politics and Social Change*, 45–46.
16. Lyndsey, "The Split-Labour Phenomenon," 123.
17. Natarajan, "Performing Multiculturalism," 705–733.
18. On the Labour government's policies toward race in this period, see Dean, "The Race Relations Policy of the First Wilson Government," 259–283.
19. Young, "Approaches to Policy Development in the Field of Equal Opportunities," 24; and Sivanandan, "Challenging Racism," 67.
20. Rex and Tomlinson, *Colonial Immigrants in a British City*, 173.
21. Young, "Approaches to Policy Development in the Field of Equal Opportunities," 26; and Wild, "'Black Was the Colour of Our Fight,'" 169–170.
22. Solomos and Back, *Race, Politics and Social Change*, 78.
23. Report of the Race Relations and Equal Opportunities Committee, "Funding of Projects Aimed at the Ethnic Minority Communities and Disabled Persons in Birmingham," presented 20 September 1985, Birmingham City Council Race Relations and Equal Opportunities Committee minutes (MS 2142/C/4/70); and Solomos and Back, *Race, Politics and Social Change*, 77.
24. Report of the City Planning Officer to the Economic Development Committee, 27 March 1985; and Race Relations and Equal Opportunities Committee, July 1984–April 1986 (MS 2142/C/4/70).
25. The County Council of West Midlands, Policy and Resources (Race Relations Sub-) Committee, 20 October 1981 (WMCC/416); and West Midlands County Council, Race Relations and Equal Opportunity Committee, 20 September 1985 (WMCC/389).
26. For an analysis of "local socialism" in Sheffield, see Payling, "'Socialist Republic of South Yorkshire,'" 602–627.
27. Barrow and Geraldine S. Cadbury Trust, 1985–6 Annual Report, 11 (MS2142/D/6), Cadbury Trust Papers.
28. Interview with David Waddington, 16 June 2011.
29. Department of Trade and Industry, *The Government's Handsworth Task Force*, 5–7, 95–96; and Andrews, "Inner-City Schemes to get 10m Cash Boost."
30. In the first two years of Thatcher's first government, expenditure by the state actually rose in light of the recession of that period. By the later 1980s this had been cut, but public expenditure as a percentage of GDP remained at a level higher than it had been in the 1950s and for much of the 1960s. See Pemberton, "The Transformation of the Economy," 181.
31. See Travis, "Oliver Letwin Blocked Help for Black Youth after 1985 Riots."
32. Report of the director of development/inner city team leader, Race Relations and Equal Opportunities Committee, 18 April 1986 (MS 2142/C/4/70); and West Midlands County Council Race Relations and Equal Opportunity Committee, 17 May 1985, agenda item 1 (WMCC/389). The black history project was applied for by John Dalton from the Trinity Arts group.
33. For more on this "black locality" in 1950s London, see Schwarz, "Claudia Jones and the *West Indian Gazette*," 272.
34. Interview with David Waddington, 16 June 2011.
35. Malik, *From Fatwa to Jihad*, 67 and 69.
36. Sivanandan, "Race, Class and the State," 362.

37. In Birmingham, claims of corruption were made against James Hunte, a black councilor representing Handsworth and the vice chairman of the Race Relations Subcommittee. Hunte's role on the "small grants committee" coincided with his playing an active role in campaigning against a pyramid scheme that particularly affected the black community, and he was also accused of nepotism with respect to his conduct while serving on the committee. See Solomos and Back, *Race, Politics and Social Change*, 71; and Henry, "The Growth of Corporate Black Identity Among Afro-Caribbean People in Birmingham, England," 288.

38. See Hick, *An Autobiography*, 170–172.

39. Burkett, *Constructing Post-Imperial Britain*, 60 and 197. See also Skinner, *The Foundations of Anti-Apartheid*; and Williams, *The Politics of Race in Britain and South Africa*.

40. Hall with Schwarz, *Familiar Stranger*, 11.

41. Hain, *Don't Play with Apartheid*, 186.

42. For example, in 1973 in a by-election in West Bromwich, a district neighboring Handsworth, an NF candidate retained his deposit for the first time, with 16 percent of the vote. Three years later roughly half the NF candidates put forward in the May local elections won 10 percent of the vote. See Fielding, *The National Front*, 26; and Walker, *The National Front*, 198.

43. Renton, *When We Touched the Sky*, 38, 175.

44. Gilroy, *There Ain't No Black in the Union Jack*, 119 and 134.

45. Weaver, "Political Groups and Young Blacks in Handsworth," 16.

46. All Faiths for One Race, Annual Report 1976–77, 1 (MS 1579/2/3/1/5), All Faiths for One Race papers (hereafter cited as AFFOR papers).

47. Interview with Clare Short, 13 February 2009.

48. Quoted in AFFOR *Newsletter* (Spring 1978), 8 (MS 1579/2/3/1/5), AFFOR papers.

49. Holden, *So What Are You Going to Do about the National Front?*, 3; and AFFOR *Newsletter* (Spring 1980), 2 (MS 2478/B/3/2, DBA).

50. Hick, *An Autobiography*, 173; and Holden, *From Race to Politics*, 3.

51. By 1984 AFFOR had received a total of £40,265 from grants and other donations, including the Cadbury Trust and the Birmingham Inner-City Partnership Fund. See AFFOR Annual Report 1983–84, 4 (MS 2478/B/3/2, DBA).

52. AFFOR Annual Report, 1977–78 (MS 2478/B/3/2, DBA), 1, 6–8; and AFFOR Annual Report 1983–84, 8.

53. Brown, *Shades of Grey*. Brown had previously published *A Theory of Police/Immigrant Relations* (Cranfield, 1974).

54. For a detailed analysis of the local newspaper's reporting of this episode, see Cashmore, *Rastaman*, 220.

55. Brown, *Shades of Grey*, 3. Gilroy's discussion of Brown's report can be found in Gilroy, "Police and Thieves," in CCCS, ed., *The Empire Strikes Back*, 160–163.

56. Short, in AFFOR and Carlton Green, *Talking Blues*, 4. See also AFFOR et al., *Talking Chalk*.

57. AFFOR Annual Report 1983–84, 20–21. Unemployment in Handsworth/Lozells was 41.1 percent in 1985. See Bhavnani et al., *A Different Reality*, 30.

58. The classic text that encapsulated the ideals of this movement is Bailey and Brake, *Radical Social Work*. For a historical reflection of this movement, see Lavalette, *Radical Social Work Today*.

59. Rex and Tomlinson, *Colonial Immigrants in a British City*, 256.

60. Rex and Tomlinson, *Colonial Immigrants in a British City*, 256.

61. AFFOR Annual Report 1976–77, 1; and AFFOR *Newsletter* (Spring 1978), 1.

62. Ramamurthy, *Black Star*, 35. For a detailed history of the emergence of the IWAs in Britain, see Josephides, "Principles, Strategies, Anti-racist Campaigns," in Goulbourne, ed., *Black Politics in Britain*, 115–129.

63. Constitution of the IWA, ca. 1979 (MS 2142/A/1/7/1), papers of Avtar Jouhl and the Indian Workers' Association (hereafter cited as AJA); *Asian Youth News*, December 1985, 1, Tandana Asian Youth Movement Archive, www.tandana.org/archives (accessed 22 October 2011).

64. Ramamurthy, *Black Star*, 70–71. Issue 5 of *Asian Youth News* also featured a front-page article on Singh. See *Asian Youth News*, April 1986, no. 5 (01/04/04/01/14/07), "Handsworth" file, Institute of Race Relations Black History Collection (hereafter cited as IRR).

65. Quoted in *Lalkar*, June 1981, 8 (MS 2141/A/5/1/1), papers of the Indian Workers' Association (hereafter cited as IWA). On the British Black Power reading of Marxism-Leninism, see Bunce and Field, "Obi B. Egbuna, CLR James and the Birth of Black Power in Britain," 401.

66. T. Mehmood, quoted in Deol, "The Myth of a Black Consciousness," 46.

67. Wild, "'Black Was the Colour of Our Fight,'" 241.

68. Quoted in *Lalkar*, October 1985, 4 (MS 2141/A/5/1/1, IWA).

69. *Asian Youth News*, September 1985, 2–3, Tandana Asian Youth Movement Archive, http://www.tandana.org/Search.html (accessed 29 August 2018).

70. Sivanandan, "Challenging Racism," 67–68; and interview with Bhopinder Basi, 20 January 2010.

71. A. Sivanandan, "From Resistance to Rebellion," in Sivanandan, ed., *A Different Hunger*, 47; *Asian Youth News*, December 1985, 1; and Bhopinder Basi, quoted in Ramamurthy, "The Politics of Britain's Asian Youth Movements," 46.

72. Sivanandan, "Liberation of the Black Intellectual," 329–343; and Ramamurthy, *Black Star*, 80–81.

73. Memo from A. Brar to all branch secretaries of the IWA, 23 October 1982 (MS 2142/A/1/3/3/7, AJA).

74. Dar, "Welfare and Other Activities"; and Josephides, "Principles, Strategies, Anti-racist Campaigns," 116. It has been estimated that between 1955 and 1957, 70 percent of Indian migrants to Britain arrived using invalid or forged documents. See Wills, *Lovers and Strangers*, 206.

75. IWA leaflet, 3 October 1986 (MS 2141/A/5/3/8, IWA).

76. On the issue of domestic violence within black communities in London, see Mama, "Woman Abuse in London's Black Communities," in James and Harris, eds., *Inside Babylon*, 97–134.

77. Interview with Surinder Guru, 9 March 20; Ramamurthy, *Black Star*, 86, 95; and Ramamurthy, "The Politics of Britain's Asian Youth Movements," 51. On the issue of race and the women's movement specifically, see Sudbury, *"Other Kinds of Dreams"*; and Thomlinson, *Race, Ethnicity and the Women's Movement in England*. See also Lent, *British Social Movements Since 1945*, 154.

78. Archival material on the Birmingham Black Sisters is scarce, and it is consequently difficult to give an exact date of the group's formation. The first issue of its newsletter did not appear until 1988, but some have suggested the group was formed in the 1970s. See Fisher, *What's Left of Blackness*. For an account of the activities of the Southall Black Sisters, see Gupta, *From Homebreakers to Jailbreakers*. See also Williams, "We Are a Natural Part of Many Different Struggles," in James and Harris, eds., *Inside Babylon*, 153–178.

79. Parmar, "Gender, Race and Class," in CCCS, ed., *The Empire Strikes Back*, 250.

80. Thomlinson, *Race, Ethnicity and the Women's Movement*, 76. For a contemporaneous account of this issue, see Carby, "White Women Listen!," 212–235.

81. For more on the Organisation of Women of Asian and African Descent, see Bryan, Dadzie, and Scafe, *The Heart of the Race*, 164–174.

82. Interview with Surinder Guru, 9 March 2011.

83. Birmingham Black Sisters, *Newsletter*, no. 2 (May–June 1988): 1–2 (01/04/04/01/14/07, IRR).

84. For more on the effects of the 1988 Immigration Act and deportation figures, see Bloch and Schuster, "At the Extremes of Exclusion," 495–496. For an overview of the Conservative Party's electoral strategy with respect to black and Asian communities generally in the 1980s, see Francis, "Mrs Thatcher's Peacock Blue Sari," 274–293.

85. Ramamurthy, *Black Star*, 104

86. *Asian Youth News*, Immigration supplement, December 1985, Tandana Asian Youth Movement Archive, www.tandana.org/data/pg/PDF/MH/MH216.PDF (accessed 12 September 2016); and Ramamurthy, *Black Star*, 113–114.

87. Parmar, "Gender, Race and Class," 245.

88. Ramamurthy, *Black Star*, 94.

89. Interview with Surinder Guru, 9 March 2011; Birmingham Black Sisters, "Free Iqbal Begum" leaflet, 1982, 2, Tandana Asian Youth Movement Archive, www.tandana.org/data/pg/PDF/SC/SC130.PDF (accessed 22 October 2011); and Thomlinson, *Race, Ethnicity and the Women's Movement*, 81.

90. Halliburton, "Lost in Translation."

91. Ramamurthy, *Black Star*, 94–95.

92. K. Rajniti, "Women Bound by the Chains of a Restrictive Social System," *Asian Youth News*, December 1985, 1, Tandana Asian Youth Movement Archive, www.tandana.org/data/pg/PDF/SC/SC130.PDF (accessed 22 October 2011).

93. See Lent, *British Social Movements Since 1945*, 156–157; Solomos, *Race and Racism in Britain*, 65; and Ramamurthy, *Black Star*, 97. In the 1960s West Indians made up just 15 percent of all deportees. See Bailkin, *The Afterlife of Empire*, 203.

94. Interview with Surinder Guru, 9 March 2011; and Bryan, Dadzie, and Scafe, *The Heart of the Race*, 165.

95. Sondhi, *Asian Resource Centre*, 3.

96. Interview with Anil Bhalla, 6 February 2010.

97. Interview with Ranjit Sondhi, 11 May 2009.

98. Asian Resource Centre, www.asianresource.org.uk/ (accessed 31 March 2010).

99. Interview with Ranjit Sondhi, 11 May 2009.

100. Interview with Anil Bhalla, 6 February 2010. On the issue of homelessness among the elderly Asian community, see Mays, "Elderly South Asians in Britain," 83.

101. Bhattacharyya, *Across All Boundaries*, 12.

102. Asian Resource Centre Annual Report, 1978–1979 (01/04/04/01/14/07, IRR); and Asian Resource Centre, Management Committee minutes, 2 April 1991 (uncatalogued Asian Resource Centre records held at ARC, 110 Hamstead Road, Handsworth).

103. Asian Resource Centre, Management Committee minutes, 30 September 1980 and 6 June 1981 (uncatalogued Asian Resource Centre records held at ARC, 110 Hamstead Road, Handsworth).

104. Ramamurthy, *Black Star*, 158–159, 171.

105. *Sunday Telegraph*, 10 December 1972, quoted in Henry, "The Growth of Corporate Black Identity Among Afro-Caribbean People in Birmingham, England," 293, 472.

106. Rex and Tomlinson, *Colonial Immigrants in a British City*, 258.

107. Marcus Garvey Foundation, *Charity Magazine*, ca. late-1980s (MS2192/C/D/1/1/1), Vanley Burke Archive (hereafter cited as VBA). For more on the humanitarian and aid sectors in this period more generally, see, for example, Hilton, "International Aid and Development NGOs in Britain and Human Rights since 1945," 449–472.

108. Matera, *Black London*, 42, 55.

109. See Killingray, "'To Do Something for the Race,'" 60.

110. See Rex and Moore, *Race, Community and Conflict*, 20.

111. In the early 1960s it was estimated that less than 1 percent of the council house population was black. See Webster, *Imagining Home*, 174.

112. Henry, "Homelessness and a Particular Response Among Young West Indians in Handsworth, Birmingham," 15–30; and Henry, "The Growth of Corporate Black Identity Among Afro-Caribbean People in Birmingham, England," 496.

113. Report in the Birmingham *Evening Mail*, 17 June 1976, quoted in Henry, "The Growth of Corporate Black Identity Among Afro-Caribbean People in Birmingham, England," 254.

114. Interview with Maurice Andrews, 16 June 2010; Harambee's aims and objectives, quoted in Henry, "Homelessness and a Particular Response Among Young West Indians in Handsworth, Birmingham," 30. On the problem of black youth being made homeless in Handsworth more generally, see John, *Race in the Inner City*, 30–31.

115. See Hines, *How Black People Overcame Fifty Years of Repression in Britain*; and Jones, *The Black House*.

116. Harambee's aims and objectives, quoted in Henry, "Homelessness and a Particular Response Among Young West Indians in Handsworth, Birmingham," 34–35; and Harambee Annual Report, 1973–1974 (CK3/97), The National Archives (hereafter cited as TNA).

117. *Evening Mail*, 13 March 1975, quoted in Henry "The Growth of Corporate Black Identity Among Afro-Caribbean People in Birmingham, England," 266.

118. Harambee's ideological stance, quoted in Rex and Tomlinson, *Colonial Immigrants in a British City*, 260–262; and interview with Maurice Andrews, 16 June 2010.

119. Henry, "The Growth of Corporate Black Identity Among Afro-Caribbean People in Birmingham, England," 461.

120. Memo from senior community relations officer of CRC to Mrs. T. Hasnain, regional development officer, 29 April 1975 (CK3/106, TNA). Harambee also obtained funds from

the Cadbury Trust, the British Council of Churches, and the Community Relations Council.

121. Harambee Annual Report, 1973–1974 (CK3/97, TNA).

122. Interview with Maurice Andrews, 16 June 2010.

123. Brown gives the date of ACSHO's establishment as 1964, but elsewhere it is given as 1966. In either case, it is significant that this predates the 1967 establishment of the UCPA, which is often seen as marking the birth of Black Power in Britain.

124. "Joint Attack by the Labour Party and Conservative Party," *Jomo*, no. 2 (March 1989): 11 (MS 2192/C/D/1/1, VBA); and interview with Bini Brown, 15 December 2009.

125. Rex and Tomlinson, *Colonial Immigrants in a British City*, 257–258.

126. Wild, "'Black Was the Colour of Our Fight,'" 8.

127. Stokely Carmichael, quoted in Ramdin, *The Making of the Black Working Class in Britain*, 376; and Henry, "The Growth of Corporate Black Identity Among Afro-Caribbean People in Birmingham, England," 476.

128. Rex and Tomlinson, *Colonial Immigrants in a British City*, 258. On the introductory training sessions of the British Black Panthers, see Bunce and Field, "Obi B. Egbuna, CLR James and the Birth of Black Power in Britain," 406.

129. Interview with Bini Brown, 15 December 2009.

130. John, *Race in the Inner City*, 33.

131. Bergman and Coard, "Trials and Tribulations of a Self-Help Group," 112–114.

132. Myers and Grosvenor, "Exploring Supplementary Education," 508.

133. Ramdin, *The Making of the Black Working Class*, 250; Dove, 'The Emergence of Black Supplementary Schools," 435.

134. Ramdin, *The Making of the Black Working Class*, 248.

135. Coard, *How the West Indian Child Is Made Educationally Subnormal in the British School System*, 38. See also Gerrard, "Self Help and Protest," 32–58.

136. Myers and Grosvenor, "Exploring Supplementary Education," 509.

137. Beckles, "'We Shall Not Be Terrorized Out of Existence,'" 63.

138. A similar school in Bristol is described in Pryce, *Endless Pressure*, 169.

139. ACSHO, "Tuesday Meetings" leaflet, ca. late 1970s (MS 2192/C/D/1/1, VBA).

140. Inner-London Education Authority, *Multi-Ethnic Education*, 1977, quoted in Connolly, "Splintered Sisterhood," 53.

141. ACSHO, "Pan African Congress Movement," promotional leaflet, 1990, 4 (MS 2192/C/D/1/1, VBA).

142. For a qualitative analysis of the success of black supplementary schools in the early 1980s, see Dove, 'The Emergence of Black Supplementary Schools," 430–446.

143. ACSHO, "Tuesday Meetings" leaflet, 4; and interview with Bini Brown, 15 December 2009.

144. Grosvenor, *Assimilating Identities* 157–158.

145. ACSHO, "Tuesday Meetings" leaflet, 5.

146. ACSHO, "Dem Invade Handsworth Again Me Friend," 1985 (MS 2192/C/D/1/1, VBA).

147. ACSHO, "Tuesday Meetings" leaflet, 5; and ACSHO, "Dem Invade Handsworth Again Me Friend," 1985. For a detailed account of the "Mangrove nine" case, see Bunce and Field, *Darcus Howe*, 105–135.

148. ACSHO, "Pan African Congress Movement," 3.

149. "Garveyism and the Lessons from History," *Jomo*, no. 2 (March 1989) (MS 2192 /C/D/1/1, VBA).

150. Interview with Bini Brown, 15 December 2009.

151. ACSHO, "Tuesday Meetings" leaflet, 2.

152. Dennis, *Behind the Frontlines*, 119.

153. Bini Brown, letter to Tuesday seminar attendees, 12 December 1995 (MS2192/C/D/1/1/1, VBA); and undated ACSHO promotional leaflet, ca. 1980 (MS 2192/C/D/1/1, VBA).

154. For a discussion of the gender dynamics of London-based organizations, see Wild, "'Black Was the Colour of Our Fight,'" 135–136.

155. ACSHO, "Tuesday Meetings," 1994, 3–4 (MS 2192/C/D/1/1, VBA)

156. This account comes from Murphy, *Tales From Two Cities,* 177. Murphy does not explicitly mention ACSHO by name but does explain that the male attendees were members of a militant black organization that had been established in Handsworth some twenty years earlier, which suggests that the ACSHO is the group in question.

157. Dennis, *Behind the Frontlines,* 117.

158. ACSHO, "Tuesday Meetings," 1994, 3–4.

159. Quoted in *Here and Now*, episode 167, "Handsworth: What Went Wrong" (Central Television, 1985). From Media Archive of Central England (hereafter cited as MACE), University of Lincoln, www.macearchive.org/Archive/Title/here-and-now-programme-167 /MediaEntry/664.html (accessed 22 October 2011).

160. Interview with Bini Brown, 15 December 2009.

161. Henry, "The Growth of Corporate Black Identity Among Afro-Caribbean People in Birmingham, England," 142.

162. ACSHO, Handsworth Defence Campaign leaflet, October 1985 (01/04/04/01/14/07, IRR).

163. ACSHO, Handsworth Defence Campaign leaflet, October 1985.

164. Dear, *Handsworth/Lozells September 1985*, 49.

165. See Brady, "The Fight to Save Harambee."

166. Interview with Surinder Guru, 9 March 2011.

167. The County Council of West Midlands, Policy and Resources Race Relations Sub-Committee, 8 December 1983, Report of County Treasurer and County Personnel Officer, agenda item 1, Large Grant Scheme 1983/84 (WMCC/416); and The County Council of West Midlands, Race Relations and Equal Opportunity Committee, 20 September 1985 (WMCC/389).

168. Andrews, "The Problem of Political Blackness," 2060–2078.

169. Interview with Ranjit Sondhi, 11 May 2009.

170. See Malik, *From Fatwa to Jihad*, 1–35.

CHAPTER 2. VISUALIZING HANDSWORTH

1. Rushdie, "Songs Don't Know the Score," in Procter, ed., *Writing Black Britain*, 263.

2. Hall, "Songs of Handsworth Praise," in Procter, ed., *Writing Black Britain*, 264.

3. Hall, "Songs of Handsworth Praise," in Procter, ed., *Writing Black Britain*, 264.

4. Howe, "The Language of Black Culture," in Procter, ed., *Writing Black Britain*, 264–265.

5. Ward, introduction to *British Culture and the End of Empire*, 11; Courtman, "A Journey through the Imperial Gaze," in Faulkner and Ramamurthy, eds., *Visual Culture and Decolonisation in Britain*, 128.

6. Enwezor, "Coalition Building," in Eshun and Sagar, eds., *The Ghost of Songs*, 108. On the work of this generation of artists more generally, see Chambers, *Black Artists in British Art*.

7. Hall, "Reconstruction Work," 106–13; and Perry, *London Is the Place for Me*, 71.

8. For a discussion of the work of Riis and Hines, see Marien, *Photography*, 202–208. Riis in particular had highly problematic views on race and often contextualized his subjects in a manner that drew on his own racialized stereotypes. See O'Donnell, "Pictures vs. Words?," 7–26.

9. See Gilroy, *Black Britain*, 94.

10. Enoch Powell, 20 April 1968. The full text of the speech is available at http://www.telegraph.co.uk/comment/3643823/Enoch-Powells-Rivers-of-Blood-speech.html (accessed 18 January 2011); Hall et al., *Policing the Crisis*.

11. Margaret Thatcher, speech to the 1922 Committee, 20 July 1984, MTF, www.margarettthatcher.org/document/105563 (accessed 14 November 2014).

12. Gilroy, "Police and Thieves," 173; and Gilroy, *There Ain't No Black in the Union Jack*, 228.

13. For historical work on documentary photography, see, for example, Moran, "Imagining the Street in Post-War Britain," 166–186; Brooke, "Revisiting Southam Street," 453–496; and Allberson, "Visualizing Wartime Destruction and Postwar Reconstruction," 532–578. Susan Sontag's influential essays on photography, published in the early 1970s in *New York Review of Books*, were collated in Sontag, *On Photography*. Berger's critical intervention came in the 1972 television series *Ways of Seeing* and the accompanying book of the same name.

14. On self-fashioning see, for example, Houlbrook, "'A Pin to See the Peepshow,'" 215–249. On photography and self-fashioning, see Hanna, "Reading Irish Women's Lives in Photograph Albums," 89–109.

15. Hall, "Cultural Identity and Diaspora," in Rutherford, ed., *Identity*, 225.

16. Workers' Film and Photo League founding manifesto, quoted in Grosvenor and Macnab, "Photography as an Agent of Transformation," 127–128; and Forbes, "The Worker Photography Movement in Britain, 1934–1939," in Ribalta, ed., *The Worker Photography Movement*, 206.

17. On alternative theater, the underground press, and the background to the emergence of Arts Labs in Britain, see Marwick, *The Sixties*, 340–353; and Donnelly, *Sixties Britain*, 125–127.

18. Jim Haynes, "Arts Laboratory," letter dated 28 October 1969, www.thecentreofattention.org/dgartslab.html (accessed 18 July 2016). See also Haynes, *Thanks for Coming!*.

19. See Kelly, *Community, Art and the State*, 10.

20. See Grosvenor and Macnab, "Photography as an Agent of Transformation," 119–123; and De Cuyper, "On the Future of Photographic Representation in Anthropology," 5–7.

21. On the obscenity trials see, for example, Sutherland, *Offensive Literature*.

22. Interview with Trevor Fisher, 17 June 2013.

23. Eley, *A Crooked Line*, 51–52. See also Gwinn, "'History Should Become Common Property,'" 96–117.

24. The Birmingham Arts Lab had been established in 1968 and by this period was located in close proximity to what is now the Aston University campus. See Birmingham Museums and Art Gallery, *Birmingham Arts Lab*.

25. Quoted in Bishton and Homer, "People Power?," 7. See also Spence, "The Politics of Photography," 1.

26. Bishton and Homer, "People Power?," 7.

27. Hu, "Community Photography," 280. For a discussion of WELD's nonphotographic activities, see Rex and Tomlinson, *Colonial Immigrants in a British City*, 256–257.

28. Grosvenor and Macnab, "Photography as an Agent of Transformation," 121.

29. Jon Stewart, quoted in Bishton and Homer, "People Power?," 7.

30. See, for example, Anderson, *Reporting Back*.

31. Brooke, "Revisiting Southam Street," 469.

32. Hanna, "Reading Irish Women's Lives in Photograph Albums," 93.

33. Berger, *About Looking*, 52.

34. See Bishton and Homer, "People Power?," 7–8.

35. Jon Stewart, quoted in Bishton and Homer, "People Power?," 7–8.

36. Sharon Smith, quoted in Bishton and Homer, "People Power?," 8.

37. Bishton and Homer, "People Power?," 7–8.

38. Sharon Smith, quoted in Bishton and Homer, "People Power?," 7–8.

39. Bishton, "Local Colour," *Sunday Times Magazine*, 21 September 1980, 96.

40. Bishton and Homer, "People Power?," 8.

41. Sontag, *On Photography*, 7.

42. Murphy, *Tales from Two Cities*, 242.

43. Attie, *Russian Self-Portraits*, 4.

44. Interview with Derek Bishton, 1 February 2009.

45. Margaret Thatcher, "TV Interview for Granada World in Action," 27 January 1968, MTF, www.margaretthatcher.org/document/103485 (accessed 22 October 2014).

46. Bishton, "Handsworth Self Portrait Project," 2; Bishton, Homer, and Reardon, quoted in Grosvenor et al., eds., *Making Connections*, 78.

47. I curated the final exhibition of photographs, which was staged at the University of Birmingham in summer 2010, and also took part in the shoots. The re-created Self-Portrait Project was run by Brian Homer in collaboration with another photographer, Timm Sonnenschein. Neither Bishton nor Reardon was directly involved.

48. Long, Baig-Clifford, and Shannon, "'What We're Trying to Do Is Make Popular Politics,'" 80. On the birth of Channel 4 more specifically, see Hobson, *Channel 4*.

49. Kelly, *Community, Art and the State*, 10; Chapman, "Welcome to Ikon," in Watkins, ed., *This Could Happen to You*, 125.

50. John Akomfrah, quoted in Dickenson, ed., *Rogue Rebels*, 312; Akomfrah, "Black Independent Film-Making," in Eshun and Sagar, eds., *The Ghosts of Songs*, 145.

51. Akomfrah, "Black Independent Film-Making," 144–145.

52. Schaffer, *The Vision of a Nation*, 209.

53. On *Pressure* see, for example, Pines, "The Cultural Context of Black British Cinema," in Baker, Diawara, and Lindeborg, eds., *Black British Cultural Studies*, 188.

54. Schaffer, *The Vision of a Nation*, 261.

55. Eshun, "Drawing the Forms of Things Unknown," in Eshun and Sagar, eds., *The Ghosts of Songs*, 179.

56. Quoted in Eshun, "Drawing the Forms of Things Unknown," 179. On Lugard specifically and his status as an "archetypal man of the British Empire," see Vernon, *Modern Britain*, 401.

57. Dickenson, *Rogue Rebels*, 309–311. On the GLC in the 1980s, see Brooke, "Space, Emotions and the Everyday," 110–142.

58. Perry, *London Is the Place for Me*, 3.

59. See Hughes and Seton, "Birmingham Violence Spreads to New Areas," 1. Government documents recently released under the thirty-year rule have shown the extent to which some in government were anxious about making increased levels of funding available to inner-city areas because of a belief that the riots were caused by the "character" of its black inhabitants. This is discussed in more detail in chapter 1.

60. Dyer, *White*, 82; Eshun. "Drawing the Forms of Things Unknown," 88.

61. Enwezor, "Coalition Building," 51.

62. Eshun, "Untimely Meditations," 40.

63. Dickenson, *Rogue Rebels*, 316.

64. Having seen the highly problematic way in which black characters were portrayed in the film, Robeson eventually disowned it. See Matera, *Black London*, 286–289. See also Paul Robeson, *Here I Stand*.

65. Mercer, "Post-Colonial Trauerspiel," in Eshun and Sagar, eds., *The Ghosts of Songs*, 44.

66. For more on Michael X and his role in the British Black Power movement, see Bunce and Field, "Obi B. Egbuna, C. L. R. James and the Birth of Black Power in Britain," 391–414.

67. For example, Julien and Mercer, "De Margin and De Centre," 2–11.

68. See McRobbie, "Stuart Hall," 665–683.

69. Enwezor, "Coalition Building," 120.

70. See Bunce and Field, *Darcus Howe*, 32–41.

71. Gilroy, "Police and Thieves," 173.

72. Gysin, "War on the Streets," 1; Rees, "Handsworth Ablaze Again after Night of Horror," 1; Parker, "Sun Names Black Bomber," 1.

73. Parker, "Sun Names Black Bomber," 1.

74. Rushdie, "Songs Don't Know the Score," 263.

75. Rushdie, introduction to Bishton and Reardon, *Home Front*, 6–7. For a parallel documentary project, undertaken by a resident of Handsworth and later a contributor to *Ten.8*, see "Hinterland: B21," 1981–1990, in the Darryl Georgiou collection.

76. See Mercer, *Black Film/British Cinema*.

77. Hall, "Vanley Burke and the 'Desire for Blackness,'" in Sealy, ed., *Vanley Burke*, 12.

78. Interview with Vanley Burke, 25 March 2008.

79. See Hobson, *Channel 4*, 68.

80. "Black on Black" postfilm script, London Weekend Television, 1985 (MS2192/C/F/1/2, VBA).

81. Interview with Vanley Burke, 25 March 2008.

82. Hall, "Vanley Burke and the 'Desire for Blackness,'" 13.

83. Interview with Vanley Burke, 25 March 2008.

84. See Jones, *The Black House*.

85. Vanley Burke, "Artist Statement," *Ten.8 Photographic Magazine*, no. 2 (Summer 1979): 7.

86. Brooke, "Revisiting Southam Street," 483; Connell, "Race, Prostitution and the New Left," 301–340.

87. Editorial, "The Unity of a Great Time for Queen and Country," 6.

88. Courtman, "A Journey Through the Imperial Gaze," 145.

89. On the lack of mainstream media coverage of the African Liberation Day march, see Henry, "The Growth of Corporate Black Identity Among Afro-Caribbean People in Birmingham, England," 475.

90. Chambers, *Black Artists in British Art*, 45.

91. Burke, "Here I Stand," in Sealy, ed., *Vanley Burke*, 31.

92. Morris, ed., *Vanley Burke* 18, 26, 51.

93. Interview with Vanley Burke, 25 March 2008.

94. Fagan, "'That's Me in the Picture': Winford Fagan in Handsworth, Birmingham, 1970."

95. Interview with Vanley Burke, 25 March 2008.

96. For an example of Caesar's work outside Handsworth, see Caesar, *Sparkbrook Pride*.

97. Caesar, quoted in BBC, "Handsworth Riots: How Deep are the Scars 25 Years On?"

98. Rushdie, "Songs Don't Know the Score," 263.

99. Burke, "Here I Stand," 31.

100. Dear, *Handsworth/Lozells September 1985*, 19.

101. Burke, "Here I Stand," 31.

102. Interview with Derek Bishton, 1 February 2009.

103. Rushdie, introduction to Bishton and Reardon, *Home Front*, 6–7.

104. Alongside his *Handsworth Songs* review and introduction to *Home Front*, see also Rushdie, "The New Empire Within Britain," in Rushdie, *Imagining Homelands*, 129–138.

105. See Gilroy, *After Empire?*

106. Hall, "New Ethnicities," 447.

107. See Watkins, ed., *At Home with Vanley Burke*.

108. Bannister, "Coventry Photographer Masterji Gets 'New Lease of Life' after First Exhibition Aged 94."

109. Particularly important here is the work of the Birmingham photographer Mahtab Hussain. A selection of Hussain's series on British Muslim identities was featured in Connell and Hilton, *50 Years On*. Also relevant are the photographs of the British *bhangra* scene by Gursharan Singh Chana (aka "Boy Chana"), which were first displayed in an exhibition in Birmingham in 2005. Artists of South Asian descent were operating in the 1980s, working across a range of mediums including batik and the moving image, though not tied to a specific locale (whether Handsworth or elsewhere). For an overview of this work see Chambers, *Black Artists in British Art*, 91–104.

110. Bishton, *Black Heart Man*. For a brief discussion of Bishton's work in relation to wider questions of black diasporic identities, see Hall, "Cultural Identity and Diaspora," 232.

111. Burkett, *Constructing Post-Imperial Britain*, 60, 197.

CHAPTER 3. DREAD CULTURE

1. See Hebdige, *Cut 'n' Mix*, 79.
2. De Koningh and Griffiths, *Tighten Up!*, 159.
3. See Barrett, *The Rastafarians*, 111.
4. Campbell, "Rastafari," 6.
5. The term itself was first used in Gilroy, *There Ain't No Black in the Union Jack*, 197.
6. Putnam, *Radical Moves*, 3. See also Matera, *Black London*, 145–199.
7. Barrett, *The Rastafarians*, 138.
8. Hall, "Negotiating Caribbean Identities," 9.
9. See Cashmore, *Rastaman*, 20.
10. Hobsbawm, "Inventing Traditions," in Hobsbawm and Ranger, eds., *The Invention of Traditions*, 9.
11. Ross, *Fast Cars, Clean Bodies*.
12. Anderson, *Imagined Communities*.
13. See Brocken, *The British Folk Revivial*.
14. Charles Parker, quoted in Filewood and Watt, *Workers' Playtime*, 86; Parker, "Banner," *New Statesman*, 11 October 1974 (MS 1611/A/4, Banner Theatre of Actuality archive, hereafter cited as BTA).
15. Review of *The Great Divide*, in *Banner Theatre of Actuality Report, 1976–78* (MS1611/A/4/2, BTA).
16. Handsworth Community Theatre Project, introductory leaflet, ca. 1979 (MS1611/C, BTA).
17. Interview with Chris Rogers, 3 October 2009.
18. Interview with Milton Godfrey, 28 May 2009.
19. Banner Theatre internal memo, 28 March 1984 (MS1611/A/1/10, BTA).
20. Interview with Milton Godfrey, 28 May 2009.
21. Waters, "Representations of Everyday Life," 121–150.
22. Dennis, *Behind the Frontlines*, 97.
23. For an account of the Greenham Peace camps see, for example, Cook and Kirk, *Greenham Women Everywhere*. See also Moores, "RAGE against the Obscene," 204–227.
24. Interview with Milton Godfrey, 28 May 2009.
25. Ramdhanie, "African Dance in England—Spirituality and Continuity," 2:215–216.
26. Interview with Bob Ramdhanie, 18 February 2009.
27. Ramdhanie, "African Dance in England," 2:216 and 221.
28. Bob Ramdhanie, quoted in Walia, *African Oasis*.
29. The group came across the word in the *Caribbean Times*. Interview with Bob Ramdhanie, 29 July 2009.
30. *The History of the Drum* program, 1992 (KDTA, KO/E/7, Kokuma Dance Company archive, hereafter cited as KA).
31. *The History of the Drum* program, 1992 (KDTA, KO/E/7, KA).
32. In 1988/1989 Kokuma received £45,000 from West Midlands Arts. By the year 1989/1990 this had increased to £60,000. See Ramdhanie, "African Dance in England," 2:244.
33. Travis, "Rates Grant for Rain Dance Lessons in Ghana," 10.

34. Ramdhanie, "African Dance in England," 2:225–226.

35. The notion of "African dance" is self-evidently a vague concept; however, as Carty argues, "there is a clear genre of movements that are common across African dance forms and lead us to the basics of African dance technique." See Carty, "Black Dance in England," in Adewole et al., eds., *Voicing Black Dance*, 18–19; and "Kokuma Performing Arts," introductory pamphlet, 1988, 1 (KDTA, KO/H/5, KA).

36. Quoted in Walia, *African Oasis*.

37. Ursula Walker (née Lawrence), quoted in Grimley, "Beating the Drum for Brum," 18.

38. Interview with Ursula Walker, 8 July 2009.

39. On Rastafarianism and gender, see Campbell, "Rastafari," 18.

40. Henry, "The Growth of Corporate Black Identity Among Afro-Caribbean People in Birmingham, England," 488.

41. Interview with Ursula Walker, 8 July 2009.

42. *The Awakening* programme, March 1994 (KDTA, KO/E/7, KA).

43. Ramdhanie, "African Dance in England," 2:215.

44. On the historical independence of Ethiopia, see Tibebu, "Ethiopia," 414–430; and Marcus, *A History of Ethiopia*. For an account of the life and legacy of Selassie, see Asserate, *King of Kings*.

45. Cashmore, *Rastaman*, 22.

46. Hiro, *Black British, White British*, 72.

47. Marcus Garvey, quoted in Hiro, *Black British, White British*, 71. In 1948 Selassie made five hundred acres of land in the Shashamene district of Ethiopia available to potential Rastafarian settlers living elsewhere in the diaspora.

48. Hiro, *Black British, White British*, 72.

49. Hall, "Negotiating Caribbean Identities," 14.

50. Campbell, "Rastafari," 7–12.

51. Hall with Schwarz, *Familiar Stranger*, 49.

52. Perry, *London Is the Place for Me*, 81. See also Hall, "Negotiating Caribbean Identities," 6–7. For one of the earliest academic studies of Rastafarianism in Jamaica, see Nettleford's classic *Mirror Mirror*.

53. Interview with Rose Clarke, 30 September 2006.

54. Henry, "Homelessness and a Particular Response Among Young West Indians in Handsworth, Birmingham," 15–30.

55. Hebdige, "Reggae, Rastas and Rudies," 7.

56. On Selassie's visit to Jamaica, see Asserate, *King of Kings*, 257–259.

57. Hebdige, *Cut 'n' Mix*, 75–81.

58. Interview with Basil Gabbidon, 15 July 2009.

59. Hebdige, *Subculture*, 36.

60. For an early example of the mainstream media's interest in reggae, see "Reggae, Reggae, Reggae," *Sunday Times Magazine*, 4 February 1973, front page. For a general overview of subcultures in postwar Britain, see Osgerby, "Youth Culture," in Addison and Jones, eds., *A Companion to Contemporary Britain 1939–2000*, 127–144.

61. Hebdige, *Subculture*, 43.

62. Mercer, "Black Hair/Style Politics," 40–41.

63. Hiro, *Black British, White British*, 72.
64. Hebdige, *Cut 'n' Mix*, 98.
65. Gilroy, "Steppin' Out of Babylon," in CCCS, ed., *The Empire Strikes Back*, 290–292.
66. Barrett, *The Rastafarians*, 139.
67. Hebdige, "Reggae, Rastas and Rudies," 9 and 37–38.
68. Hall, "Negotiating Caribbean Identities," 12.
69. Willory (surname not provided), Trinity Arts Oral History Project, 1984. For an extended sociological study into the relationship between older and younger black generations in Britain, see Pryce, *Endless Pressure*.
70. Interview with Brian Bennett, 22 May 2009.
71. Interview with Brian Bennett, 22 May 2009.
72. C. Sealy, Trinity Arts Oral History Project, 1984.
73. Bob Marley and the Wailers, *Exodus*.
74. Misty in Roots, "Jah Jah Bless Africa," and Aswad, "Back to Africa." "Babylon Makes the Rules" was a track on Steel Pulse's second album, *A Tribute to the Martyrs*.
75. Quoted in Silverton, "No Jah-Bubble in-a Birmingham."
76. Hebdige, "Reggae, Rastas and Rudies," 12.
77. Gilroy, "You Can't Fool the Youths," 216.
78. Basil Gabbidon, quoted in Velk, *Handsworth Evolution*.
79. Interview with Basil Gabbidon, 15 July 2009. Jonathan Dimbleby's influential documentary *Ethiopia: the Unknown Famine* was broadcast on ITV in 1973.
80. Hebdige, *Cut 'n' Mix*, 100.
81. Steel Pulse, *Handsworth Revolution*.
82. Quoted in Silverton, "No Jah-Bubble in-a Birmingham."
83. Steel Pulse, *Handsworth Revolution*.
84. Gilroy, *There Ain't No Black in the Union Jack*, 168; and De Koningh and Griffiths, *Tighten Up!*, 210. For an online archive of material relating to defunct Birmingham music venues, see www.birminghammusicarchive.com/ (accessed 1 August 2017).
85. Interview with Amlak Tafari, 22 May 2009.
86. Gilroy, *There Ain't No Black in the Union Jack*, 18; and Stolzoff, *Wake the Town and Tell the People*, 99.
87. Wood, "'A Design for Social Living,'" in Macpherson et al., eds., *Sub/versions*, 165; and Stolzoff, *Wake the Town and Tell the People*, 41.
88. See, for example, "Police Clamp Down on Shebeens," *Birmingham Post*, 19 September 1969, quoted in Morris, ed., *Vanley Burke*, 134.
89. Bishton and Reardon, *Home Front*, 37. On the ritualized nature of sound system clashes in Jamaica, see Stolzoff, *Wake the Town and Tell the People*, 8–9.
90. Promotional flier, Birmingham, 28 May 1979, Digbeth Civic Hall. This flier was obtained by the author from John Dalton, a community arts worker who in the early 1980s was helping James Brown, a cricketer at Handsworth Cricket Club, write his memoirs. Brown had attempted to handwrite his memoirs on the back of these fliers. There is a full discussion of the importance of cricket in black Handsworth in chapter 4 of this book.
91. Tyler, "Dawn of the Dread."
92. Stolzoff, *Wake the Town and Tell the People*, 55.

93. See Rush, *Bonds of Empire*, 45.

94. Johnson sketched an early idea of what "dub poetry" was in relation to the wider reggae scene in an article for *Race and Class*. See Johnson, "Jamaican Rebel Music," 397–412. For an analysis of Johnson's work, see Morris, "A Note on 'Dub Poetry,'" 66–69; and Hitchcock, "'It Dread Inna Inglan,'" 1–11.

95. On Johnson's role in the *Race Today* collective, see Bunce and Field, *Darcus Howe*, 150.

96. Zephaniah, *Rasta*.

97. Zephaniah, *The Dread Affair*, 7, 79.

98. Zephaniah, *The Dread Affair*, 47.

99. Zephaniah, "Propaganda," in *The Dread Affair*, 57.

100. Zephaniah, "African Culture," in *The Dread Affair*, 92.

101. Zephaniah, "Living and Dread," in *The Dread Affair*, 40.

102. See Stolzoff, *Wake the Town and Tell the People*, 185.

103. Zephaniah, "Dis Policeman Keeps on Kicking me to Death," in *The Dread Affair*, 96.

104. Newman, "Exploring Birmingham's Sound System Culture."

105. Interview with Brian Bennett, 22 May 2009. On the conception of clashes in militaristic language, see Stolzoff, *Wake the Town and Tell the People*, 9, 52–53.

106. Michael La Rose, quoted in Harris and White, eds. *Changing Britannia*, 126.

107. Interview with Brian Bennett, 22 May 2009.

108. Interview with Brian Bennett, 22 May 2009.

109. Interview with Ras Tread, 12 June 2009.

110. On sound system crews, see Stolzoff, *Wake the Town and Tell the People*, 198.

111. Interview with Ras Tread, 12 June 2009.

112. Interview with Brian Bennett, 22 May 2009.

113. Interview with Ras Tread, 12 June 2009.

114. Interview with Ras Tread, 12 June 2009.

115. Gilroy, *There Ain't No Black in the Union Jack*, 170.

116. Interview with Ras Tread, 12 June 2009; and Bishton and Reardon, *Home Front*, 101.

117. Interview with Ras Tread, 12 June 2009.

118. Basil Gabbidon, quoted in "The Basil Gabbidon Story."

119. Dudrah, "Drum 'n' Dhol," 375; and Dudrah, *Bhangra*, 14.

120. On Kapur's work as a form of "intermezzo" culture, see Back, "X Amount of *Sat Siri Akal!*," in Harris and Rampton, eds., *The Language, Ethnicity and Race Reader*, 329. On "multicultural drift," see Hall, "From Scarman to Stephen Lawrence," 186.

121. Quoted in Plummer, *Movement of Jah People*, 48.

122. Interview with Ursula Walker, 8 July 2009.

123. The silence of the early sociologies of subcultures about the place of women and girls was highlighted by McRobbie, "Settling Accounts with Subcultures," in Bennett et al., eds., *Culture, Ideology and Social Process*, 111–123. On the overemphasis on generational schisms in accounts of Rastafarianism, see Gilroy, "Steppin' Out of Babylon," 293.

124. On the misogynistic elements within the Jamaican dance-hall music of the 1990s, see Stolzoff, *Wake the Town and Tell the People*, 109–110.

125. On Lovers' Rock specifically, see Hebdige, *Cut 'n' Mix*, 129; and Palmer, "'Ladies A Your Time Is Now!,'" 177–192.

126. Dennis, *Behind the Frontlines*, 103; and Campbell, "Rastafari," 18.

127. In the mid-1990s the most popular woman DJ in Jamaica was Lady Shaw. The first years of the twenty-first century witnessed the appearance of an increasing number of women MCs in the UK hip-hop, garage, and grime scenes. Alongside Leshurr, this included the London-based artists Ms. Dynamite and Lady Sovereign. See May, "Nothing Like Words Spoken," 611–649.

128. Hebdige, *Cut 'n' Mix*, 100.

129. Hall, "Negotiating Caribbean Identities," 13.

CHAPTER 4. LEISURE AND SOCIABILITY

1. James, *Beyond a Boundary*, 88, 159; and James, "Rohan Kanhai". See also James, "Garfield Sobers," in Grimshaw, ed., *The CLR James Reader*, 379–389.

2. In the 1930s James had coestablished the International Africa Friends of Ethiopia campaign group in London, and was an active player in London's "black internationalist" scene. See Matera, *Black London*, 62–63. James was expelled from the United States in 1953. There are numerous biographies of his life; see, for example, Dhondy, *CLR James*; and Renton, *CLR James*.

3. As Bill Schwarz has noted, the similarities between James's interests and cultural studies were present in James' earlier work, at least in his 1949–1950 work on American popular culture, eventually published as *American Civilisation*. See Schwarz, "Black Metropolis, White England," 193. See also Howe, "C. L. R. James," in Schwarz, ed., *West Indian Intellectuals in Britain*, 153–174; and Smith, "'Beyond a Boundary,'" 95–112.

4. James, *Beyond a Boundary*, 34, 36, 81.

5. On the nebulousness of the everyday and the problem this poses for its analysis, see Highmore, *Everyday Life and Cultural Theory*, 1–16.

6. Clarke, "Defending Ski-Jumpers," in Gray et al., eds., *CCCS Selected Working Papers*, 2:231.

7. Rosenwein, *Emotional Communities in the Early Middle*, 24. On emotional communities in a contemporary British context, see Barron and Langhamer, "Feeling through Practice," 3.

8. Rush, *Bonds of Empire*, 2. On the tendency to overlook the importance of this ideology to immigrant generations, see Howe, "C. L. R. James." See also Schwarz, "Crossing Seas," in Schwarz, ed., *West Indian Intellectuals in Britain*, 7, 12.

9. On the changing nature of the West Indian identity, see Hall, "What Is a West Indian?," in Schwarz, ed., *West Indian Intellectuals in Britain*, 31–50. On residual colonial Victorianism, see Gikandi, "The Embarrassment of Victorianism," in Kucich and Sadoff, eds., *Victorian Afterlife*, 158.

10. As has been argued, a much larger proportion of postwar immigration from the Caribbean was middle class in nature than has commonly been recognized. See Rush, *Bonds of Empire*, 12.

11. Bourdieu, *Distinction*; and Bourdieu, *The Logic of Practice*.

12. Collins, "Pride and Prejudice," 403.

13. James, "Immigrants to Britain," 15–16.

14. Brown, "Continental Cricket Club" (ca. 1980), 1. The memoirs were submitted in handwritten form to Trinity Arts Centre in Small Heath, Birmingham, in the early 1980s, and were obtained by the author from John Dalton, a former employee of the center.

15. On working-class memoirists see Jones, *The Working Class in Mid-Twentieth-Century England*, 36. On the "ordinary" in working-class narratives, see Savage, Bagnall, and Longhurst, "Ordinary, Ambivalent and Defensive," 875–892.

16. Constantine, *Cricketers' Carnival*, 79. For an assessment of Constantine's pioneering spell in the Lancashire town of Nelson in the 1930s, see Calder, "A Man for All Cultures," 19–42.

17. Interview with Francis Nation, 12 December 2009.

18. McKibbin, *Classes and Cultures*, 335–337; Holt, *Sport and the British*, 98–99.

19. James, *Beyond a Boundary*, 34. James was educated at Queen's Royal College in Port of Spain.

20. McKibbin, *Classes and Cultures*, 338; and Holt, *Sport and the British*, 222.

21. Midgett, "Cricket and Calypso," 244.

22. "The Fourth Test Match," *Times*, 16 Aug 1950, 7.

23. Phillips and Phillips, *Windrush*, 95 and 102–103. On the relationship between cricket and calypso music, see Midgett, "Cricket and Calypso," 241; and Westall, "'This Thing Goes Beyond the Boundary,'" in Bateman and Bale, eds., *Sporting Sounds*, 222–236.

24. Austin, *Urban Life in Kingston, Jamaica*, 123.

25. Hall with Schwarz, *Familiar Stranger*, 27.

26. Interview with Francis Nation, 12 December 2009. On black cricket clubs as a form of resistance, see Carrington, "Sport, Masculinity and Black Cultural Resistance," 284.

27. Midgett, "Cricket and Calypso," 241; Schwarz, "Crossing Seas," 13. On the West Indian Federation specifically, see Duke, *Building a Nation*.

28. James, "Rohan Kanhai"; and Burton, *Afro-Creole*, 184.

29. Holt, *Sport and the British*, 222; Midgett, "Cricket and Calypso," 40; and Burton, *Afro-Creole*, 183–184.

30. Continental Cricket Club, *Handsworth Cricket Trinidad Tour*, 5–7.

31. There are many examples of postwar cricketing journalism that, prior to the West Indian team's rise to global ascendancy from the mid-1970s onward, presented a narrative of "calypso cricket." See, for example, Manning, "It's Their Job to Entertain Us Before the Real Cricket," 12. See also Williams, *Cricket and Race*, 118; and Lister, *Fire in Babylon*, 58. On the racial stereotypes of cricket journalism in the early twentieth century, see Bateman, *Cricket, Literature and Culture*, 160.

32. Burton, *Afro-Creole*, 179. The seminal anthropological work on Caribbean street culture is Abrahams, *The Man-of-Words in the West Indies*. For an overview of the representation of this culture in the fiction of John and Naipaul, see Westall, "Men in the Yard and on the Street," 1–14.

33. Brown, "Continental Cricket Club," 6; and Handsworth Cricket Club, *Handsworth Cricket Trinidad Tour*, 20.

34. Handsworth Cricket Club, *Handsworth Cricket Trinidad Tour*, 47, 53. On the advertising featured in the *Gazette*, see Schwarz, "Claudia Jones and the *West Indian Gazette*," 277.

35. Williams, *Cricket and England*, 8–9.
36. Handsworth Cricket Club, *Handsworth Cricket Trinidad Tour*, 13, 21.
37. On the ethnic makeup of South Asian clubs, see Williams, *Cricket and Race*, 176.
38. Duke, *Building a Nation*, 5 and 25. There is evidence of similar processes among Caribbean migrants to the United States. See Kasinitz, *Caribbean New York*, 56–57.
39. James, "Migration, Racism and Identity Formation," 240.
40. Viv Richards, quoted in Handsworth Cricket Club, *Handsworth Cricket Trinidad Tour*, 11.
41. Interview with Frances Nation, 12 December 2009.
42. Carrington, "Sport, Masculinity and Black Cultural Resistance," 290.
43. Interview with Frances Nation, 12 December 2009.
44. Brown, "Continental Cricket Club," 7.
45. Smith, "Fearsome Four Have No Regrets," 29.
46. Viv Richards, quoted in Williams, *Cricket and Race*, 135, and in Riley, *Fire in Babylon*. See also Westall, "Men in the Yard and on the Street," 9.
47. Michael Holding, quoted in Riley, *Fire in Babylon*.
48. For example, Burton, *Afro-Creole*, 18; and Tiffin, "Cricket, Literature and the Politics of Decolonisation," in Beckles and Stoddard, eds., *Liberation Cricket*, 367.
49. James, *Beyond a Boundary*, 51–52.
50. Interview with Frances Nation, 12 December 2009.
51. Brown, "Continental Cricket Club," 7.
52. James, *Beyond a Boundary*, 34.
53. Interview with Frances Nation, 12 December 2009; interview with Johnson Gowane, 16 September 2011; and interview with Len Gidden, 18 January 2010.
54. Schwarz, "Crossing Seas," 7; and Rush, *Bonds of Empire*, 2.
55. H. Sutcliffe (1933), quoted in Williams, *Cricket and England*, 2; and interview with Frances Nation, 12 December 2009.
56. Evans, *Afro-Creole*, 160.
57. Mass Observation, *The Pub and the People*, 301–302.
58. Austin, "Culture and Ideology in the English-Speaking Caribbean," 231. On the history of dominoes more generally, see Taylor, *Played at the Pub*, 144. See also *Caribbean Domino Club*.
59. Interview with Burt Williams, 12 October 2011; and interview with Anita Witter, 17 June 2006.
60. Taylor, *Played at the Pub*, 147; and interview with Burt Williams, 12 October 2011.
61. Interview with Roy Richards, 18 June 2010; interview with Anita Witter, 17 June 2006; and *Caribbean Domino Club*.
62. Austin, "Culture and Ideology in the English-Speaking Caribbean," 231; and Taylor, *Played at the Pub*, 148.
63. Interview with Burt Williams, 12 October 2011; interview with Roy Richards, 18 June 2010; and interview with Len Gidden, 18 January 2010.
64. Interview with Johnson Gowane, 16 September 2011.
65. Interview with Johnson Gowane, 16 September 2011.
66. *Caribbean Domino Club*.

67. See, for example, Hey, *Patriarchy and Pub Culture*. For an account that examines women drinkers in public houses during World War II, see Langhamer, "'A Public House Is for All Classes, Men and Women Alike,'" 423–443.

68. Anonymous interviewee, 12 October 2011; interview with J. Gowane, 16 September 2011; and *Caribbean Domino Club*.

69. Interview with Don Williams, 12 October 2011.

70. Murphy, *Tales from Two Cities*, 214–217.

71. Henry, "The Growth of Corporate Black Identity Among Afro-Caribbean People in Birmingham, England," 443.

72. Murphy, *Tales from Two Cities*, 217.

73. Interview with Roy Richards, 18 June 2010; and interview with Althea Crawford, 13 June 2011.

74. *Caribbean Domino Club*.

75. Henry, "The Growth of Corporate Black Identity Among Afro-Caribbean People in Birmingham, England," 443.

76. See Phillips and Phillips, *Windrush*, 99–100; and O'Connell, *Credit and Community*, 227–230. See also Bryan, Dadzie, and Scafe, *The Heart of the Race*, 131.

77. O'Connell, *Credit and Community*, 229.

78. This is the date given for the league's establishment by its secretary, Althea Crawford. In other places the date is given as 1992.

79. Davies, "Pub Games".

80. R. Taylor, quoted in *Caribbean Domino Club*.

81. Interview with Andrea Williams, 16 September 2010. On the growing number of women players, see Taylor, *Played at the Pub*, 149; and Davies, "Pub Games."

82. Elkes, "Angry Planners Approve Handsworth Pub's Conversion into Mosque."

83. Anglo-Caribbean Dominoes League and Guinness, "The Domino Effect," 1, 17.

84. Interview with Althea Crawford, 13 June 2011; and interview with Johnson Gowane, 16 September 2011.

85. Murphy, *Tales from Two Cities*, 160–166.

86. Hill, "From Church to Sect," 114.

87. Rush, *Bonds of Empire*, 52.

88. See Parsons, "Filling a Void?," in Parsons, ed., *The Growth of Religious Diversity*, 1:246–247.

89. Anderson, "Writing the Pentecostal History of Africa, Asia and Latin America," 141; and Austin, *Urban Life in Kingston, Jamaica*, 107.

90. O'Brien and Church of England, *Faith in the City of Birmingham*, 26.

91. On the emergence of mosques in Birmingham, see, for example, Gale, "The Multicultural City and the Politics of Religious Architecture," 30–44.

92. Interview with Gerald Edmund, February 2011; and Bethel Church, "Congratulations on Your Golden Jubilee," 2

93. Parsons, "Filling a Void?," 246–247; Clarke, "Old Wine and New Skins," 147. For an early sociology of black Pentecostal churches in Britain, see Calley, *God's People*.

94. Rex and Tomlinson, *Colonial Immigrants in a British City*, 264–265.

95. Reddie, "Faith, Stories and the Experience of Black Elders," in Jagessar and Reddie, eds., *Black Theology in Britain*, 56.

96. Pryce, *Endless Pressure*, 198–199; Murphy, *Tales from Two Cities*, 160–16; and Hill, "From Church to Sect," 118.

97. Rex and Tomlinson, *Colonial Immigrants in a British City*, 265.

98. Parsons, "Filling a Void?," 253–255; Toulis, *Believing Identity*, 80; and "Sister Louis," quoted in Toulis, *Believing Identity*, 201.

99. Anonymous speakers, quoted in Smith, "Mary in the Kitchen, Martha in the Pew,", 67, 97; Pryce, *Endless Pressure*, 208; and Toulis, *Believing Identity*, 115.

100. Interview with Esme Mignott, 8 June 2011.

101. Toulis, *Believing Identity*, 197–198.

102. Hill, "From Church to Sect," 116; Austin, *Urban Life in Kingston, Jamaica*, 104; Toulis, *Believing Identity*, 101; and Rush, *Bonds of Empire*, 53.

103. See Lancaster, *My Journeys Through Life*, 123–132.

104. Henry, "The Growth of Corporate Black Identity Among Afro-Caribbean People in Birmingham, England," 403.

105. Langhamer, *Women's Leisure in England 1920–1960*.

106. Alexander, "'A Mouse in a Jungle,'" in Jarrett-Macauley, ed., *Reconstructing Womanhood, Reconstructing Feminism*, 87–89. See also Bryan, Dadzie, and Scafe, *The Heart of the Race*, 131–132.

107. Toulis, *Believing Identity*, 231–233; Parsons, "Filling a Void?," 251; and Alexander, "'A Mouse in a Jungle,'" 96.

108. Toulis, *Believing Identity*, 233.

109. In 1999 it was estimated that 75 percent of the pastors in the New Testament Church of God, for example, were aged fifty-five or above. See Clarke, "Old Wine and New Skins," 149.

110. Interview with Icilda Smith, Cannon Street Memorial Baptist Church Oral History Project, 2006 (MM-025); and interview with K. Gordon, Cannon Street Memorial Baptist Church Oral History Project, 2006 (MM-032).

111. Interview with K. Gordon, Cannon Street Memorial Baptist Church Oral History Project, 2006 (MM-032).

112. Parsons, "Filling a Void?," 251.

113. Murphy, *Tales from Two Cities*, 169. See also James, "Migration, Racism and Identity Formation," 254.

114. Wood, "Matthew 7, Verse 1," in Ross and Brissett, eds., *Whispers in the Walls*, 37.

115. Interview with Jacko Rankin, 9 June 2011; and interview with D. Smith, Cannon Street Memorial Baptist Church Oral History Project, 2006 (MM-004).

116. Brown, *Religion and Society in Twentieth-Century Britain*, 291.

117. Interview with Esme Mignott, 8 June 2011. See Rush, *Bonds of Empire*, 10, 52.

118. Hall, "Reconstruction Work," 106–113.

119. For a detailed discussion of this studio photography, see Courtman, "A Journey through the Imperial Gaze," 139; Newman, "Harry Jacobs," in Ashton and Kean, eds., *People and Their Pasts*, 260–270; Hall, "Reconstruction Work," 254; Connell, "Photographing Handsworth," 128–152.

120. Campt, "Imagining Diaspora," 5.

121. Hill, "From Church to Sect," 120–121.

122. Interview with Merisse Crooks, 25 August 2011.

123. Cohen, *Household Gods*, 121 and 125; Giles, *The Parlour and the Suburb*, 18.

124. Interview with Esme Mignott, 8 June 2011.
125. Rex and Tomlinson, *Colonial Immigrants in a British City*, 145–147.
126. Austin, *Urban Life in Kingston, Jamaica*, 43, 76.
127. Clarke, "Letters A Yard," in Ross and Brissett, eds., *Whispers in the Walls*, 18.
128. In the early 1980s the Polaroid One-Step had become the most-sold camera in the world. See Buse, "Polaroid into Digital," 218.
129. Quoted in Webster, *Imagining Home*, 165.
130. Tolla-Kelly, "Locating Processes of Identification," 317.
131. Murphy, *Tales from Two Cities*, 163.
132. Interview with Esme Mignott, 8 June 2011.
133. Interview with James Pogson, 21 November 2011.
134. Highmore, *The Great Indoors*, 26.
135. On the business rationale behind Tupperware parties see, for example, Cialdini, "Harnessing the Science of Persuasion," 74. On the history of the Tupperware party, see Bax, "Entrepreneur Brownie Wise," 171–180.
136. Interview with James Pogson, 21 November 2011
137. Hoggart, *The Uses of Literacy*, 35.
138. Noble, "'A Room of Her Own,'" in McMillan, ed., *The Front Room*, 89.
139. Interview with Jacko Rankin, 9 June 2011; and interview with Joe Aldred, 22 June 2011.
140. McMillan, "The 'West Indian' Front Room," 64.
141. Interview with James Pogson, 21 November 2011
142. Hall, "The 'West Indian' Front Room," in M. McMillan, ed., *The Front Room*, 23.
143. See Webster, *Imagining Home*, 123–127.
144. See Langhamer, *Women's Leisure in England*, 134.
145. Perry, *London Is the Place for Me*, 78. See also Noble, "'A Room of Her Own,'" 88.
146. For a discussion of Boyce's work, see Chambers, *Black Artists in British Art*, 143.
147. Webster, *Imagining Home*, 131; and McMillan, "The 'West Indian' Front Room," 53.
148. McMillan, "The 'West Indian' Front Room," 67.
149. Schaffer, *The Vision of a Nation*, 211. See also Schaffer, "*Till Death Do Us Part* and the BBC," 454–477; Long, "Representing Race, and Place," 262–277; and Bebber, "*Till Death Us Do Part*," 253–274.
150. Abbensetts, *Empire Road*, 93, 106.
151. Noble, "'A Room of Her Own,'" 89.
152. Abbensetts, *Empire Road*, 106.
153. Hall, "The 'West Indian' Front Room," 20.
154. McMillan, "The 'West Indian' Front Room," 50.
155. Mrs. Brown, Leticia, and Anonymous, in *The West Indian Front Room* comments book, Geffrye Museum of the Home exhibition archives, London; and 'Kunjufu', User on Blacknet forum, www.bnvillage.co.uk/village-square/79543-west-indian-front-room.html (accessed 28 July 2011);
156. Interview with Merisse Crooks, 25 August 2012.
157. Grant, Levine, and Trentmann, introduction to *Beyond Sovereignty*, 2–3.
158. R. Butcher, quoted in Smith, "Roland the First."

159. James, "Immigrants to Britain," 191.

160. Perry, *London Is the Place for Me*, 49.

161. See Phillips and Phillips, *Windrush*, and the accompanying television series of the same name. For an anthropological study of a Muslim diasporic formation in Britain, see, for example, Werbner, *Imagined Diasporas among Manchester Muslims*.

162. Schwarz, "Crossing Seas," 3; and Schwarz, "Black Metropolis, White England," 194.

EPILOGUE

1. James, "Immigrants to Britain," 15–16.

2. See Trilling, *Bloody Nasty People*; and Ford and Goodwin, *Revolt on the Right*. On Farage's admiration for Powell, see Mason, "Nigel Farage Backs 'Basic Principle' of Enoch Powell's Immigration Warning."

3. Gilroy, *After Empire?*.

4. "Theresa May's Conference Speech in Full.". See also Hutton, "Never Before in My Adult Life Has the Future Seemed So Bleak for Progressives."

5. Gilroy, *After Empire?*, 5, 76, 89.

6. Amin, "Ethnicity and the Multicultural City," 959–980; Wise and Velayutham, *Everyday Multiculturalism*; Neal et al., "Living Multiculture," 308–323. For a European perspective, see Buettner, *Europe After Empire*, 412–414.

7. Stuart Hall, quoted in *The Stuart Hall Project*.

8. On the significance of the terrorist attacks in Europe to perceptions of multiculturalism and the increasingly "civilisational" register of these debates, see Chin, "Turkish Women, West German Feminists, and the Gendered Discourse on Muslim Cultural Difference," 557–581; and Chin, *The Crisis of Multiculturalism in Europe*.

9. On the enduring problem of housing in Handsworth, see Cole and Ferrari, "Connectivity of Place and Housing," in Flint and Robertson, eds., *Community Cohesion in Crisis?*, 57–79. On the 2005 riots in Handsworth/Lozells specifically, see Vulliamy, "Rumours of a Riot.". For the landmark report on the Metropolitan Police's handling of the Lawrence murder, see Macpherson *The Stephen Lawrence Inquiry*. For an overview of the profound inequalities facing ethnic minorities more generally at the turn of the millennium, see Parekh, *The Future of Multi-Ethnic Britain*.

10. Hall with Schwarz, *Familiar Stranger*, 199.

BIBLIOGRAPHY

ARCHIVAL COLLECTIONS

Asian Resource Centre, 110 Hamstead Road, Handsworth
    Committee meeting minutes, financial records, and other material relating to the
Darryl Georgiou collection (https://artslabinternational.com)
    Photographic material relating to "'Hinterland: B21,'" 1981–1990 project
Geffrye Museum of the Home, London
    The West Indian Front Room exhibition material
Institute for Race Relations Black History Collection, London
    Files relating to community groups in Handsworth.
Library of Birmingham
    All Faiths for One Race papers
    Avtar Jouhl and the Indian Workers' Association papers
    Banner Theatre of Actuality papers
    Birmingham City Council papers
    Cadbury Trust Papers
    Derek Bishton archive
    Indian Workers' Association papers
    Local newspaper archives
    Vanley Burke Archive
    West Midlands County Council papers
Margaret Thatcher Foundation archive
Media Archive of Central England, University of Lincoln
    Local news report archives
National Archive, Kew Gardens
    Birmingham Community Relations Council papers and bid applications

National Resource Centre for Dance, University of Surrey
    Kokuma Dance Company papers, publicity material, and videos
Tandana Asian Youth Movement Archive (http://www.tandana.org/archives)
    Antideportation campaign leaflets
    Copies of *Asian Youth News*
Trinity Arts Centre, Birmingham
    James Brown, "Continental Cricket Club." Unpublished memoir, ca. 1980.
    Trinity Arts Oral History Project, 1984

NEWSPAPERS AND PERIODICALS

Birmingham Evening Mail
Birmingham Post
Daily Express
Daily Mail
Daily Mirror
Evening Dispatch
Express and Star
The Guardian
The Sun
The Sunday Times
Time Out
The Times

ORAL HISTORIES

Existing Collections

Birmingham Black Oral History Project, 1990
Cannon Street Memorial Baptist Church Oral History Project, Handsworth, 2005
"Millennibrum" Oral History Project, Birmingham City Council, 2000

Conducted by the Author

Joe Aldred, 22 June 2011
Maurice Andrews, 16 June 2010
Bhopinder Basi, 20 January 2010
Errol Beaumont, 7 May 2011
Brian Bennett, 22 May 2009
Anil Bhalla, 6 February 2010
Derek Bishton, 1 February 2009
Bini Brown, 15 December 2009
Vanley Burke, 25 March 2008
Eric Cameron, 28 September 2006
Maeve Clarke, 26 June 2011
Rose Clarke, 30 September 2006

Althea Crawford, 13 June 2011
Merisse Crooks, 25 August 2011
Bishop Gerald Edmund, 9 February 2011
Basil Gabbidon, 15 July 2009
Len Gidden, 18 January 2010
Milton Godfrey, 28 May 2009
Johnson Gowane, 16 September 2011
Surinder Guru, 9 March 2011
Jackie Guy, 7 May 2009
John Hick, 6 May 2009
Brian Homer, 27 February 2009
Pete James, 12 June 2009
Steven Kapur (aka Apache Indian), 14 October 2009
Tony Martin, 12 March 2011
Esme Mignott, 8 June 2011
Lord Bill Morris, 13 November 2008
Francis Nation, 12 December 2009
James Pogson, 21 November 2011
Bob Ramdhanie, 18 February 2009
Jacko Rankin (aka Jacko Melody), 9 June 2011
Roy Richards, 18 June 2010
Chris Rogers, 3 October 2009
Dave Rogers, 26 May 2009
Clare Short, 13 February 2009
Norman Smith, 5 January 2007
Ranjit Sondhi, 11 May 2009
Amlak Tafari, 22 May 2009
Ras Tread (formerly Colin Braham), 12 June 2009
Lord David Waddington, 16 June 2011
Yugesh Walia, 16 November 2009
Barbara Walker, 17 June 2011
Ursula Walker (née Lawrence Lawrence), 8 July 2009
Andrea Williams, 16 September 2011
Bert Williams, 16 September 2011
Don Williams, 12 October 2011
Anita Witter, 17 June 2011
Benjamin Zephaniah, 20 May 2009

FILM, TELEVISION, AND MUSIC

Aswad, "Back to Africa," *Aswad* (Mango Records, 1976).
Babylon (Franco Rosso, 1980).
Black Christmas (BBC Television, 1977).
Empire Road (BBC Television, 1978–1979).

Fire in Babylon (Stevan Riler, 2010).
Handsworth Songs (John Akomfrah,1987).
Inside Out, West Midlands (BBC television, October 2010).
Bob Marley and the Wailers, *Catch a Fire* (Island Records, 1973).
———, *Exodus* (Island Records, 1977).
Misty in Roots. "Jah Jah Bless Africa" (People Unite, 1981).
Judy Mowatt, *Black Woman* (Shanachie, 1980).
Steel Pulse, *Handsworth Revolution* (Island Records,1978).
———, *A Tribute to the Martyrs* (Mango Records, 1979).
———, *Caught You* (Mango Records, 1980).
———, *True Democracy* (Elektra, 1982).
———, *Babylon the Bandit* (Mango Records, 1986).
The Stuart Hall Project (John Akomfrah, 2013).
African Oasis (Yugesh Walia, 1982). (Birmingham Film Workshop, 1982).
Benjamin Zephaniah, *Rasta* (Upright, 1982).

WORKS CITED

Abbensetts, Michael. *Empire Road*. St. Albans: Granada Publishing, 1979.
Abernethy, Graeme. "'Not Just an American Problem': Malcolm X in Britain." *Atlantic Studies* 7, no. 3 (2010): 285–307.
Abrahams, Roger D. *The Man-of-Words in the West Indies*. Baltimore, MD, and London: Johns Hopkins University Press, 1983.
Adewole, Funmi, Dick Matchett, and Colin Prescod, eds. *Voicing Black Dance: The British Experience, 1930s–1990s*. London: The Association of Dance and the African Diaspora, 2007.
Adi, Hakim. *Pan-Africanism and Communism: The Communist International, Africa and the Diaspora, 1919–1939*. Trenton, NJ: Africa World Press, 2013.
Akomfrah, John. "Black Independent Film-Making: A Statement by the Black Audio Film Collective," 1983. In *The Ghosts of Songs: The Film art of the Black Audio Film Collective, 1982–1998*, edited by Kodwo Eshun and Anjalika Sagar, 144–145. Liverpool: Liverpool University Press, 2007.
Alexander, Valentina. "'A Mouse in a Jungle': The Black Christian Woman's Experience in the Church and Society in Britain." In *Reconstructing Womanhood, Reconstructing Feminism*, edited by Delia Jarrett-Macauley, 87–110. London and New York: Routledge, 1996.
All Faiths for One Race (AFFOR) and Carlton Green. *Talking Blues: The Black Community Speaks about Its Relationship with the Police*. Birmingham, UK: AFFOR, 1978.
All Faiths for One Race (AFFOR), Laxmi Jamdaigni, Mal Phillips-Bell, and Job Ward. *Talking Chalk: Black Pupils, Parents and Teachers Speak about Education*. Birmingham, UK: AFFOR, 1982.
Allberson, T. "Visualizing Wartime Destruction and Postwar Reconstruction: Herbert Mason's Photograph of St. Paul's Reevaluated." *Journal of Modern History* 87, no. 3 (2015): 532–578.
Ames, Eric. *Carl Hagenbeck's Empire of Entertainments*. Seattle: University of Washington Press, 2009.

Amin, Ash. "Ethnicity and the Multicultural City: Living with Diversity." *Environment and Planning A* 34 (2002): 959–980.
Anderson, Allan. "Writing the Pentecostal History of Africa, Asia and Latin America." *Journal of Beliefs and Values* 25, no. 2 (2004): 139–151.
Anderson, Benedict. *Imagined Communities: Reflections on the Origin and Spread of Nationalism*. London: Verso, 1983.
Anderson, Hurvin. *Reporting Back*. Birmingham, UK: Ikon Gallery, 2013.
Andrews, G. "Inner-City Schemes to Get 10m Cash Boost." *Guardian*, 28 April 1987.
Andrews, Kehinde. "The Problem of Political Blackness: Lessons from the Black Supplementary School Movement." *Ethnic and Racial Studies* 39, no. 11 (2016): 2060–2078.
Angelo, Anne-Marie. "The Black Panthers in London, 1967–1972: A Diasporic Struggle Navigates the Black Atlantic." *Radical History Review* 103 (2009): 17–35.
Anglo-Caribbean Dominoes League and Guinness. "The Domino Effect." Promotional leaflet, ca. 2000.
Asserate, Asfa-Wossen. *King of Kings: The Triumph and Tragedy of Emperor Haile Selassie I of Ethiopia*. London: Faber, 2015.
Attie, David. *Russian Self-Portraits*. London: Thames and Hudson, 1977.
Auguiste, Reece. "*Handsworth Songs*: Some Background Notes." *Framework*, no. 35 (1988): 4–8.
Austin, Diane. J. "Culture and Ideology in the English-Speaking Caribbean: A View from Jamaica." *American Ethnologist* 10, no. 2 (1983): 223–240.
———. *Urban Life in Kingston, Jamaica: The Culture and Class Ideology of the Two Neighbourhoods*. New York: Gordon and Breach Science Publishers, 1984.
Back, Les. "X Amount of *Sat Siri Akal*! Apache Indian, Reggae Music and Intermezzo Culture," 1995. In *The Language, Ethnicity and Race Reader*, edited by Roxy Harris and Ben Rampton, 328–345. London and New York: Routledge, 2003.
Bailey, Roy, and Mike Brake, eds. *Radical Social Work*. London: Edward Arnold, 1975.
Bailkin, Jordanna. *The Afterlife of Empire*. Berkeley: University of California Press, 2012.
Ball, Wendy, and John Solomos, eds. *Race and Local Politics*. Basingstoke: Macmillan, 1990.
Bannister, A. "Coventry Photographer Masterji Gets 'New Lease of Life' after First Exhibition Aged 94." *Coventry Telegraph*, 19 November 2016. Accessed 31 July 2017. www.coventrytelegraph.net/incoming/coventry-photographer-masterji-gets-new-12201203.
Barker, Martin. *The New Racism: Conservatives and the Ideology of the Tribe*. London: Junction Books, 1981.
Barrett, Leonard. *The Rastafarians*. Boston: Beacon Press, 1988.
Barron, Hester, and Claire Langhamer. "Feeling through Practice: Subjectivity and Emotion in Children's Writing." *Journal of Social History* 51, no. 1 (2016): 1–23.
Barthes, Roland. *Camera Lucida*. London: Flamingo, 1984.
"Basil Gabbidon Story, The." 2006. Accessed 26 May 2011. http://andybrouwer.co.uk/basil.html.
Bateman, Anthony. *Cricket, Literature and Culture*. Farnham: Ashgate, 2009.
Bax, Christina E. "Entrepreneur Brownie Wise: Selling Tupperware to America's Women in the 1950s." *Journal of Women's History* 22, no. 2 (2010): 171–180.
BBC. "Handsworth Riots: How Deep are the Scars 25 Years On?" October 25, 2010. Accessed 12 October 2011. http://news.bbc.co.uk/local/birmingham/hi/people_and_places/news id_9118000/9118723.stm.

Bebber, Brett. "*Till Death Us Do Part*: Political Satire and Social Realism in the 1960s and 1970s." *Historical Journal of Film, Radio and Television* 34, no. 2 (2014): 253–274.
Beckles, Colin A. "'We Shall Not Be Terrorized Out of Existence': The Political Legacy of England's Black Bookshops." *Journal of Black Studies* 29, no. 1 (1998): 51–72.
Bell, Amy Helen. *Murder Capital: Suspicious Deaths in London, 1933–53*. Manchester: Manchester University Press, 2015.
Berger, John. *About Looking*. London: Writers and Readers, 1980.
Bergman, Jim, and Bernard Coard. "Trials and Tribulations of a Self-Help Group." *Race Today* 4, no. 4 (1972): 112–114.
Bethel Church. "Congratulations on Your Golden Jubilee." Pamphlet produced for the Bethel United Church of Jesus Christ by *The Voice* newspaper, 18 July 2005.
Bhattacharyya, Gargi. *Across All Boundaries: 25 Years of the Asian Resource Centre in Birmingham*. Birmingham, UK: Asian Resource Centre, 2003. Accessed 22 October 2011. www.asianresource.org.uk/anniv-book.pdf.
Bhavnani, R., Paul Gilroy, Stuart Hall, Herman Ouseley, and Keith Vaz. *A Different Reality: An Account of Black People's Experiences and Their Grievances before and after the Handsworth Rebellions of 1985*. Birmingham, UK: West Midlands County Council, 1986.
Birmingham City Council. *Handsworth/Soho/Lozells: Inner Area Study 1985/6*. Birmingham, UK: Birmingham City Council, 1986.
Birmingham Evening Mail. "Independence Day Festival." 6 June 1977, 4.
Birmingham Museums and Art Gallery. *Birmingham Arts Lab: The Phantom of Liberty*. Birmingham, UK: Birmingham Museum and Art Gallery, 1998.
Bishton, Derek. "Handsworth Self Portrait Project." *Ten.8 Photographic Magazine* 4 (Spring 1980): 3–4.
———. "Local Colour." *Sunday Times Magazine*, 21 September 1980, 96.
———. *Black Heart Man: A Journey into Rasta*. London: Chatto and Windus, 1986.
Bishton, Derek, and Brian Homer. "People Power?" *Ten.8 Photographic Magazine* 1 (February 1979): 6–7.
Bishton, Derek, and John Reardon. *Home Front*. London: Jonathan Cape, 1984.
Bloch, Alice, and Liza Schuster. "At the Extremes of Exclusion: Deportation, Detention and Dispersal." *Ethnic and Racial Studies* 28, no. 3 (2005): 495–496.
Bocking-Welch, Anna. *British Civic Society at the End of Empire: Decolonization, Globalization and International Responsibility*. Manchester: Manchester University Press, 2018.
Bourdieu, Pierre. *Distinction: A Social Critique of the Judgment of Taste*. Cambridge, MA: Harvard University Press, 1984.
———. *The Logic of Practice*. Stanford: Stanford University Press, 1990.
Bourne, Jenny. "Cheerleaders and Ombudsman: The Sociology of Race Relations in Britain." *Race and Class* 21 (1979): 331–352.
———. "The Life and Times of Institutional Racism." *Race and Class* 43, no. 2 (2001): 7–22.
Brady, P. "The Fight to Save Harambee." *Voice*, 18 January 2010. Accessed 17 March 2011. www.voice-online.co.uk/content.php?show=16929.
Brah, Avtar. "Difference, Diversity and Differentiation." In *Race, Culture and Difference*, edited by James Donald and Ali Rattansi, 126–145. London: Sage, 1992.
Brocken, Michael. *The British Folk Revivial, 1944–2002*. Aldershot: Ashgate, 2003.

Brooke, Stephen. "Living in 'New Times': Historicizing 1980s Britain." *History Compass* 12, no. 1 (2014): 20–32.
———. "Revisiting Southam Street: Class, Generation, Gender, and Race in the Photography of Roger Mayne." *Journal of British Studies* 53 (2014): 453–496.
———. "Space, Emotions and the Everyday: The Affective Ecology of 1980s London." *Twentieth Century British History* 28, no. 1 (2016): 110–142.
Brown, Callum G. *Religion and Society in Twentieth-Century Britain*. Edinburgh: Pearson Education, 2006.
Brown, Jaqueline Nassey. *Dropping Anchor, Setting Sail: Geographies of Race in Black Liverpool*. Princeton, NJ: Princeton University Press, 2005.
Brown, James. "Continental Cricket Club." Unpublished memoir, ca. 1980.
Brown, John. *A Theory of Police/Immigrant Relations*. Cranfield: Cranfield Institute of Technology, 1974.
———. *Shades of Grey: A Report on Police-West-Indian Relations in Handsworth*. Bedford: Cranfield Institute of Technology, 1977.
———. *Policing by Multi-Racial Consent: The Handsworth Experience*. London: Bedford Square Press, 1982.
Brown, P., and N. Deakin. "The Bleeding Heart of England." *Guardian*, 11 September 1985, 15.
Bryan, Beverly, Stella Dadzie, and Suzanne Scafe. *The Heart of the Race: Black Women's Lives in Britain*. London: Virago, 1985.
Buettner, Elizabeth. *Europe After Empire: Decolonization, Society, and Culture*. Cambridge, UK: Cambridge University Press, 2016.
Bunce, R. E. R., and Paul Field. "Obi B. Egbuna, C. L. R. James and the Birth of Black Power in Britain: Black Radicalism in Britain 1967–72." *Twentieth Century British History* 22, no. 3 (2011): 391–414.
Bunce, Robin, and Paul Field. *Darcus Howe: A Political Biography*. London; New York: Bloomsbury, 2015.
Burke, Vanley. "Artist Statement." *Ten.8 Photographic Magazine*, no. 2 (Summer 1979): 7.
———. "Here I Stand." In *Vanley Burke: A Retrospective*, edited by Mark Sealy, 30–34. London: Lawrence and Wishart, 1993.
Burkett, Jodi. *Constructing Post-Imperial Britain: Britishness, "Race" and the Radical Left in the 1960s*. Basingstoke: Palgrave Macmillan, 2013.
Burton, Antoinette M. *After the Imperial Turn? Thinking with and through the Nation*. Durham, NC: Duke University Press, 2003.
Burton, Richard D. *Afro-Creole: Power, Opposition and Play in the Caribbean*. Ithaca, NY, and London: Cornell University Press, 1997.
Buse, Peter. "Polaroid into Digital: Technology, Cultural Form, and the Social Practices of Snapshot Photography." *Continuum: Journal of Media and Cultural Studies* 24, no. 2 (2010): 215–230.
Caesar, Pogus. *Sparkbrook Pride*. Birmingham, UK: Punch, 2011.
Calder, Angus. "A Man for All Cultures: The Careers of Learie Constantine." *Culture, Sport, Society* 6, no. 1 (2003): 19–42.
Calley, Malcolm J. C. *God's People: West Indian Pentecostal Sects in England*. London and New York: Oxford University Press/Institute for Race Relations, 1965.

Campbell, Horace. "Rastafari: Culture of Resistance." *Race and Class* 22, no. 1 (1980): 1–22.

Campt, Tina. "Imagining Diaspora: Race, Photography, and the Ernest Dyche Archive." *The SemiAnnual Newsletter of the Robert Penn Warren Centre for the Humanities* 16, no. 2 (2008): 1–7.

Carby, Hazel. "White Women Listen! Black Feminism and the Boundaries of Sisterhood." In *The Empire Strikes Back: Race and Racism in Contemporary Britain*, edited by Centre for Contemporary Cultural Studies, 212–235. London: Hutchinson, 1982.

Caribbean Domino Club. BBC Radio 4 documentary, 18 April 2014. Accessed 28 September 2016. www.bbc.co.uk/programmes/b04olthj.

Carrington, Ben. "Sport, Masculinity and Black Cultural Resistance." *Journal of Sport and Social Issues* 22, no. 3 (1998): 275–298.

Carty, Hilary. "Black Dance in England: The Pathway Here." In *Voicing Black Dance: The British Experience, 1930s–1990s*, edited by Funmi Adewole, Dick Matchett, and Colin Prescod, 11. London: The Association of Dance and the African Diaspora, 2007.

Cashmore, Ernest. *Rastaman: The Rastafari movement in England*. 2nd ed. London: Unwin, 1983.

Centre for Contemporary Cultural Studies, ed. *The Empire Strikes Back: Race and Racism in 70s Britain*. London: Hutchinson, 1982.

Chambers, Eddie. *Black Artists in British Art: A History since the 1950s*. London: I. B. Tauris, 2014.

Chapman, Simon. "Welcome to Ikon." In *This Could Happen to You: Ikon in the 1970s*, edited by Jonathan Watkins, 125. Birmingham, UK: Ikon, 2010.

Chin, Rita. "Turkish Women, West German Feminists, and the Gendered Discourse on Muslim Cultural Difference." *Public Culture* 22, no. 3 (2010): 557–581.

———. *The Crisis of Multiculturalism in Europe: A History*. Princeton, NJ: Princeton University Press, 2017.

Cialdini, Robert B. "Harnessing the Science of Persuasion." *Harvard Business Review* (October 2001): 72–79.

Clarke, Clifton R. "Old Wine and New Skins: West Indian and the New North African Pentecostal Churches in Britain and the Challenge of Renewal." *Journal of Pentecostal Theology* 19, no. 1 (2010): 143–154.

Clarke, Gary. "Defending Ski-Jumpers: A Critique of Theories of Youth Sub-cultures," 1981. In *CCCS Selected Working Papers*, edited by Ann Gray, Jan Campbell, Mark Erickson, Stuart Hanson, and Helen Wood, 2:230–256. London: Routledge, 2007.

Clarke, Maeve. "Letters A Yard." In *Whispers in the Walls: New Black and Asian Voices from Birmingham*, edited by Leone Ross and Yvonne Brissett, 13–30. Birmingham, UK: Tindal St Press, 2001.

Coard, Bernard. *How the West Indian Child Is Made Educationally Subnormal in the British School System: The Scandal of the Black Child in Schools in Britain*. London: New Beacon Books, 1971.

Cohen, Deborah. *Household Gods: The British and Their Possessions*. New Haven, CT: Yale University Press, 2006.

Cole, Ian, and Ed Ferrari. "Connectivity of Place and Housing: The Case of Birmingham." In *Community Cohesion in Crisis? New Dimensions of Diversity and Difference*, edited by John Flint and David Robertson, 57–79. Bristol: Policy, 2008.

Collins, Marcus. "Pride and Prejudice: West Indian Men in Mid-Twentieth Century Britain." *Journal of British Studies* 40, no. 3 (2001): 391–418.
Connell, Kieran. "Photographing Handsworth: Photography, Meaning and Identity in a British Inner City." *Patterns of Prejudice* 46, no. 2 (2012): 128–152.
———. "Review Essay: *Policing the Crisis* 35 Years On." *Contemporary British History* 29, no. 2 (2015): 273–283.
———. "Race, Prostitution and the New Left: The Post-war Inner City through Janet Mendelsohn's 'Social Eye.'" *History Workshop Journal* 83, no. 1 (2017): 301–340.
Connell, Kieran, and Matthew Hilton, eds. *50 Years On: The Centre for Contemporary Cultural Studies* (exhibition catalog). Birmingham, UK: Homer Creative, 2014.
———. "The Working Practices of Birmingham's Centre for Contemporary Cultural Studies." *Social History* 40, no. 3 (2015): 287–311.
———, eds. *Cultural Studies 50 Years On*. London: Rowman and Littlefield International, 2016.
Connolly, Clara. "Splintered Sisterhood: Antiracism in a Young Women's Project." *Feminist Review* 36 (Autumn 1990): 52–64.
Constantine, Learie. *Cricketers' Carnival*. London: Stanley Paul, 1948.
Continental Cricket Club. *Handsworth Cricket Trinidad Tour: Official Tour Brochure*. Birmingham, UK: Handsworth Cricket, 1986.
Cook, Alice, and Gwyn Kirk. *Greenham Women Everywhere: Dreams, Ideas and Actions from the Women's Peace Movement*. London: Pluto, 1983.
Corthorn, Paul. *Enoch Powell: Politics and Ideas in Modern Britain*. Oxford: Oxford University Press, 2019.
Cottle, Simon. *TV News, Urban Conflict and the Inner City*. Leicester: Leicester University Press, 1993.
Courtman, Sandra. "What Is Missing from the Picture?" *Wasafiri* 29 (1999): 9–15.
———. "A Journey through the Imperial Gaze: Birmingham's Photographic Collections and Its Caribbean Nexus." In *Visual Culture and Decolonisation in Britain*, edited by Simon Faulkner and Anandi Ramamurthy, 127–153. Aldershot: Ashgate, 2006.
Critcher, Chas. "Action Not Words: Neighbourhood Activism and Cultural Studies." In *Cultural Studies 50 Years On*, edited by Kieran Connell and Matthew Hilton, 247–256. London: Rowman and Littlefield International, 2016.
Critcher, Chas, Margaret Parker, and Ranjit Sondhi. *Race in the Provincial Press—A Case Study of Five West Midlands Newspapers*. Birmingham, UK: University of Birmingham/Centre for Contemporary Cultural Studies, 1975.
Daly, Macdonald, and Alexander George, eds. *Margaret Thatcher in Her Own Words*. Harmondsworth: Penguin, 1987.
Dar, Sarah. "Welfare and Other Activities." Accessed 24 March 2010. www.connectinghistories.org.uk/Learning%20Packages/Social%20Justice/social_justice_lp_02c.asp.
Davies, Dan. "Pub Games: Dominoes." *Time Out*, 9 May 2006. Accessed 29 October 2011. www.timeout.com/london/features/307/Pub_games-dominoes.html.
Davies, Pauline. "Trapped! Unmarried West Indian Mothers in Handsworth." Papers on Community and Youth Work 2. Birmingham, UK: Westhill College, ca. 1975.
De Certeau, Michel. *The Practice of Everyday Life*. Berkeley: University of California Press, 1984.

De Cuyper, Shiela. "On the Future of Photographic Representation in Anthropology: Lessons Front the Practice of Community Photography in Britain." *Visual Anthropology Review* 13, no. 2 (1997–1998): 2–18.

De Koningh, Michael, and Marc Griffiths. *Tighten Up! The History of Reggae in the UK.* London: Sanctuary, 2003.

Dean, Dennis. "The Race Relations Policy of the First Wilson Government." *Twentieth Century British History* 11, no. 3 (2000): 259–283.

Dear, Geoffrey. *Handsworth/Lozells September 1985.* Birmingham, UK: West Midlands Police, 1985.

Dennis, Ferdinand. *Behind the Frontlines: Journey into Afro-Britain.* London: Victor Gollancz, 1988.

Deol, Amardeep. "The Myth of a Black Consciousness." MA diss., University of Birmingham, 2008.

Department for Trade and Industry. *The Government's Handsworth Task Force: An Evaluation Report.* London: Department for Trade and Industry, 1989.

Dhondy, Farrukh. *CLR James: Cricket, the Caribbean and World Revolution.* London: Weidenfeld and Nicolson, 2001.

Dick, Malcolm. "Locality and Diversity: Minority Ethnic Communities in the Writing of Birmingham's History." In *New Directions in Local History Since Hoskins*, edited by Christopher Dyer, Andrew Hopper, Evelyn Lord, Andrew James Hopper, and Nigel Tringham, 85–97. Hatfield: University of Hertfordshire Press, 2011.

Dickenson, Margaret, ed. *Rogue Rebels: Oppositional Film in Britain, 1945–90.* London: BFI, 1999.

Dixon, David. "Thatcher's People: The British Nationality Act 1981." *Journal of Law and Society* 10, no. 2 (1983): 161–180.

Donnelly, Mark. *Sixties Britain: Culture, Society and Politics.* Harlow: Pearson, 2005.

Dove, Nah (Dorothy) E. "The Emergence of Black Supplementary Schools: Resistance to Racism in the United Kingdom." *Urban Education* 27, no. 4 (1993): 430–447.

Dudrah, Rajinder K. "Drum 'n' Dhol: British Bhangra Music and Diasporic South Asian Formation." *European Journal of Cultural Studies* 5, no. 3 (2002): 363–383.

———. *Bhangra: Birmingham and Beyond.* Birmingham, UK: Birmingham City Council, 2007.

Duke, Eric D. *Building a Nation: Caribbean Federation in the Black Diaspora.* Gainesville: Florida University Press, 2016.

Dworkin, Dennis. *Cultural Marxism in Postwar Britain: History, the New Left, and the Origins of Cultural Studies.* Durham, NC: Duke University Press, 1997.

Dyer, Richard. *White.* London: Routledge, 1997.

Editorial. "The Unity of a Great Time for Queen and Country." *Birmingham Evening Mail*, 6 June 1977, 6.

Edwards, Brent Hayes. *The Practice of Diaspora: Literature, Translation, and the Rise of Black Internationalism.* Cambridge, MA: Harvard University Press, 2003.

Eley, Geoff. *A Crooked Line: From Cultural History to the History of Society.* London: University of Michigan, 2005.

———. "The Trouble with 'Race': Migrancy, Cultural Difference and the Remaking of Europe." In *After the Nazi Racial State: Difference and Democracy in Germany and*

Europe, edited by Rita Chin, Heide Fehrenbach, Geoff Eley, and Atina Grossmann, 137–182. Ann Arbor: University of Michigan Press, 2009.

Elkes, N. "Angry Planners Approve Handsworth Pub's Conversion into Mosque." *Birmingham Mail*, 18 May 2009. Accessed 11 April 2017. www.birminghammail.co.uk/news/local-news/angry-planners-approve-handsworth-pubs-93496.

Enwezor, Okwui. "Coalition Building: Black Audio Film Collective and Transnational Postcolonialism." In *The Ghosts of Songs—The Film Art of the Black Audio Film Collective*, edited by Kodwo Eshun and Anjalika Sagar, 106–129. Liverpool: Liverpool University Press, 2007.

Eshun, Kodwo. "Untimely Meditations: Reflections on the Black Audio Film Collective." *Nka Journal of Contemporary African Art* 19 (2004): 38–45.

———. "An Absence of Ruins—John Akomfrah in Conversation with Kodwo Eshun." In *The Ghosts of Songs—The Film Art of the Black Audio Film Collective*, edited by Kodwo Eshun and Anjalika Sagar, 130–139. Liverpool: Liverpool University Press, 2007.

———. "Drawing the Forms of Things Unknown." In *The Ghosts of Songs—The Film Art of the Black Audio Film Collective*, edited by Kodwo Eshun and Anjalika Sagar, 74–105. Liverpool: Liverpool University Press, 2007.

Eshun, Kodwo, and Anjalika Sagar, eds. *The Ghosts of Songs—The Film Art of the Black Audio Film Collective*. Liverpool: Liverpool University Press, 2007.

Fagan, Winford. "'That's Me in the Picture': Winford Fagan in Handsworth, Birmingham, 1970." *Guardian*, 11 September 2015. Accessed 19 July 2016. www.theguardian.com/artanddesign/2015/sep/11/winford-fagan-handsworth-photograp-vanley-burke.

Fanon, Frantz. *Black Skins, White Masks*. New ed. New York: Grove Press, 2008.

Fielding, Nigel. *The National Front*. London: Routledge and Kegan Paul, 1981.

Filewood, Alan, and David Watt. *Workers' Playtime: Theatre and the Labour Movement since 1970*. Strawberry Hills: Currency Press, 2001.

Fisher, Tracy. *What's Left of Blackness: Feminisms, Transracial Solidarities, and the Politics of Belonging in Britain*. New York: Palgrave Macmillan, 2012.

Forbes, Duncan. "The Worker Photography Movement in Britain, 1934–1939." In *The Worker Photography Movement (1926–1939): Essays and Documents*, edited by J. Ribalta, 206–217. Madrid: Museo Nacional Centro De Arte Reina Sofia, 2011.

Ford, Robert, and Matthew Goodwin. *Revolt on the Right: Explaining Support for the Radical Right in Britain*. Abingdon: Routledge, 2014.

Francis, Matthew. "Mrs Thatcher's Peacock Blue Sari: Ethnic Minorities, Electoral Politics and the Conservative Party, c. 1974–86." *Contemporary British History* 31, no. 2 (2017): 274–293.

Fryer, Peter. *Staying Power: The History of Black People in Britain*. London: Pluto Press, 1984.

Fukunishi, Yumiko. "British Photojournalism in the 1930s: An Analysis of Selected Works by Stefan Lorant, Humphrey Spender and Bill Brandt." MPhil thesis, University of Birmingham, 2003.

Gaffney, John. *Interpretations of Violence: The Handsworth Riots of 1985*. Coventry: Centre for Research in Ethnic Relations, University of Warwick, 1987.

Gale, Richard. "The Multicultural City and the Politics of Religious Architecture: Urban Planning, Mosques and Meaning-making in Birmingham, UK." *Built Environment* 31, no. 1 (2004): 30–44.

Geiss, Imanuel. *The Pan-African Movement: A History of Pan-Africanism in America, Europe and Africa*. London: Methuen, 1974.

Gerrard, Jessica. "Self Help and Protest: The Emergence of Black Supplementary Schooling in England." *Race, Ethnicity and Education* 16, no. 1 (2013): 32–58.

Gikandi, Simon. "The Embarrassment of Victorianism: Colonial Subjects and the Lure of Englishness." In *Victorian Afterlife: Postmodern Culture Rewrites the Nineteenth Century*, edited by John Kucich and Diane F. Sadoff, 157–185. Minneapolis: University of Minnesota Press, 2000.

Giles, Judy. *The Parlour and the Suburb: Domestic Identities, Class, Femininity and Modernity*. Oxford; New York: Berg, 2004.

Gilroy, Paul. "You Can't Fool the Youths . . . Race and Class Formation in the 1980s." *Race and Class* 23 (1981): 207–222.

———. "Police and Thieves." In *The Empire Strikes Back: Race and Racism in 70s Britain*, edited by Centre for Contemporary Cultural Studies, 143–182. London: Hutchinson, 1982.

———. "Steppin' Out of Babylon—Race, Class and Autonomy." In *The Empire Strikes Back: Race and Racism in 70s Britain*, edited by Centre for Contemporary Cultural Studies, 290–292. London: Hutchinson, 1982.

———. *There Ain't No Black in the Union Jack*. London: Unwin Hyman, 1987.

———. *The Black Atlantic: Modernity and Double Consciousness*. Cambridge, MA: Harvard University Press, 1993.

———. "Climbing the Racial Mountain: A Conversation with Isaac Julien." In *Small Acts: Thoughts on the Politics of Black Cultures*, edited by Paul Gilroy, 166–172. London: Serpent's Tail, 1993.

———. "Wearing Your Art on Your Sleeve: Notes Towards a Diaspora History of Black Ephemera." In *Small Acts: Thoughts on the Politics of Black Cultures*, edited by Paul Gilroy, 237–257. London: Serpent's Tail, 1993.

———. "One Nation under a Groove: The Cultural Politics of 'Race' and Racism in Britain." In *Becoming National: A Reader*, edited by Geoff Eley and Ronald G. Suny, 352–369. New York: Oxford University Press, 1996.

———. *After Empire? Postcolonial Melancholia or Convivial Culture?* London: Routledge, 2004.

———. *Black Britain: A Photographic History*. London: Saqi/Getty, 2007.

Gilroy, Paul, and Jim Pines. "Handsworth Songs: Audiences/Aesthetics/Independence: Interview with the Black Audio film Collective." *Framework* 35 (1988): 9–18.

Ginzburg, Carlo. "Microhistory: Two or Three Things I Know about It." *Critical Inquiry* 20, no. 1 (1993): 10–35.

Goulbourne, Harry. *Black Politics in Britain*. Basingstoke: Macmillan, 1998.

Grant, Kevin, Philippa Levine, and Frank Trentmann, eds. *Beyond Sovereignty: Britain, Empire and Transnationalism, c. 1880–1950*. Basingstoke: Palgrave Macmillan, 2007.

Green, E. H. H. *Thatcher*. London: Hodder Arnold, 2006.

Grimley, T. "Beating the Drum for Brum." *Birmingham Post*, 24 September 1992, 18.

Grossberg, Larry. "On Postmodernism and Articulation: An Interview with Stuart Hall." In *Stuart Hall: Critical Dialogues in Cultural Studies*, edited by. David Morley and Kuan-Hsing Chen, 131–150. London: Routledge, 1995.

Grosvenor, Ian. *Assimilating Identities: Racism and Educational Policy in Post-1945 Britain.* London: Lawrence and Wishart, 1997.

Grosvenor, Ian, and Natasha Macnab. "Photography as an Agent of Transformation." *Paedagogica Historica: International Journal of the History of Education* 51, nos. 1–2 (2015): 117–135.

Grosvenor, Ian, Rita McLean, and Sian Roberts, eds. *Making Connections: Birmingham Black International History.* Birmingham, UK: Black Pasts, Birmingham Futures Group, 2002.

Gunning, Dave. *Race and Antiracism in Black British and Asian Literature.* Liverpool: Liverpool University Press, 2010.

Gupta, Rahila, ed. *From Homebreakers to Jailbreakers: Southall Black Sisters.* London: Zed Books, 2003.

Guy, Jackie. "Developing Audiences for African and Caribbean Dance." *Dance Dates* (Summer 1994). Accessed 5 September 2018. https://www.communitydance.org.uk/DB/animated-library/the-future-of-black-british-dance?ed=14052.

Gwinn, Ian. "'History Should Become Common Property': Raphael Samuel, History Workshop, and the Practice of Socialist History, 1966–1980." *Socialist History* 51 (Spring 2017): 96–117.

Gysin, C. "War on the Streets." *Daily Mirror*, 11 September 1985, 1.

Hain, Peter. *Don't Play with Apartheid: The Background to the Stop the Seventy Tour Campaign.* London: George Allen and Unwin, 1971.

Hall, Catherine. "Rethinking Imperial Histories: The Great Reform Act of 1867." *New Left Review* 208 (November–December 1994): 3–29.

———. "What Is a West Indian?" In *West Indian Intellectuals in Britain*, edited by Bill Schwarz, 153–174. Manchester: Manchester University Press, 2003.

Hall, Catherine, and Keith McClelland. *Race, Nation and Empire.* Manchester: Manchester University Press, 2010.

Hall, Catherine, and Sonya O. Rose, eds. *At Home with Empire: Metropolitan Culture and the Imperial World.* Cambridge, UK: Cambridge University Press, 2007.

Hall, Stuart. "The Social Eye of Picture Post." *Working Papers in Cultural Studies* 2 (Spring 1972): 71–120.

———. "The Great Moving Right Show." *Marxism Today* (January 1979): 14–20.

———. "Cultural Identity and Diaspora." In *Identity: Community, Culture, Difference*, edited by Jonathan Rutherford, 222–237. London: Lawrence and Wishart, 1990.

———. "Reconstruction Work." *Ten.8 Photographic Magazine* 2, no. 3 (1992): 106–113.

———. "Vanley Burke and the 'Desire for Blackness.'" In *Vanley Burke: A Retrospective*, edited by Mark Sealy, 12–15. London: Lawrence and Wishart, 1993.

———. "Negotiating Caribbean Identities." *New Left Review* 209 (1995): 3–14.

———. "New Ethnicities." In *Stuart Hall: Critical Dialogues in Cultural Studies*, edited by David Morley and Kuan-Hsing Chen, 441–449. London: Routledge, 1995.

———. "From Scarman to Stephen Lawrence." *History Workshop Journal* 48 (Autumn 1999): 187–197.

———. "Songs of Handsworth Praise," 1986. In *Writing Black Britain, 1948–1998: An Interdisciplinary Anthology*, edited by John Procter, 264–265. Manchester: Manchester University Press, 2000.

———. "The 'West Indian' Front Room." In *The Front Room: Migrant Aesthetics in the Home*, edited by Michael McMillan, 16–23. London: Black Dog Publishing, 2009.

Hall, Stuart, Chas Critcher, Tony Jefferson, John Clarke, and Brian Roberts, eds. *Policing the Crisis—Mugging, the State and Law and Order*. 2nd ed. Basingstoke: Palgrave Macmillan, 2002.

Hall, Stuart, and Martin Jacques, eds. *The Politics of Thatcherism*. London: Lawrence and Wishart/Marxism Today, 1983.

Hall, Stuart, and Tony Jefferson, eds. *Resistance Through Rituals: Youth Subcultures in Postwar Britain*. London: Hutchinson, 1976.

Hall, Stuart, John Rex, Bhikhu Parekh, Alan Little, and Trevor Huddleston. *Five Views of Multi-Racial Britain: Talks on Race Relations Broadcast by BBC TV*. London: Commission for Racial Equality, 1978.

Hall, Stuart, with Bill Schwarz. *Familiar Stranger: A Life between Two Islands*. London: Allen Lane, 2017.

Halliburton, R. "Lost in Translation." *Independent*, 7 May 1996. accessed 12 September 16. www.independent.co.uk/news/uk/lost-in-the-translation-1346248.html.

Hanna, Erika. "Reading Irish Women's Lives in Photograph Albums: Dorothy Stokes and Her Camera, 1926–53." *Cultural and Social History* 11, no. 1 (2014): 89–109.

Hansen, Randall. "The Politics of Citizenship in 1940s Britain: The British Nationality Act." *Twentieth Century British History* 10, no. 1 (1999): 67–95.

Harris, Roxy, and Sarah White, eds. *Changing Britannia: Life Experience with Britain*. London: New Beacon Books, 1999.

Haynes, Jim. *Thanks for Coming!* London: Faber and Faber, 1984.

Hebdige, Dick. "Reggae, Rastas and Rudies: Style and the Subversion of Form." Centre for Contemporary Cultural Studies Stencilled Occasional Paper. Birmingham, UK: University of Birmingham, ca. 1975.

———. *Subculture: The Meaning of Style*. London/New York: Methuen, 1979.

———. *Cut 'n' Mix: Culture, Identity and Caribbean Music*. London: Routledge, 1990.

Henry, Beresford Ivan. "Homelessness and a Particular Response Amongst Young West Indians in Handsworth, Birmingham." MA thesis, University of Birmingham, 1974.

———. "The Growth of Corporate Black Identity Among Afro-Caribbean People in Birmingham, England." PhD thesis, Warwick University, 1982.

Henry, William (Lez). *What the Deejay Said: A Critique from the Street!* London: Nu-Beyond, 2006.

Hey, Valerie. *Patriarchy and Pub Culture*. London: Tavistock, 1986.

Hick, John. *Faith and Knowledge: A Modern Introduction to the Problem of Religious Knowledge*. New York: Cornell University Press, 1957.

———. *An Autobiography*. Oxford: One World, 2002.

Higgins, John. *Raymond Williams: Literature, Marxism and Cultural Materialism*. London: Routledge, 1999.

Highmore, Ben. *Everyday Life and Cultural Theory: An Introduction*. London: Routledge, 2002.

———. *The Great Indoors: At Home in the Modern British House*. London: Profile, 2014.

Hill, Clifford S. *West Indian Migrants and the London Churches.* London: Oxford University Press, 1963.

———. "From Church to Sect: West Indian Religious Sect Development in Britain." *Journal for the Scientific Study of Religion* 10, no. 2 (1971): 114–123.

Hill, Jeffrey. "League Cricket in the North and Midlands, 1900–1940." In *Sport and the Working Class in Modern Britain*, edited by Richard Holt, 121–141. Manchester: Manchester University Press, 1990.

Hilton, Matthew. "The Banality of Consumption." In *Citizenship and Consumption*, edited by Frank Trentmann and Kate Soper, 87–103. London: Palgrave, 2008.

———. "Politics Is Ordinary: Non-governmental Organizations and Political Participation in Contemporary Britain." *Twentieth Century British History* 22, no. 2 (2011): 230–268.

———. "International Aid and Development NGOs in Britain and Human Rights since 1945." *Humanity: An International Journal of Human Rights, Humanitarianism and Development* 3, no. 3 (2012): 449–472.

Hilton, Matthew, Chris Moores, and Florence Sutcliffe-Braithwaite. "New Times Revisited: Britain in the 1980s." *Contemporary British History* 31, no. 2 (2017): 145–165.

Hines, Vince. *How Black People Overcame Fifty Years of Repression in Britain, 1945–1995.* London: Zulu Books, 1998.

Hiro, Dilip. *Black British, White British: A History of Race Relations in Britain.* London: Grafton, 1991.

Hitchcock, Peter. "'It Dread Inna Inglan': Linton Kwesi Johnson, Dread and Dub Identity." *Postmodern Culture* 4, no. 1 (1993): 1–11.

Hobsbawm, Eric. "Inventing Traditions." In *The Invention of Traditions*, edited by Eric Hobsbawm and Terance Ranger, 1–15. Cambridge, UK: University of Cambridge, 1983.

Hobson, Dorothy. *Channel 4: The Early Years and the Jeremy Isaacs Legacy.* London: I. B. Tauris, 2008.

Hoggart, Richard. *The Uses of Literacy: Aspects of Working Class Life, with Special Reference to Publications and Entertainments.* Harmondsworth: Penguin, 1957.

Holden, Tony. *So What Are You Going to Do about the National Front?* Birmingham, UK: All Faiths For One Race/Sidelines, 1978.

———. *From Race to Politics.* Birmingham, UK: All Faiths For One Race/Sidelines, 1979.

Holmes, Colin. *John Bull's Island: Immigration and British Society, 1871–1971.* Basingstoke: Macmillan, 1988.

Holt, Richard. *Sport and the British: A Modern History.* Oxford: Oxford University Press, 1989.

Holt, Richard, ed. *Sport and the Working Class in Modern Britain.* Manchester: Manchester University Press, 1990.

hooks, bell. *Killing Rage: Ending Racism.* London: Penguin, 1996.

Houlbrook, Matt. *Queer London: Perils and Pleasure in the Sexual Metropolis, 1918–1957.* Chicago: Chicago University Press, 2005.

———. "'A Pin to See the Peepshow': Culture, Fiction and Selfhood in Edith Thompson's Letters, 1921–22." *Past and Present* 207, no. 1 (2010): 215–249.

Howe, Darcus. "The Language of Black Culture." In *Writing Black Britain, 1948–1998: An Interdisciplinary Anthology*, edited by James Procter, 265. Manchester: Manchester University Press, 2000.

Howe, Stephen. "C. L. R. James: Visions of History, Visions of Britain." In *West Indian Intellectuals in Britain*, edited by Bill Schwarz, 153–174. Manchester: Manchester University Press, 2003.

Hu, Z. "Community Photography: An Assessment of Its Ideas and Practices, with Particular Reference to Birmingham and the West Midlands." PhD thesis, Birmingham City University, 2009.

Hughes, Colin, and Craig Seton. "Birmingham Violence Spreads to New Areas." *Times*, 11 September 1985, 1.

Hulme, Tom. *After the Shock City: Urban Culture and the Making of Modern Citizenship*. Woodbridge: Boydell and Brewer, 2019.

Hutton, Will. "Never Before in My Adult Life Has the Future Seemed So Bleak for Progressives." *Guardian*, 7 May 2017. Accessed 26 July 2017. www.theguardian.com/commentisfree/2017/may/06/never-in-my-adult-life-has-future-seemed-so-bleak-for-progressives.

Jagessar, Michael, and Antony Reddie, eds. *Black Theology in Britain: A Reader*. London: Equinox, 2007.

Jamdagni, Laxmi, Mal Phillips-Bell, and Job Ward. *Talking Chalk: Black Pupils, Parents and Teachers Speak about Education*. Birmingham, UK: AFFOR, 1982.

James, C. L. R. *Beyond a Boundary*. London: Yellow Jersey Press, 1963.

———. "Rohan Kanhai: A Study in Confidence." *New World* (1966). Accessed 9 May 2011. www.guyanaundersiege.com/leaders/kanhai.htm.

———. "Immigrants to Britain: Formerly Colonial Peoples." *Caribbean Quarterly* 35, no. 4 (1989): 15–34.

———. *American Civilisation*. Cambridge and Oxford, UK: Blackwell, 1993.

———. "Black Power," 1967. In *The C. L. R. James Reader*, edited by Anna Grimshaw, 362–374. Oxford: Blackwell, 1993.

———. "Garfield Sobers," 1969. In *The CLR James Reader*, edited by Anna Grimshaw, 379–389. Oxford: Blackwell 1993.

James, Leslie. *George Padmore and Decolonization from Below: Pan-Africanism, the Cold War, and the End of Empire*. Basingstoke: Palgrave Macmillan 2015.

James, Winston. "Migration, Racism and Identity Formation: The Caribbean Experience in Britain." In *Inside Babylon: The Caribbean Diaspora in Britain*, edited by Winston James and Clive Harris, 231–288. London: Verso, 1993.

James, Winston, and Clive Harris, eds. *Inside Babylon: The Caribbean Diaspora in Britain*. London: Verso, 1993.

Jefferson, Tony, and John Clarke. "Down These Mean Streets . . . the Meaning of Mugging." Centre for Contemporary Cultural Studies Stencilled Occasional Paper. Birmingham, UK: University of Birmingham, 1973.

———. "Mugging and Law 'n' Order." Centre for Contemporary Cultural Studies Stencilled Occasional Paper. Birmingham, UK: University of Birmingham, 1975.

John, Gus. *Race in the Inner City: A Report from Handsworth, Birmingham*. London: Runnymede Trust, 1970.

John, Gus, and Derek Humphry. *Because They're Black*. Harmondsworth: Penguin, 1972.

Johnson, Cedric. "From Popular Anti-imperialism to Sectarianism: The African Liberation Support Committee and Black Power Radicals." *New Political Science* 25, no. 4 (2003): 477–507.

Johnson, Linton Kwesi. "Jamaican Rebel Music." *Race and Class* 17, no. 4 (1976): 397–412.
Jones, Ben. *The Working Class in Mid-Twentieth-Century England: Community, Identity and Social Memory*. Manchester: Manchester University Press, 2012.
Jones, Colin. *The Black House*. London: Prestal Publishing, 2006.
Jones, E. Jean Johnson. "The *Choreographic Notebook*: A Dynamic Documentation of the Choreographic Process of Kokuma Dance Theatre, an African-Caribbean Dance Company." In *Dance in the Field: Theory, Methods and Issues in Dance Ethnography*, edited by T. J. Buckland, 100–110. Basingstoke: Palgrave, 1999.
Josephides, Sasha. "Principles, Strategies, Anti-racist Campaigns: The Case of the Indian Workers' Association." In *Black Politics in Britain*, edited by Harry Goulbourne, 115–129. Hants: Gower, 1990.
Julien, Isaac, and Kobena Mercer. "De Margin and De Centre." *Screen* 29, no. 4 (1988): 2–11.
Kasinitz, Phillip. *Caribbean New York: Black Immigrants and the Politics of Race*. Ithaca, NY, and London: Cornell University Press, 1992.
Keith, Michael. *Race, Riots and Policing: Lore and Disorder in a Multi-racist Society*. London: UCL Press, 1990.
Kelly, Owen. *Community, Art and the State: Storming the Citadels*. London: Comedia, 1984.
Killingray, David. "'To Do Something for the Race': Harold Moody and the League of Coloured Peoples." In *West Indian Intellectuals in Britain*, edited by Bill Schwarz, 51–70. Manchester: Manchester University Press, 2003.
Kruse, Kevin M. *White Flight: Atlanta and the Making of Modern Conservatism*. Princeton, NJ: Princeton University Press, 2005.
Kundnani, Arun. *The End of Tolerance: Britain in the 21st Century*. London: Pluto Press, 2007.
Kushner, Tony. *We Europeans?* Aldershot: Ashgate, 2004.
Laite, Julia. *Common Prostitutes and Ordinary Citizens: Commercial Sex in London, 1885–1960*. Houndmills: Palgrave Macmillan, 2012.
Lancaster, Esme. *My Journeys Through Life*. Willenhall: Birches, 2006.
Lane, Jeremy F. *Pierre Bourdieu: A Critical Introduction*. London: Pluto, 2000.
Langhamer, Claire. *Women's Leisure in England 1920–60*. Manchester: Manchester University Press, 2000.
Langhamer, Claire. "'A Public House Is for All Classes, Men and Women Alike': Women, Leisure and Drink in Second World War England." *Women's History Review* 12, no. 3 (2011): 423–443.
Langhamer, Claire. "Feeling through Practice: Subjectivity and Emotion in Children's Writing." *Journal of Social History* 51, no. 1 (2016): 3.
Lavalette, Michael. *Radical Social Work Today: Social Work at the Crossroads*. Chicago: University of Chicago Press, 2011.
Lawrence, Daniel. *Black Migrants, White Natives: A Study of Race Relations in Nottingham*. London: Cambridge University Press, 1974.
Lawrence, Errol. "'In the Abundance of Water the Fool Is Thirsty': Sociology and Black 'Pathology.'" In *The Empire Strikes Back: Race and Racism in Seventies Britain*, edited by Centre for Contemporary Cultural Studies, 95–142. London: Hutchinson, 1982.
Lawrence, Jon. "Class, 'Affluence' and the Study of Everyday Life in Britain, c. 1930–64." *Cultural and Social History* 10, no. 2 (2013): 273–299.

Layton-Henry, Zig. *The Politics of Race in Britain*. London: Allen and Unwin, 1984.
Layton-Henry, Zig, and Paul B. Rich, eds. *Race, Government and Politics in Britain*. London: Macmillan, 1986.
Lent, Adam. *British Social Movements Since 1945: Sex, Colour, Peace and Power*. Basingstoke: Palgrave, 2001.
Lewis, Gordon. "Race Relations in Britain: A View from the Caribbean." *Race Today* 1, no. 3 (1969): 78–80.
Lister, Simon. *Fire in Babylon: How the West Indies Cricket Team Brought a People to Its Feet*. London: Yellow Jersey Press, 2015.
Long, Paul. "Representing Race, and Place: Black Midlanders on Television in the 1960s and 1970s." *Midland History* 36, no. 2 (2011): 262–77.
Long, Paul, Yasmeen Baig-Clifford, and Roger Shannon. "'What We're Trying to Do Is Make Popular Politics': The Birmingham Film and Video Workshop." *Historical Journal of Film, Radio and Television* 33, no. 3 (2013): 377–395.
Lyndsey, Lydia. "The Split-Labour Phenomenon: Its Impact on West Indian Workers as a Marginal Working Class in Birmingham, England, 1948–1962." *Journal of African American History* 87 (2002): 119–145.
Macpherson, William. *The Stephen Lawrence Inquiry: Report of an Inquiry by Sir William Macpherson of Cluny*. London, Stationary Office, 1999.
Malik, Kenan. *From Fatwa to Jihad: The Rushdie Affair and Its Legacy*. London: Atlantic Books, 2009.
Mama, Amina. "Woman Abuse in London's Black Communities." In *Inside Babylon: the Caribbean Diaspora in Britain*, edited by Winston James and Clive Harris, 97–134. London: Verso, 1993.
Manning, J. L. "It's Their Job to Entertain us Before the Real Cricket." *Daily Mail*, 4 July 1966, 12.
Marcus, Harold G. *A History of Ethiopia*. Berkeley: University of California Press, 1994.
Marien, Mary Warner. *Photography: A Cultural History*. London: Laurence King, 2006.
Marwick, Arthur. *The Sixties: Cultural Revolution in Britain, France, Italy and the United States, c. 1958–1974*. Oxford: Oxford University Press, 1998.
Mason, Rowena. "Nigel Farage Backs 'Basic Principle' of Enoch Powell's Immigration Warning." *Guardian*, 5 January 2014. www.theguardian.com/politics/2014/jan/05/nigel-farage-enoch-powell-immigration.
Mason, Tony, ed. *Sport in Britain: A Social History*. Cambridge, UK: Cambridge University Press, 1989.
Mass Observation *The Pub and the People: A Worktown Study*. London: Victor Gollancz, 1943.
Matera, Marc. *Black London: The Imperial Metropolis and Decolonization in the Twentieth Century*. Oakland: University of California Press, 2015.
Mathur, Saloni. "Living Ethnological Exhibits: The Case of 1886." *Cultural Anthropology* 15, no. 4 (2001): 492–524.
May, Claudia. "Nothing Like Words Spoken: Black British 'Femcees' and the Sampling of Hip Hop as a Theoretical Trope." *Cultural Studies* 27, no. 4 (2013): 611–649.
Mays, Nicholas. "Elderly South Asians in Britain: A Survey of Relevant Literature and Themes for Future Research." *Ageing and Society* 3, no. 1 (1983): 71–97.

McKibbin, Ross. *Classes and Cultures: England 1918–1951*. Oxford: Oxford University Press, 1998.
McMillan, Michael. "The 'West Indian' Front Room: Reflections on a Diasporic Phenomenon." *Kunapipi* 30, no. 2 (2008): 44–70.
———, ed. *The Front Room: Migrant Aesthetics in the Home*. London: Black Dog Publishing, 2009.
———. "Migrant Aesthetics in the Front Room." In *The Front Room: Migrant Aesthetics in the Home*, edited by Michael McMillan, 8–15. London: Black Dog Publishing, 2009.
McRobbie, Angela. "Settling Accounts with Subcultures: A Feminist Critique." In *Culture, Ideology and Social Process: A Reader*, edited by Tony Bennett, Graham Martin, Colin Mercer, and Jane Woollacott, 111–123. London: Open University Press, 1981.
———. "Stuart Hall: Art and the Politics of Black Cultural Production." *The South Atlantic Quarterly* 115, no. 4 (2016): 665–683.
Mercer, Kobena, "Black Hair/Style Politics." *New Formations* 3 (1987): 33–54.
———, ed. *Black Film/British Cinema*. London: Institute of Contemporary Arts, 1988.
———. "Post-Colonial Trauerspiel." In *The Ghosts of Songs: The Film Art of the Black Audio Film Collective, 1982–1998*, edited by Kodwo Eshun and Anjalika Sagar, 43–59. Liverpool: Liverpool University Press, 2007.
Midgett, Douglas. "Cricket and Calypso: Cultural Representation and Social History in the West Indies." *Culture, Sport, Society* 6, nos. 2–3 (2003): 239–268.
Moores, Chris. "RAGE against the Obscene: Opposition to the Greenham Peace Camps and Political Activism in 1980s Britain." *History Workshop Journal* 78, no. 1 (2014): 204–227.
Moran, Joe. "Imagining the Street in Post-War Britain." *Urban History* 39, no. 1 (2012): 166–186.
Morley, David, and Kuan-Hsing Chen, eds. *Critical Dialogues in Cultural Studies*. London: Routledge, 1995.
Morris, Lynda, ed. *Vanley Burke: By the Rivers of Birminam*. Birmingham, UK: MAC, 2012.
Morris, Mervyn. "A Note on 'Dub Poetry.'" *Wasafiri* 13, no. 26 (1997): 66–69.
Mort, Frank. *Capital Affairs: London and the Making of the Permissive Society*. New Haven, CT: Yale University Press, 2010.
Mead, Matthew. "*Empire Windrush*: The Cultural Memory of an Imaginary Arrival." *Journal of Postcolonial Writing* 45, no. 2 (2000): 137–149.
Miles, Robert. *Racism*. London: Routledge, 1989.
Modood, Tariq. *Multicultural Politics: Racism, Ethnicity and Muslims in Britain*. Edinburgh: Edinburgh University Press, 2005.
Murphy, Dervla. *Tales from Two Cities: Travel of Another Sort*. London: Murray, 1987.
Myers, Kevin. *Struggles for a Past: Irish and Afro-Caribbean Histories in England, 1951–2000*. Manchester: Manchester University Press, 2015.
Myers, Kevin, and Ian Grosvenor. "Exploring Supplementary Education: Margins, Theories and Methods." *History of Education* 40, no. 4 (2011): 501–521.
Natarajan, Radhika. "Performing Multiculturalism: The Commonwealth Arts Festival of 1965." *Journal of British Studies* 53, no. 3 (2014): 705–733.
Neal, Sarah, Katy Bennett, Allan Cochrane, and Giles Mohan. "Living Multiculture: Understanding the New Spatial and Social Relations of Ethnicity and Multiculture in England." *Environment and Planning C: Government and Policy* 31, no. 2 (2013): 308–323.

Neale, Matt. "Research in Urban History: Recent Theses on Crime in the City, 1750–1900." *Urban History* 40, no. 3 (2013): 567–577.

Nettleford Rex. *Mirror Mirror: Identity, Race and Protest in Jamaica.* Kingston: Collins Sangster, 1970.

Newman, A. "Exploring Birmingham's Sound System Culture." *Sabotage Times*, 23 July 2015. Accessed 19 August 2016. http://sabotagetimes.com/music/exploring-birminghams-sound-system-culture.

Newman, Jon. "Harry Jacobs: The Studio Photographer and the Visual Archive." In *People and Their Pasts: Public History Today*, edited by Paul Ashton and Hilda Kean, 260–270. London: Palgrave, 2009.

Noble, Denise. "'A Room of Her Own': Gendering the Front Room." In *The Front Room: Migrant Aesthetics in the Home*, edited by Michael McMillan, 84–93. London: Black Dog Publishing, 2009.

O'Brien, Richard, and Church of England. *Faith in the City of Birmingham: An Examination of Problems and Opportunities Facing a City.* Exeter: Paternoster Press, 1988.

O'Connell, Sean. *Credit and Community: Working-class Debt in the UK since 1880.* Oxford: Oxford University Press, 2009.

O'Donnell Edward T. "Pictures vs. Words? Public History, Tolerance, and the Challenge of Jacob Riis." *Public Historian* 26, no. 3 (2004): 7–26.

Osgerby, Bill. "Youth Culture." In *A Companion to Contemporary Britain 1939–2000*, edited by Paul Addison and Harriet Jones, 127–144. Oxford: Blackwell, 2005.

Owusu, Kwesi, ed. *Black British Culture and Society: A Text Reader.* London: Routledge, 1999.

Palmer, Lisa Amanda. "'Ladies A Your Time Is Now!' Erotic Politics, Lovers' Rock and Resistance in the UK." *African and Black Diaspora: An International Journal* 4, no. 2 (2011): 177–192.

Parekh, Bikhu. *The Politics of Race Relations.* London: Routledge, 1998.

Parker, A. "Sun Names Black Bomber." *Sun*, September 13, 1985, 1.

Parmar, Pratibha. "Gender, Race and Class: Asian Women in Resistance." In *The Empire Strikes Back: Race and Racism in Contemporary Britain*, edited by Centre for Contemporary Cultural Studies, 236–275. London: Hutchinson, 1982.

Parsons, Gerald. "Filling a Void? Afro-Caribbean Identity and Religion." In *The Growth of Religious Diversity: Britain from 1945*, vol. 1, *Traditions*, edited by Gerald Parsons, 243–273. London: Routledge/the Open University, 1993.

Patterson, Tiffany Ruby, and Robin D. G. Kelley. 'Unfinished Migrations: Reflections on the African Diaspora and the Making of the Modern World." *African Studies Review* 43, no. 1 (2000): 11–45.

Paul, Kathleen. *Whitewashing Britain: Race and Citizenship in the Post-war Era.* London: Cornell University Press, 1997.

Payling, Daisy. "'Socialist Republic of South Yorkshire': Grassroots Activism and Left-Wing Solidarity in 1980s Sheffield." *Twentieth Century British History* 25, no. 4 (2014): 602–627.

Pemberton, Hugh. "The Transformation of the Economy." In *A Companion to Contemporary Britain 1939–2000*, edited by Paul Addison and Harriet Jones, 180–202. Oxford: Blackwell, 2005.

Peplow, Simon. "'A Tactical Manoeuvre to Apply Pressure': Race and the Role of Public Inquiries in the 1980 Bristol 'Riot.'" *Twentieth Century British History* 29, no. 1 (2018): 129–155

Perks, Robert, and Alistair Thompson, eds. *The Oral History Reader*. London: Routledge, 2006.

Perry, Kennetta Hammond. *London Is the Place for Me: Black Britons, Citizenship and the Politics of Race*. Oxford: Oxford University Press, 2015.

Phillips, Mike. *London Crossings: A Biography of Black Britain*. London: Continuum, 2001.

Phillips, Trevor, and Mike Phillips. *Windrush: The Irresistible Rise of Multi-racial Britain*. London: HarperCollins, 1999.

Pines, Jim. "The Cultural Context of Black British Cinema." In *Black British Cultural Studies: A Reader*, edited by Houston A. Baker Jr., Manthia Diawara, and Ruth H. Lindeborg, 183–193. Chicago: Chicago University Press, 1996.

Plummer, John. *Movement of Jah People: The Growth of the Rastafarians*. Birmingham, UK: Press Gang, 1978.

Pomeranz, Kenneth. "Histories for a Less National Age." *American Historical Review* 119, no. 1 (2014): 1–22.

Pryce, Ken. *Endless Pressure: A Study of West-Indian Lifestyle in Bristol*. Harmondsworth: Penguin, 1979.

Putnam, Lara. "To Study the Fragments/Whole: Microhistory and the Atlantic World." *Journal of Social History* 39, no. 3 (2006): 615–630.

———. *Radical Moves: Caribbean Migrants and the Politics of Race in the Jazz Age*. Chapel Hill: University of North Carolina Press, 2013.

Qureshi, Sadiah. *Peoples on Parade: Exhibitions, Empire and Anthropology in Nineteenth-Century Britain*. Chicago: University of Chicago Press, 2011.

Ramamurthy, Anandi. "The Politics of Britain's Asian Youth Movement." *Race and Class* 48, no. 2 (2006): 38–60.

———. *Black Star: Britain's Asian Youth Movements*. London: Pluto Press, 2013.

Ramdhanie, Bob. "African Dance in England—Spirituality and Continuity." PhD thesis, University of Warwick, 2005.

Ramdin, Ron. *The Making of the Black Working Class in Britain*. Aldershot: Gower, 1987.

Ratcliffe, Peter. *Racism and Reaction: A Profile of Handsworth*. London: Routledge and Kegan Paul, 1981.

Reddie, Anthony. "Faith, Stories and the Experience of Black Elders." In *Black Theology in Britain: A Reader*, edited by Michael Jagessar and Anthony Reddie, 192–199. London: Equinox, 2007.

Rees, A. "Handsworth Ablaze Again after Night of Horror." *Daily Express*, 11 September 1985, 1.

Renton, Dave. *When We Touched the Sky: The Anti-Nazi League, 1977–81*. Cheltenham: New Clarion Press, 2006.

———. *CLR James: Cricket's Philosopher King*. London: Haus Books, 2007.

Rex, John, and Robert Moore. *Race, Community and Conflict: A Study of Sparkbrook*. London: Oxford University Press, 1967.

Rex, John, and Sally Tomlinson. *Colonial Immigrants in a British City: A Class Analysis*. London: Routledge and Kegan Paul, 1979.

Roberts, Robert. *The Classic Slum: Salford in the First Quarter of the Century*. Manchester: Manchester University Press, 1971.

Robeson, Paul. *Here I Stand*. London: Dennis Dobson, 1958.

Robinson, Emily, Camilla Schofield, Florence Sutcliffe-Braithwaite, and Natalie Thomlinson. "Telling Stories about Post-War Britain: Popular Individualism and the 'Crisis' of the 1970s." *Twentieth Century British History* 28, no. 2 (2017): 268–304.

Rose, E. J. B., and Nicholas Deakin. *Colour and Citizenship: A Report on British Race Relations*. London: Oxford University Press, 1969.

Rosenwein, Barbara H. *Emotional Communities in the Early Middle Ages*. New York: Cornell University Press, 2006.

Ross, Kristin. *Fast Cars, Clean Bodies: Decolonization and the Reordering of French Culture*. London: MIT Press, 1996.

Rush, Anne Spry. *Bonds of Empire: West Indians and Britishness from Victoria to Decolonization*. Oxford: Oxford University Press, 2011.

Rushdie, Salman. "Songs Don't Know the Score," 1986. In *Writing Black Britain, 1948–1998: An Interdisciplinary Anthology*, edited by James Procter, 263–264. Manchester: Manchester University Press, 2000.

———. "The New Empire Within Britain," 1982. In *Imagining Homelands*, 129–138. London: Vintage, 2010.

Savage, Mike, Gaynor Bagnall, and Brian Longhurst. "Ordinary, Ambivalent and Defensive: Class Identities in the North West of England." *Sociology* 39, no. 5 (2005): 875–892.

Scarman, Lord. *The Scarman Report: The Brixton Disorders 10–12 April 1981*. London: HMSO, 1981.

Schaffer, Gavin. "*Till Death Do Us Part* and the BBC: Racial Politics and the Working Classes 1965–75." *Journal of Contemporary History* 45, no. 2 (2010): 454–477.

———. *The Vision of a Nation: Making Multiculturalism on British Television, 1960–80*. Basingstoke: Palgrave MacMillan, 2014.

Schofield, Camilla. *Enoch Powell and the Making of Post-Colonial Britain*. Cambridge, UK: Cambridge University Press, 2013.

Schwarz, Bill. "Black Metropolis, White England." In *Modern Times: Reflections on a Century of English Modernity*, edited by Mica Nava and Alan O'Shea, 176–207. London and New York: Routledge, 1996.

———, ed. *West Indian Intellectuals in Britain*. Manchester: Manchester University Press, 2003.

———. "Crossing Seas." In *West Indian Intellectuals in Britain*, edited by Bill Schwarz, 1–30. Manchester: Manchester University Press, 2003.

———. "Claudia Jones and the *West Indian Gazette*: Reflections on the Emergence of Postcolonial Britain." *Twentieth Century British History* 14, no. 3 (2003): 264–285.

———. *Memories of Empire*. Vol. 1, *The White Man's World*. Oxford: Oxford University Press, 2011.

Sealy, Mark, ed. *Vanley Burke: A Retrospective*. London: Lawrence and Wishart, 1993.

Silverman, Julius. *The Handsworth Riots, 9, 10, 11 September: A Report of an Inquiry of Julius Silverman Presented to Birmingham City Council*. Birmingham, UK: Birmingham City Council, 1986.

Silverton, Pete. "No Jah-Bubble in-a Birmingham." *Sounds*, 22 April 1978. Accessed 18 June 2010. www.rocksbackpages.com/article.html?ArticleID=11490.

Sivanandan, Ambalavaner. "Race, Class and the State: The Black Experience in Britain." *Race and Class* 17 (1976): 347–368.

———. "Liberation of the Black Intellectual." *Race and Class* 18, no. 4 (1977): 329–343

———. *A Different Hunger*. London: Pluto Press, 1982.

———. "From Resistance to Rebellion." In *A Different Hunger: Writings on Black Resistance*, edited by Ambalavaner Sivanandan, 47. London: Pluto Press, 1982.

———. "UK Commentary—Britain's Gulags." *Race and Class* 27 (1986): 81–85.

———. *Communities of Resistance*. London: Verso, 1990.

———. "Race and Resistance: The IRR Story." *Race and Class* 50, no. 2 (2008): 1–30.

Skinner, Rob. *The Foundations of Anti-Apartheid: Liberal Humanitarians and Transnational Activists in Britain and the United States, c. 1919–64*. Basingstoke: Palgrave, 2010.

Smith, Andrew. "'Beyond a Boundary' (of a 'Field of Cultural Production'): Reading C. L. R. James with Bourdieu." *Theory, Culture and Society* 23, no. 4 (2006): 95–112.

Smith, Anna Marie. *New Right Discourse on Race and Sexuality*. Cambridge, UK: Cambridge University Press, 1994.

Smith, Helen. "Working-Class Ideas and Experiences of Sexuality in Twentieth-Century Britain: Regionalism as a Category of Analysis." *Twentieth Century British History* 29, no. 1 (2018): 58–78.

Smith, Jennifer H. "Mary in the Kitchen, Martha in the Pew: Patterns of Holiness in a Methodist Church." MPhil thesis, University of Birmingham, 2005.

Smith, Norman. *Bad Friday*. London: New Beacon Books, 1985.

Smith, P. "Roland the First." *Daily Mail*, 22 August 1980, n.p.

Smith, P. "Fearsome Four Have No Regrets." *Daily Mail*, 13 August 1984, 29.

Solomos, John. *Race and Racism in Contemporary Britain*. Basingstoke: Macmillan Education, 1989.

Solomos, John, and Les Back. *Race, Politics and Social Change*. London: Routledge, 1995.

Sondhi, Ranjit. *Asian Resource Centre: Problems, Perspectives and Progress*. Birmingham, UK: Asian Resource Centre, 1979.

Sontag, Susan. *On Photography*. Harmondsworth: Penguin, 1979.

Spence, Jo. 'The Politics of Photography'. *Camerawork* 1 (February 1976), 1–3.

———. *Putting Myself in the Picture*. London: Camden, 1986.

Stoby, Michelle. "Black British Drama after *Empire Road*." *Wasafiri* 17, no. 35 (2002): 3–8.

Stolzoff, Norman C. *Wake the Town and Tell the People: Dancehall Culture in Jamaica*. Durham, NC: Duke University Press, 2000.

Street, Joe. "Malcolm X, Smethwick, and the Influence of the African American Freedom Struggle on British Race Relations in the 1960s." *Journal of Black Studies* 38, no. 6 (2008): 932–950.

Sturge, Mark. *Look What the Lord Has Done!* Milton Keynes: Scripture Union Publishing, 2005.

Sudbury, Julia. *"Other Kinds of Dreams": Black Women's Organisations and the Politics of Transformation*. London: Routledge, 1997.

Sutherland, John. *Offensive Literature: Decensorship in Britain 1960–1982*. London: Junction Books, 1982.

Tabili, Laura. "The Construction of Racial Difference in Twentieth-Century Britain: the Special Restriction (Coloured Alien Seamen) Order, 1925." *Journal of British Studies* 33, no. 1 (1994): 54–98.

———. *Global Migrants, Local Culture: Natives and Newcomers in Provincial England, 1841–1939*. London: Palgrave Macmillan, 2011.

Tagg, John. *The Burden of Representation: Essays on Photographs and Histories*. London: Macmillan, 1988.

Taylor, Arthur. *Played at the Pub: The Pub Games of Britain*. Swindon: English Heritage, 2009.

Telegraph. "Theresa May's Conference Speech in Full." 5 October 2016. Accessed 26 July 2017. www.telegraph.co.uk/news/2016/10/05/theresa-mays-conference-speech-in-full/.

Thomlinson, Nathalie. *Race, Ethnicity and the Women's Movement in England, 1968–1993*, London: Palgrave, 2016.

Thompson, Robert Farris. *Flash of the Spirit: African and Afro-American Art and Philosophy*. New York: Vintage, 1983.

Tibebu, Teshale. "Ethiopia: The 'Anomaly' and 'Paradox' of Africa." *Journal of Black Studies* 26, no. 4 (1996): 414–430.

Tiffin, Helen. "Cricket, Literature and the Politics of Decolonisation: The Case of C. L. R. James." In *Liberation Cricket: West Indies Cricket Culture*, edited by Hilary Beckles and Brian Stoddard, 356–370. Manchester: Manchester University Press, 1995.

Times. "The Fourth Test Match." 16 August 1950, 7.

Tolla-Kelly, Divya P. "Locating Processes of Identification: Studying the Precipitates of Rememory Through Artefacts in the British Asian Home." *Transactions of the Institute of British Geographers* 29, no. 3 (2004): 314–329.

Tonkin, Elizabeth. *Narrating Our Pasts: The Social Construction of Oral History*. Cambridge, UK: Cambridge University Press, 1992.

Toulis, Nicole Rodriguez. *Believing Identity: Pentecostalism and the Mediation of Jamaican Ethnicity and Gender in England*. Oxford: Berg, 1997.

Travis, A. "Rates Grant for Rain Dance Lessons in Ghana." *Evening Mail*, 26 June 1983, 10.

Travis, A. "Oliver Letwin Blocked Help for Black Youth after 1985 Riots." *Guardian*, 29 December 2015. Accessed 13 September 2018. www.theguardian.com/politics/2015/dec/30/oliver-letwin-blocked-help-for-black-youth-after-1985-riots.

Trilling, Daniel. *Bloody Nasty People: The Rise of Britain's Far Right*. London: Verso: 2012.

Troyna, Barry, and Jenny Williams. *Racism, Education and the State*. London: Biddles, 1986.

Tyler, K. "Dawn of the Dread." *Guardian*, 4 October 2008. Accessed 17 August 2016. www.theguardian.com/music/2008/oct/04/babylon.franco.rosso.

Velk, Robin. *Handsworth Evolution*. Radio documentary for Birmingham Music Heritage, October 2010. Accessed 24 May 2011. http://radiotogo.blogspot.com/2010/10/handsworth-evolution-documentary.html.

Vernon, James. "The History of Britain Is Dead; Long Live a Global History of Britain." *History Australia* 13, no. 1 (2016): 19–34.

———. *Modern Britain: 1750-present*. Cambridge, UK: Cambridge University Press, 2017.

Vulliamy, Ed. "Rumours of a Riot." *Guardian*, 29 November 2005. Accessed 27 July 2017. www.theguardian.com/uk/2005/nov/29/race.world.

Walker, Martin. *The National Front*. London: Fontana, 1978.
Walkowitz, Judith. *City of Dreadful Delight: Narratives of Sexual Danger in Late-Victorian London*. Chicago: Chicago University Press, 1992.
Ward, Stuart, ed. *British Culture and the End of Empire*. Manchester: Manchester University Press, 2001.
Waters, Chris. "'Dark Strangers' in Our Midst: Discourses of Race and Nation in Britain, 1947–1963." *Journal of British Studies* 36, no. 2 (1997): 207–238.
———. "Representations of Everyday Life: L. S. Lowry and the Landscape of Memory in Postwar Britain." *Representations* 65 (1999): 121–150.
Watkins, Jonathan, ed. *This Could Happen to You: Ikon in the 1970s*. Birmingham, UK: Ikon, 2010.
———. *At Home with Vanley Burke*. Birmingham, UK: Ikon Gallery, 2015.
Weaver, Gordon. "Political Groups and Young Blacks in Handsworth." Faculty of Commerce and Social Science discussion paper. University of Birmingham, 1980.
Webster, Wendy. *Imagining Home: Gender, "Race" and National Identity, 1945–64*. London and New York: Routledge, 2003.
Werbner, Pnina. *Imagined Diasporas among Manchester Muslims*. Oxford: James Currey, 2002.
West Midlands Probation Service. *After the Disturbances, Not Back to Normal: A Report of the West Midlands Probation Service Following the Lozells and Handsworth Disturbances of September 1985*. Birmingham, UK: West Midlands Probation Service, 1986.
Westall, Claire. "Men in the Yard and on the Street: Cricket and Calypso in *Moon on a Rainbow Shawl* and *Miguel Street*." *Anthurium: A Caribbean Studies Journal* 3. no. 2 (2005): 1–14.
———. "'This Thing Goes Beyond the Boundary': Cricket, Calypso, the Caribbean and Their Heroes." In *Sporting Sounds: Relationships between Sport and Music*, edited by Anthony Bateman and John Bale, 222–236. Abingdon: Routledge, 2009.
Wetherell, Sam. "Painting the Crisis: Community Arts and the Search for the 'Ordinary' in 1970s and 80s London." *History Workshop Journal* 76, no. 1 (2013): 235–249.
Whipple, Amy. "Revisiting the 'Rivers of Blood' Controversy: Letters to Enoch Powell." *Journal of British Studies* 48, no. 3 (2009): 717–735.
Whitall, Daniel. "Creolising London: Black West Indian Activism and the Politics of Race and Empire in Britain, 1931–1948." PhD thesis, Royal Holloway University of London, 2012.
White, Jerry. *Rothschild Buildings: Life in an East End Tenement Block 1887–1920*. London: Routledge & Kegan Paul,1980.
Wild, Rosalind Elizabeth. "'Black Was the Colour of Our Fight': Black Power in Britain, 1955–76." PhD thesis, University of Sheffield, 2008.
Wilkinson, P. "The Tinderbox Towns about to Erupt." *Daily Mail*, 11 September 1985, 6.
Williams, Claudette. "We Are a Natural Part of Many Different Struggles: Black Women Organising." In *Inside Babylon: The Caribbean Diaspora in Britain*, edited by Winston James and Clive Harris, 153–178. London: Verso, 1993.
Williams, Elizabeth M. *The Politics of Race in Britain and South Africa: Black British Solidarity and the Anti-Apartheid Struggle*. London and New York: I. B. Tauris, 2015.

Williams, Jack. "Cricket." In *Sport in Britain: A Social History*, edited by Tony Mason, 116–145. Cambridge, UK: Cambridge University Press, 1989.

———. *Cricket and Race*. Oxford: Berg, 2001.

Williams, Raymond. "Culture Is Ordinary." In *Conviction*, edited by Norman Mackenzie, 74–92. London: MacGibbon & Kee, 1958.

———. *Culture and Society*. Harmondsworth: Chatto and Windus, 1961.

———. *The Long Revolution*. London: Chatto and Windus, 1961.

———. *Marxism and Literature*. Oxford: Oxford University Press, 1977.

———. *Politics and Letters: Interviews with the New Left Review*. London: New Left Books, 1979.

———. *Towards 2000*. Harmondsworth: Pelican, 1983.

Wills, Clair. *Lovers and Strangers: An Immigrant History of Post-war Britain*. London: Allen Lane, 2017.

Wise Amanda, and S. Velayutham, eds. *Everyday Multiculturalism*. Basingstoke: Palgrave Macmillan, 2009.

Wood, Andrew. "'A Design for Social Living': Sound System Culture from JA to UK." In *Sub/versions: Cultural Status, Genre and Critique*, edited by Pauline Macpherson, Christopher Murray, Gordon Spark, and Kevin Corstorphine, 165–176. Newcastle: Cambridge Scholars Publishing, 2008.

Wood, Beverly. "Matthew 7, Verse 1." In *Whispers in the Walls: New Black and Asian Voices from Birmingham*, edited by Leone Ross and Yvonne Brissett, 31–42. Birmingham, UK: Tindal St. Press, 2001.

Woods, Robert. "Ethnic Segregation in Birmingham in the 1960s and 1970s." *Ethnic and Racial Studies* 2, no. 4 (1979): 455–475.

Yeo, Stephen. "A New Life: The Religion of Socialism in Britain, 1883–1896." *History Workshop Journal* 4 (1977): 5–56.

Young, Ken. "Approaches to Policy Development in the Field of Equal Opportunities." In *Race and Local Politics*, edited by Wendy Ball and John Solomos, 22–42. Basingstoke: Macmillan Education, 1990.

Zephaniah, Benjamin. *The Dread Affair*. London: Arena Books, 1985.

INDEX

Acapulco café, 40, 85–86, 95
African-Caribbean Self-Help Organisation (ACSHO), 18–19, 21, 40–52, 89, 157
African Liberation Day, 18–19, 80–82
All Faiths for One Race (AFFOR), 27–32, 35, 38–39, 51, 71, 95
Anderson, Hurvin, 60, 62
Angola, 10, 19, 40, 48
Anti-Apartheid Movement (AAM), 27
Anti-Nazi League (ANL), 28–29, 31
Apache Indian, musician, 116
Apartheid, 18, 44, 47, 49
Arts Labs, 58
Asian Resource Centre (ARC), 29, 38–41, 52
Asian Youth Movement (AYM), 21, 32–40, 50–51
Asian Youth News, 33–34, 37
Attie, David, 66

Babylon, film, 109–110
Balsall Heath, 79, 134, 137, 144
Banner Theatre of Actuality, 95–97
Barrow-Cadbury Trust, 24, 30, 39, 113–114
BBC: *Black and White Mistral Show* and, 69; Caribbean dominoes and, 133; Charles Parker
and, 95; *Empire Road* and, 69, 151–152; Handsworth riots and, 84; *Love Thy Neighbour* and, 69; programmes aimed at ethnic minorities, 69, 151–152

Bell, Ronald, MP, 70
Berger, John, 56, 61, 64
Bhangra, 116
Birmingham Black Sisters (BBS), 35–38
Birmingham City Council, 22, 24–25, 39, 43, 51
Bishton, Derek, 58–59, 61–68, 74, 83–90, 147
Black Audio Film Collective (BAFC), 15, 53, 55, 67–76
Black Power: African Liberation Day and, 18–19, 40; housing and, 41–43; humanitarianism and, 40; ideology and, 41–44, 47–49; relationship to south Asian political organisations and, 33, 49–50; state funding and, 43–44, 51–52; supplementary schools and, 44–47. *See also* pan-Africanism
Black Lives Matter, 160
British Nationality Act (1948), 2
British Nationality Act (1981), 4, 36
British National Party (BNP), 159
Broadside magazine, 59
Brown, Bini, 30, 44, 46–50, 52
Burke, Vanley, 12, 15, 56–57, 76–90, 134–137, 147
Butcher, Roland, 154–155

Caesar, Pogus, 76, 84–85
Calypso, 71, 99, 111, 117, 124, 126, 129, 154
Camerawork, 58–59, 68
Carmichael, Stokely, 20, 43–44, 47, 50, 72

Centre for Contemporary Cultural Studies (CCCS), 3–4, 12–13, 59
Césaire, Aimé, 70
Chaggar, Gurdip Singh, 32
Channel 4: Black Audio Film Collective and, 69, 72, 74; *Black on Black* and, 76; establishment of, 68; film and television workshops and, 68–69
Churches: Anglicanism and, 139, 141, 145; attendance among the black community in Britain and, 139–140; attendance in the Caribbean and, 139; Baptisms and, 139–141, 143–145; fictional representations of, 143; Methodism and, 139–140; Pentecostalism and, 139–146; 'Sunday best' and, 146–148
Coard, Bernard, 45
Commonwealth Arts Festival, 23, 26, 46
Conservative Party, 2–5, 19, 24, 55, 63, 70, 146
Constantine, Learie, 119, 127
Cricket: C. L. R. James and, 119–120; early development of, 123–124; Handsworth Continental Cricket Club and, 122–123, 125–131; West Indian Test team and, 124, 128–129

Dalton, John, xii, 168, 181, 184
Dennis, Ferdinand, 48, 117
Dominoes: Anglo-Caribbean Dominoes League (ACDL) and, 137–138; pubs/social clubs and, 131–136; relationship to cricket and, 130–131
Dreadlocks (hairstyle), 81, 89, 93–94, 104–107, 114, 116
Dyche, Earnest (photographic studio), 144–145

Educationally Sub-Normal (ESN) controversy, 45–46, 51
Empire Road, television series, 69, 151–152
Empire Windrush, 13, 71, 124
Ethiopia: famine and, 40; Haile Selassie and, 90, 93, 103; national colours of, 8, 89, 93–94 129; position within Rastafarianism and, 9, 15–16, 92, 94; reggae music and, 93–94, 105. See also Rastafarianism
European Union, 159–160

Fairbairn, Nicholas, MP, 4
Falklands, 2, 55
Fanon, Frantz, 9
Freitas, Michael de (Michael X), 42, 72, 78
Front room: class and, 149; fictional representations of, 147, 152; furniture and, 147–149; gender and, 148–150; photographic representations of, 147, 150–151, 153; religion and, 147–148

Gabbidon, Basil, 91, 104, 107–108, 115
Garvey, Marcus, 8, 43, 47–48, 94, 103, 114
Ghana, 1, 72, 100, 102, 115
Gilroy, Paul: Anti-Nazi League and, 28; 'Black Atlantic' and, 10; cultural studies and, 13, 73; postcolonial 'melancholia' and, 159; Powellism and, 30; Rastafarianism and, 106–107; riots and, 55
Grapevine magazine, 58–59
Greater London Council (GLC), 20, 23–24
Griffiths, Peter, 3, 19
Guy, Jackie, 98, 100, 102

Hall, Stuart: black arts movement and, 13, 53–54, 57, 73–74, 77, 88; childhood in Jamaica and, 104, 106, 125; cultural studies and, 12–13; front room and, 149; migration to Britain and, 3–4, 9, 13, 144, 160; New Left and, 27; Rastafarianism and, 94, 103, 118; Thatcherism and, 4
Hain, Peter, 27–28
Handsworth Self-Portrait Project, 64–67, 74–76
Handsworth Songs (1987), 15, 53–54, 67–72
Harambee, 42–44, 49, 51
Hick, John, 27, 29
Hinds, David, 91, 107, 116–117
History Workshop movement, 59
Hoggart, Richard, 3–4, 17, 59, 149
Homer, Brian, 58–64, 66–68, 74, 83–90
hooks, bell, 17
Howe, Darcus, 53–54, 73, 120
Hurd, Douglas, 25, 71, 84

Indian Workers' Association (IWA), 19, 21, 32–40, 50–51
International Times, 58

Jamaica: cricket and, 123, 126–127, 130; dominoes and, 132; exchange trips and, 1, 100, 102; Independence Day and, 135; migration patterns and, 11–12; Pentecostalism and, 140; Rastafarianism and, 94, 103–104, 106; reggae music and, 6, 9, 15, 91, 93, 105; sound systems and, 109, 117; Stuart Hall and, 3, 13, 106, 125
James, C.L.R.: black British identity and, 122, 154–155; Black Power and, 33, 119–120; cricket and, 119–120, 124, 126, 129–130; West Indian identity and, 121

Jazz, 93, 99, 118
Johnson, Linton Kwesi, 111
Jomo magazine, 43–44
Jones, Claudia, 19–20
Jouhl, Avtar, 33
Jungleman (sound system), 113–115

Kanhai, Rohan, 119–120, 126
Kitchener, Lord, calypso singer, 111, 124
Kokuma Dance Company, 97–103, 105–106, 115

Labour party, 23, 26, 39
Lalkar magazine, 33
Lawrence, Stephen, 6–7, 160
League of Coloured Peoples, 40–41
Leshurr, Lady, grime artist, 117
Liverpool, 11, 35, 58
London: atypicality of, 11; Black Power and, 42–48, 72, 78; Greater London Council and, 20, 23–24, 70; Lord Kitchener and, 71, 124; music scene and, 93, 106, 108, 110, 117; pan-African organisations and, 6, 15, 19, 40–41; rioting and, 3–5; Southall and, 32
Lovers' Rock, 117

Manchester, 11, 19, 37
Manchester Guardian, 126
Marley, Bob, 1, 7–8, 91, 93, 104–106, 108–109, 114
Mass Observation, 131–132
McMillan, Michael, 152–153
Mowatt, Judy, 117
Mozambique, 10, 19, 40, 48
Mugging crisis, 3–5, 12–13, 31, 55
Murphy, Dervla, 138–139, 143, 148

Namibia, 40
National Front (NF), 3–4, 28, 31,
National Union of Miners, 55

OZ magazine, 58

Pan-Africanism: Black Audio Film Collective and, 72; dance and, 1, 7, 97–103; interwar London and, 6, 15, 19, 40–41; political organisations and, 18–19, 40–52; reggae music and, 1, 6, 94, 103–117. *See also* Black Power Parker, Charles, 95–97
Patel, Maganbhai, 89, 144
Patois (Jamaican slang), 31, 45, 106, 111
Picture Post, 54–55
Policing the Crisis (Hall *et al*), 12, 159

Powell, Enoch, MP, 3–5, 27, 30, 55, 118
Pubs: closure of, 137; colour bar and, 134; dominoes and, 134–135; Rastafarians and, 134; social clubs and, 134–136

Race Relations Act (1965), 23
Race Relations Act (1976), 6, 23
Racial Adjustment Action Society (RAAS), 42, 48
Ramdhanie, Bon, 7, 97–98, 100, 102, 157
Reardon, John, 58–59, 63–68, 74, 83–90, 147
Reggae: British bands and, 12, 77, 91–93, 104, 106–109, 115–117; early development of, 91–92, 104; female performers and, 105–106, 117; Rastafarianism and, 6–7, 9–10, 15, 104–105. *See also* calypso; lovers' rock; ska
Richards, Viv, 127–129
Riots: Brixton and, 4–5, 20; Broadwater Farm and, 5; Handsworth and, 4–5, 13, 24, 26, 30, 33, 49–55, 71, 73–76, 84–86; Nottingham and, 3; Notting Hill and, 3
Robeson, Paul, 41, 72
Rock Against Racism (RAR), 28–29
Rushdie, Salman, 52–54, 56–57, 73–74, 85–87

Sadaukai, Owusu, 18
Samuel, Raphael, 59
Satanic Verses, the (Rushdie), 52–53
Scarman, Lord, 4, 20
Selassie, Haile (Ras Tafari): accession to Ethiopian throne and, 93, 103; death and, 103; emergence of Rastafarianism and, 93, 103, 114; visit to Jamaica and, 104. *See also* Rastafarianism
Shashamene (district of Ethiopia), 90
Short, Clare, 28, 30
Silver Jubilee (June 1977), 18, 51, 54, 80
Singh, Shaheed Udham, 32–33, 43
Sivanandan Ambalavener, 20, 26, 34, 38, 50
Ska, 99, 104–105, 109, 149, 154
Smethwick, 3, 19, 33
Sondhi, Ranjit, 38, 52
Sontag, Susan, 56, 61, 64
Sound systems: artistic representations of, 110; clashes and, 109–110; dub poetry and, 110–113; Jungleman and, 113–115; origins of, 109. *See also* reggae
South Africa, 10, 12, 18, 22, 27, 40, 44, 48–49, 129
Southall Black Sisters, 35
Southall Youth Movement, 33
Sparkbrook, 41

Spence, Jo, 58–59, 64, 66, 67
Steel Pulse, 12, 91–93, 104–109, 115–118, 157–158

Tafari, Amlak, 108–109, 117
Ten.8 magazine, 59–63, 77, 86
Thatcher, Margaret, MP: Falklands conflict and, 2, 55; housing policy and, 146; immigration policy and, 4, 36, 66; public expenditure and, 25; response to urban rioting and, 4, 55
There Ain't No Black in the Union Jack (Gilroy), 13, 73
Thompson, E.P., 59
Trade unions, 16, 37, 55, 95
Trinidad: calypso and, 71, 111, 117; cricket and, 119, 127–128
Tubman, Harriet, 43, 46

Unemployment, 4, 23, 31
United Kingdom Independence Party (UKIP), 159
United States: Black Power and, 18, 20, 49, 105; C. L. R. James and, 119, 155, 158; music and, 7, 115–117; race relations debates and, 4–5; supplementary schools and, 46
Universal Coloured People's Association (UCPA), 20, 44, 47–48
Uses of Literacy, the (Richard Hoggart), 16–17, 59, 149

Waddington, David, 24, 26
Walker, Maxine, 79, 150–151
West African Students' Union (WASU), 41
West Indian Federation, 125
West Indian Gazette, 20, 127
West Midlands County Council (WMCC), 24
Westminster Endeavour for Liaison and Development (WELD), 60–62, 64, 68, 67, 86–87
Williams, Raymond, 5, 8, 12–13, 17

X, Malcolm, 7, 19–20, 33, 46–47, 50, 72

Zephaniah, Benjamin, 12, 111–115
Zimbabwe, 40